Gannets, Boobies **18-19**

Cormorants, Shags **20-23**

Frigate-birds **24**

Sheathbills **25**

Phalaropes **25**

Gulls **27-40**

Skuas **26**

Terns, Noddies **41-45**

Skimmers **45**

Auks, Guillemots, Puffins **46-48**

A FIELD GUIDE TO THE
SEABIRDS
OF BRITAIN AND THE WORLD

A FIELD GUIDE TO THE
SEABIRDS
OF BRITAIN AND THE WORLD

Captain G. S. Tuck
D.S.O., Royal Navy

Illustrated by
Hermann Heinzel

COLLINS
St James's Place, London

William Collins Sons & Co Ltd
London · Glasgow · Sydney · Auckland
Toronto · Johannesburg

To

Past, present and future members

of

The Royal Naval Birdwatching Society

'I must go down to the seas again, for the call of the running tide
Is a wild call and a clear call that may not be denied;
And all I ask is a windy day and the white clouds flying,
And the flung spray and the blown spume, and the seagulls crying.'

John Masefield

First published 1978
© in the text G. S. Tuck, 1978
© in the illustrations Hermann Heinzel, 1978

ISBN 0 00 219718 9

Filmset by Jolly & Barber Ltd, Rugby, Warwickshire

Made and Printed in Great Britain by
William Collins Sons & Co Ltd Glasgow

CONTENTS

COLOUR PLATES

(between pages 133 and 227)

PREFACE

No field guide covering the world's seabirds as a whole has been published since W. B. Alexander's *Birds of the Ocean* in 1954. Since then many species have been studied intensively, primarily at breeding colonies, more recently in surveys in various ocean areas, and the general picture of seabird distribution is a good deal clearer. But the oceans over which seabirds are free to wander at will cover some seven-tenths of the whole surface of the globe; it will be many years, if ever, before these vast areas can be fully covered by seasonal observation, and then only from the decks of ships at sea.

There seemed to us a need for a guide book to help birdwatchers to identify the seabirds they see; to show a general pattern of their distribution around the world; and to provide an account for voyagers at sea along the principal ocean routes. For those who travel constantly at sea, birds provide more than purely scientific interest; they are indeed a ship's true companions in an otherwise empty vista of sea and sky. Those that arrive on board are treated as welcome visitors. Thus a few examples of notes taken, together with suggestions for the care and feeding of birds on board and simple forms for recording birds at sea, seemed worth including.

This is a practical handbook, not a work of systematics. Awesome numbers of subspecific titles have been assigned in works covering the seabirds of different countries. Many of these may well be justified. But in a book such as this the main object is to provide a guide to those seabirds which can be identified by field observation. Subspecific titles based on small taxonomic and plumage distinctions have been reduced in general to a minimum to embrace only those races whose variations are observable in the field.

Any writer on seabirds owes much to the many studies already published, and we owe a special debt, not only to W. B. Alexander's splendid book, but also to the *Preliminary Identification Manuals* published by the Smithsonian Institution; and to Captain P. P. O. Harrison's *Seabirds of the South Pacific*. The description of the sea route from New Zealand to Panama is derived largely from Captain Harrison's records. We are also grateful to many friends and correspondents for help generously given, particularly Mr. George Edwards, Mrs. M. K. Rowan, Mr. John Parslow, Dr. W. R. P. Bourne, Dr. D. L. Serventy, and Captain W. F. Mörzer-Bruyns and most of all to the members of the Royal Naval Birdwatching Society. Over a period of 18 years, ocean-going members of the R.N.B.W.S. have been sending back detailed seabird passage records of their voyages. Without this continual flow of information, much of this book could not have been compiled.

We are most grateful to Dr. C. J. O. Harrison for contributing notes on the nesting habits of seabirds. These have been incorporated in the introductions to families and in the descriptions of certain species.

In describing and compiling maps, we wish to acknowledge the help received from a study of many published works and papers on seabirds by a number of eminent ornithologists and authors. In particular we must thank Crispin Fisher for his meticulous and enthusiastic cartography. Any errors in the maps – as in the text – are the author's.

HOW TO USE THIS BOOK

The **endpapers**, inside the front and back covers, illustrate typical members of the principal seabird groups: at the front in flight, at the back standing or swimming. The numbers beside each caption refer to the colour plates on which that group is illustrated.

The **introduction**, pages xiii to xxviii, is a brief survey of the world's seabirds, their categories, physical characteristics and way of life.

The **description section**, pages 2–131, provides a systematic guide to the world's seabird species and distinct subspecies, with notes on size and measurements (see below); plumage and markings; flight and points of behaviour useful for identification; range and breeding areas. It is important to read the introductory notes given for each Family, since these are not repeated in the species descriptions. References to colour plates are given with the heading, to the world distribution maps after the notes on RANGE.

The following table has been used in quoting length. Length is measured between the tip of the bill and the tip of the longest tail feather. In tropic-birds the second measurement includes the elongated tail. Where the letter 'W' is included in captions, it indicates total wingspan.

Description	Length	
	ins	mm
Tiny	4-6	102-152
Very small	6-8	152-203
Small	8-12	203-305
Small-medium	12-16	305-406
Medium	16-20	406-508
Medium-large	20-24	508-609
Large	24-28	609-711
Very large	28-32	711-813
Outsize	above 32	813

In the case of Penguins their height has been indicated as follows:
Large: over 36 ins, over 915 mm.
Medium: 24-36 ins, 610-915 mm.
Small: 20 ins, 508 mm and below.

On the **colour plates**, between pages 133 and 229, the principal birds are painted to scale with each other; but subsidiary illustrations, e.g. to plumage and other variants, flight sketches, and other species added for the sake of comparison, are shown on a smaller scale.

The **caption pages**, facing each plate, gives the bird's names, diagnostic features, and references both to its distribution map and to the page on which it is described. Where a bird is also illustrated on another page, e.g. to show its winter or immature plumage, cross-references are given on the caption pages.

The **distribution maps,** pages 229–260, indicate the breeding, non-breeding and migratory distributions. The maps are explained on page 229, and a map to principal islands is on pages 230–231.

British seabirds. On pages 261–285 is an account by John Parslow of the seabirds of the British Isles, with maps showing the main breeding sites around our coastline and the distribution of individual species.

The **index,** pages 286–292, has references to text descriptions in normal type, to the colour plates in bold, and to the distribution maps in italic.

INTRODUCTION

This book is concerned with true or *primary* seabirds: those for which the sea is the normal habitat and principal source of food: phalaropes are included for they spend the winter months outside the breeding season entirely in the open sea. *Secondary* seabirds are those whose habitats are confined chiefly to inland lakes, rivers and lagoons, such as divers, grebes, darters and sea ducks. Although these species resort at times to sea coasts, they are not true seabirds and are outside the scope of this book. Locally, the true seabirds may be divided broadly into three zones, depending on where their principal food is obtained:

INSHORE species are those which obtain their food near the coastline or by foraging inland: pelicans, cormorants, most gulls, coastal terns, skimmers.

OFFSHORE species are those which feed on fish offshore at no great distance from the coasts: penguins (also oceanic), diving-petrels (also oceanic), gannets, boobies, frigate-birds (also oceanic) terns (except on migration), noddies, auks and allies (also oceanic). But note that the Sooty Tern and Brown-winged or Bridled Tern are frequently seen far out to sea.

PELAGIC or OCEANIC species are those which obtain their food in the open oceans: albatrosses, petrels, shearwaters, prions, storm-petrels, tropic-birds, skuas (on migration), phalaropes (outside breeding areas), kittiwakes.

Within these broad groupings the different species have their particular distribution. Each seabird species and its allied races tend to spread and breed laterally around the world within the latitude belts they favour. At the end of breeding seasons, many species disperse from their congested breeding localities to find favourable climates and feeding areas for the winter. Some, particularly those which breed in the higher latitudes, undertake enormous trans-global seasonal migrations from their breeding grounds, many crossing the equator to similar latitudes at the other end of the world where suitable feeding areas occur.

Of course, all birds have to nest and rear their young on land; so during the breeding season all seabird species may be seen at, or close off coastal breeding areas.

SEABIRD CHARACTERISTICS

In the course of evolution seabirds have developed many different characteristics both in structure and habits. These are determined primarily by the types of sea food they have become adapted to consume, and the areas where this is most abundant. This in turn is associated with their adaptability to breed in large colonies whether on cliffs where in certain cases brood patch will only allow coverage of a single egg, in colonies on sand dunes or more independently where nesting material may be collected and two or three eggs laid, or the need to escape predation by nesting in burrows or crevices where only a single egg is laid. Some indeed nest in trees. Where different species nest together in large colonies, an ecological pattern can normally be found in which each requires a different type of sea food for its offspring. In this way, the adjacent sea provides enough food for all.

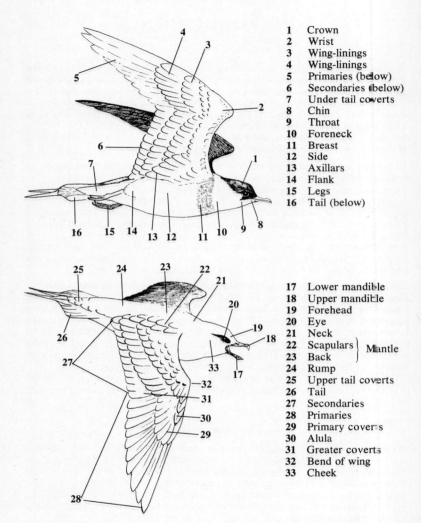

1 Crown
2 Wrist
3 Wing-linings
4 Wing-linings
5 Primaries (below)
6 Secondaries (below)
7 Under tail coverts
8 Chin
9 Throat
10 Foreneck
11 Breast
12 Side
13 Axillars
14 Flank
15 Legs
16 Tail (below)

17 Lower mandible
18 Upper mandible
19 Forehead
20 Eye
21 Neck
22 Scapulars ⎫
23 Back   ⎬ Mantle
24 Rump
25 Upper tail coverts
26 Tail
27 Secondaries
28 Primaries
29 Primary coverts
30 Alula
31 Greater coverts
32 Bend of wing
33 Cheek

While all seabirds should be capable of resting on the sea, and make use of their preening gland – or in the case of petrels oil from their nostrils – to keep their plumage oiled, a few have become less adapted to do so. Frigate-birds do not have the oiled feathers to provide buoyancy. Cormorants would become waterlogged if they did not regain land frequently to preen and dry their feathers. Sooty Terns will rarely attempt to settle for long periods on the sea. It is said that the Ivory Gull in the high Arctic avoids wetting its feathers to prevent them becoming encrusted with ice.

Heat conservation

Heat conservation is an important requirement in all birds, but particularly so in seabirds. Their closely-knit oiled outer plumage, the filoplumes of their under-bodies and underlayers of fat and blubber help to insulate them, and species which inhabit higher colder latitudes are generally found to be larger than their counter-parts in lower latitudes. More rounded contours and "built-in" necks which help to conserve heat are noticeable in such species as the penguins and auks of high latitudes.

Legs and feet

A noticeable feature in different species is the position of the legs in relation to the underbody. Those which spend much time out of the water, particularly gulls, have sturdy legs placed centrally below their underbodies providing a horizontal carriage and balance suitable for foraging for food on tidelines or inland. Species which pursue fish underwater have shorter legs placed much further aft and wider webbed feet to act as paddles or rudders. This results in a more upright stance, evident particularly in the alcids (auks and allies) and penguins. Many truly oceanic species have not retained sufficient strength in their legs to bear the weight effectively on land, and are forced to shuffle forward helped by their wings. This makes them so vulnerable to predators that many petrels, shearwaters and storm-petrels have become adapted to approaching and leaving their enclosed nesting sites under cover of darkness.

Bills

The bills of seabirds vary to meet their particular mode of life. Penguins have caruncles on tongue and palate to grasp fish firmly. The bills of albatrosses and petrels are stout and hooked at the tip, those of shearwaters generally similar but more slender. A distinguishing feature in all species of the Order Procellariiformes is the presence of the two nostrils opening together at the end of a double tube on the upper mandible. Diving-petrels also possess a distensible pouch at the base of the lower mandible. The bills of tropic-birds, gannets and boobies are stout and dagger shaped, in keeping with the streamlined outline of these species which dive from considerable heights into the sea, and well suited for grasping quite sizeable fish. Cormorants and frigate-birds both have long slender bills sharply hooked at the tip. This helps cormorants to seize and pierce the gills of the fish they pursue, and serves frigate-birds as a weapon both for harrying other seabirds, and for snatching food from the surface, and indeed fledgling birds from nesting colonies of terns, without pausing in flight. The long powerful bill of the Pelican and its huge pouch serves to seize large fish on conclusion of its headlong dives and to scoop up smaller fry after driving them into the shallows. The fine needle-shaped bills of phalaropes have been adapted to probe for small marine animals at their breeding grounds and to peck for planktonic crustaceans on the surface of the sea. Skuas with their stout hooked bills pirate other seabirds and are great scavengers of both eggs and young.

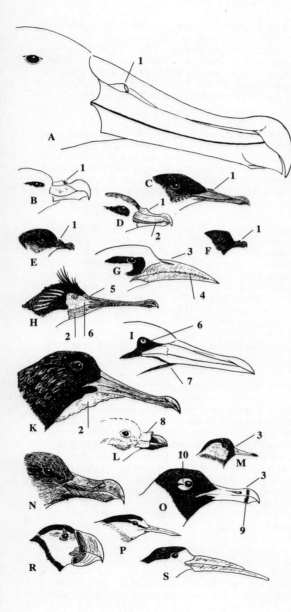

SEABIRDS' BILLS

A Albatrosses
  1 nostril

B Petrels

C Shearwaters

D Prions
  2 pouch

E Diving-petrels

F Storm-petrels

G Tropic-birds
  3 nostril
  4 saw bill

H Cormorants
  5 caruncles
  6 naked skin on face

I Gannets
  7 gular stripe naked

K Frigate-birds

L Sheathbills
  8 'sheath'

M Phalaropes

N Skuas

O Gulls
  9 under mandible
    often with red spot
  10 eye-ring

P Terns

R Puffins

S Skimmers

The strong bills of the larger gulls are equally suitable for scavenging on the tidelines, tearing at refuse and killing fledgling seabirds. The finer bills of terns are sufficient for the capture of fry and eels. Puffins have backwardly directed spines on their tongues enabling them to hold each small fish caught separately until six or more may be seen dangling crosswise in their bills. The bills of skimmers are useful for scooping up fish in flight, with the lower and longer mandible skimming below the surface while the bird maintains its flight.

FEEDING

The Oceans

The existence of life in the surface layers of the oceans depends upon the presence of dissolved nutrient salts, largely nitrates and phosphates from the deep layers of the ocean being brought to the surface. Here by a process of photosynthesis, through the energy of sunlight together with dissolved carbon dioxide and oxygen, phytoplankton multiplies. From this basis arises the food-chain of life in the upper layer of the sea. Microscopic zooplankton, crustacea, copepods and the like, and finally fish consume each other, providing food for seabirds, until the last in the food chain dies, sinks below the surface to recreate the cycle. The immense quantities of guano from the excreta of seabirds on islands also get washed into the sea to augment the nutrient salts.

To provide for these conditions, nutrient-rich deep water must be brought to the surface in circumstances known as "up-welling". Such areas occur in high polar latitudes near moving ice masses; where strong constant winds and rough weather persist; where winds or surface currents deflect surface water away from coasts; where cool currents flow past coastal land masses; in the warm tropical oceans where deep water strikes an incline around islands; and in the open oceans where converging or crossing currents occur.

While winds and currents affect particular areas in this way a broad pattern of rich surface feed zones or 'convergencies' emerges between the Poles and the Equator. These may be summarised as follows: Polar zones around the ice edge; Arctic and Antarctic convergencies at about 55 degrees latitude; Sub-arctic and Sub-antarctic zones between 55 and 35 degrees latitude; and Sub-tropical zones between 35 degrees and 10 degrees latitude. Within the doldrums near the Equator in the open oceans, the warm surface water however provides little surface feed.

As a general guide, the principal areas over which oceanic seabirds tend to feed are:

PACIFIC OCEAN. The Arctic convergence about 55° N. and into the Bering Sea. The converging currents east of Japan. Off west coast of British Columbia. Along the equatorial counter current between 6° and 8° N. Along the west coast of South America in the Humboldt Current. New Zealand seas. Around tropical pacific Islands.

INDIAN OCEAN. The south-east coast of Arabia during the south-west monsoon. The north-east coast of Arabia and Mekran coast during the north-east monsoon. Along the equatorial counter current, especially around islands. Off the west coast of Australia. Off the southern tip of South Africa.

ATLANTIC OCEAN. The confluence of the Labrador Current and the Gulf Stream. Upswellings off islands and off the north-west coast of Africa. In the Buenguela Current off the west coast of South Africa. In the Falkland Current.

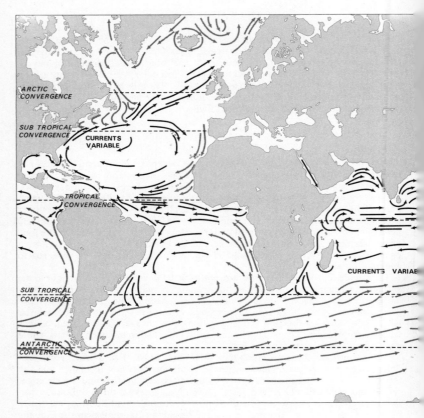

OCEAN CURRENTS AND SURFACE FEED

The map above shows the course of the principal surface currents in the world's oceans. The warm currents are indicated by solid black arrows, the cool or cold by lighter arrows.

The direction and strength of surface current result from the effects of constant winds and of the rotation of the earth. These cause the currents to circulate generally clockwise in the northern hemisphere and anti-clockwise in the southern.

Areas of turbulence and upwelling yield the richest supplies of surface feed for seabirds. Their main causes and areas are:

1. In the high latitudes near the Poles, with easterly winds and floating ice.

2. The Arctic and Antarctic convergences, with high winds and strong surface currents.

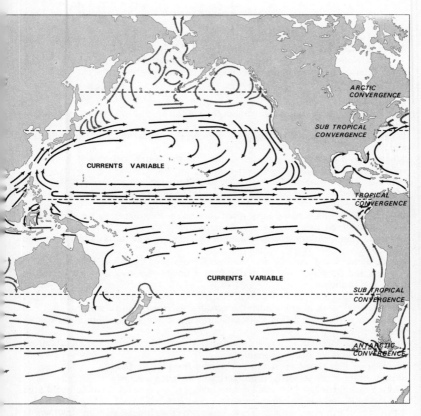

3. The subtropical convergences at about 35° Lat.

4. The cold currents flowing northwards off the southern hemisphere continents – the Humboldt Current of the west coast of South America and the weaker Falkland Current off the south-eastern coast, and the Benguela Current passing up the west coast of Africa.

5. Where opposite currents converge or overlap, e.g. off Labrador the cold, southward-flowing Labrador Current impinges on the Gulf Stream, causing considerable turbulence.

6. Currents flowing sharply away from coastlines, e.g. the strong South West Monsoon off the coast of South-east Arabia during the northern summer months causes upwelling close offshore.

7. Where currents are deflected off islands, e.g. tropical oceanic islands.

Where variable weak winds and currents occur in warm tropical and sub-tropical zones, little surface feed is present in the open ocean.

SOUTHERN OCEAN. Along the belt of the Antarctic convergence at about 55° S. Along the seaward edge of the pack-ice.

In the Sub-arctic zones certain southern hemisphere migratory petrels and shearwaters spend the northern summer months.

The Food

The following list provides a general outline of the kind of food taken by different groups:

Penguins: Fish, squid and krill, propelling themselves underwater with their flippers and using their feet as rudders.

Albatrosses: Fish, squid, garbage, settling on the water with raised wings and submerging a little way below the surface.

Petrels and **Shearwaters:** Mainly fish, squid and crustaceans, but some will also eat garbage. Food is obtained mainly from close to the surface, but they often settle and submerge freely.

Prions: Mainly small crustaceans, often obtained by running along the surface and scooping up food with their heads submerged.

Storm-petrels: Planktonic crustaceans, fish eggs, oily scum obtained from the surface.

Tropic-birds: Squid and fish near the surface obtained by diving from a height.

Gannets and **Boobies:** Fish, by diving from a height. Boobies frequently capture flying fish in the air.

Pelicans: Fish, either by diving from a height, or scooping fish into their pouches when several work in unison driving shoaling fish into shallow water.

Cormorants: Fish, by diving from the surface and propelling themselves chiefly with their legs.

Frigate-birds: Pirate other seabirds and snatch up food vomited. Snatch offal from the surface and eat fledgling seabirds.

Phalaropes: Planktonic crustaceans obtained from the surface.

Skuas: Pirate other seabirds, offal, garbage, fledgling seabirds.

Gulls: Scavenge for molluscs and worms on tide lines; feed inland on refuse. Large gulls will kill and eat fledgling seabirds.

Terns: Small fish near surface. Terns often hover with head slanting downwards searching for fish before diving just below the surface.

Noddies: Fish, probably squid also. Noddies usually fly close above the surface unlike terns.

Alcids: Fish, small squid, crustaceans, diving from the surface.

Drinking

Seabirds will drink fresh water where this is available in preference to salt water. Pelagic seabirds have become adapted to drinking sea water and have developed a salt water excreting gland in the nose which extracts the surplus salt from the water taken in and empties it back into the sea.

With a very few exceptions there is not noticeable plumage difference between the sexes of adult seabirds. Frigate-birds are a notable exception. The plumage of immature birds however is often entirely different from that of mature adults. Many immatures take several years to assume full adult plumage, and these differences are a frequent cause of perplexity to observers.

During the course of a year all birds moult their feathers, but there is a considerable variation in the extent and period in which different species elect to moult. Some species moult more than once in a year. The moult of wing and tail feathers is arranged so that not more than one or two feathers are missing from each side at one time. A common time for moulting to commence is shortly after the mating season, and this appears more applicable to the inshore and residential species. Species which undertake distant migrations immediately after the breeding season, such as the migratory shearwaters, retain their original wing and tail feathers until reaching or approaching their contra-nuptial feeding grounds. The periods and extent of moulting however varies in many cases. Penguins for example slough all their feathers at once, lose much weight and are unable to go to sea to feed for several weeks.

Most adult seabirds retain the same plumage throughout the seasons, but there are notable exceptions. In particular cormorants, phalaropes, the dark hooded gulls and terns and the auks. In the contra-nuptial season certain cormorants lose their distinctive white plumage patches, dark hooded gulls and terns lose their dark hoods and retain only dusky patches about their heads. Phalaropes assume an entirely different plumage, and many auks and murrelets shed their crests or facial adornments. At this season there is a general tendency in birds with bright coloured bills and legs to revert to duller colours.

IDENTIFYING SEABIRDS

Naturally the first object when sighting a seabird is to be able to put a name to it. As a first step it is helpful to know the general characteristics of the different Families in which seabird species are grouped:

PENGUINS. Family Spheniscidae. Medium to outsize. Stout bodied and short necked, standing upright on land on short webbed feet set very far back. Penguins differ from all other seabirds in having 'flippers' instead of quilled wings. When at the surface they swim very low in the water with only the head or part of the back showing, and are sometimes seen 'porpoising' in and out of the water. Confined to the Southern Hemisphere, except for the Galapagos Penguin.

ALBATROSSES and MOLLYMAWKS. Family Diomedeidae. Very large to outsize. Distinguished at sea by their large size, long slender wings, stout bills with upper mandible slightly hooked, short tails and characteristic gliding flight. The different colouring of the bills and pattern of the underwing margins helps to distinguish species. The smaller species are often referred to as 'Mollymawks'.

TRUE PETRELS and SHEARWATERS. Family Procellariidae. Medium size with long narrow wings held out straight or angled in flight. Fly low over the sea in tilted glides on extended wings alternating with a few wing beats. (Some 'gadfly' petrels of the genus *Pterodroma* tend to swoop and soar.) Distinguished at close quarters by their tubular nostrils.

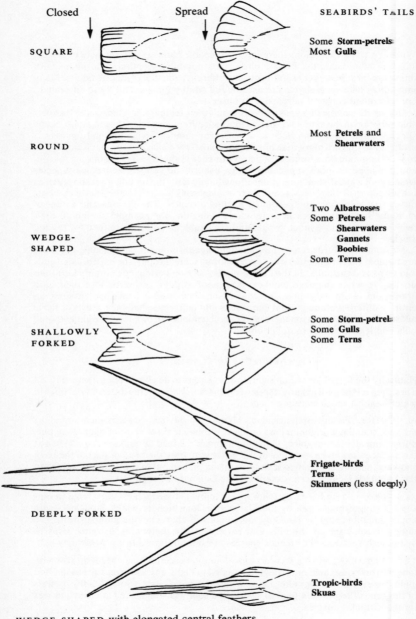

Closed   Spread   SEABIRDS' TAILS

SQUARE

Some **Storm-petrels**
Most **Gulls**

ROUND

Most **Petrels** and
Shearwaters

WEDGE-
SHAPED

Two **Albatrosses**
Some **Petrels**
    Shearwaters
    Gannets
    Boobies
Some **Terns**

SHALLOWLY
FORKED

Some **Storm-petrels**
Some **Gulls**
Some **Terns**

DEEPLY FORKED

Frigate-birds
Terns
Skimmers (less deeply)

Tropic-birds
Skuas

WEDGE-SHAPED with elongated central feathers

xxii

STORM-PETRELS. Family Hydrobatidae. Very small dark birds usually to be seen flitting back and forth close to the sea, sometimes close in the wake of a ship, or pattering the surface with their webbed feet. Tubular nostrils.

DIVING-PETRELS. Family Pelecanoididae. Small stumpy little birds, blackish above and white below with short bills and wings, legs placed far back. Usually seen in flocks resting on the surface of the water. Fly short distances with rapidly beating wings and usually dive on alighting. Confined to Southern Oceans. Tubular nostrils.

TROPIC-BIRDS. Family Phaethontidae. Medium size, graceful white birds with greatly elongated central tail feathers. High flying with quick powerful wing beats.

PELICANS. Family Pelecanidae. Outsize birds with broad rounded wings, heavy bodies and huge pouched bills. In flight heads are thrust back on shoulders. Plunge clumsily into sea for food.

GANNETS and BOOBIES. Family Sulidae. Very large. Cigar-shaped with long narrow wings, short necks and stout conical pointed bills. Flight is stately with regular wing beats. Plunge headlong into sea for food.

CORMORANTS and SHAGS. Family Phalacrocoracidae. Medium large to large. Dark birds with long necks and wings and slender hooked bills. Fly low over surface with regular wing beats. Dive from surface of water for food.

FRIGATE-BIRDS. Family Fregatidae. Very large almost black plumaged birds with very long narrow wings, long forked tails and long slender hooked bills. Circle for hours overhead, tails opening and closing scissor-fashion. Chase and pirate other seabirds.

PHALAROPES. Family Phalaropodidae. Very small delicate rather long-necked waders. Winter at sea in favoured localities. Usually seen in flocks either swimming buoyantly on the sea or flying with rapid flight for short distances.

SKUAS and JAEGERS. Family Stercorariidae. Medium size. Dark uniform brown or in the light phase with yellowish sides and neck and pale underparts. Long wings, slightly hooked bills. The Great Skua is much larger than the three Jaegers, and is uniform brown with broad rounded wings and pale wing patches. Chase and pirate other seabirds.

GULLS. Family Laridae. Medium to large. In most cases in adult plumage have head, body and tail white, and the upper wings grey or black. The tail is nearly always square. Some of the smaller gulls acquire a dark hood in the breeding season. The majority of the immature birds are mottled brown overall.

TERNS. Family Sternidae. Small to medium. Graceful seabirds distinguished by their long narrow wings, short legs and long deeply forked tails. The majority have the crown black in the breeding season and the remainder of the plumage a mixture of pale grey and white. A few species, e.g. Noddies, are mainly sooty-brown. Fly with rapid wing beats. Hover and plunge into sea for food.

SKIMMERS. Family Rhynchopidae. Medium size. Somewhat like large terns with very long narrow wings; short legs and slightly forked tails. Blackish above with white foreheads and underparts and long bills usually orange or yellow with dark tips, the lower mandible extending well beyond the upper.

AUKS. Family Alcidae. Small to medium size. Short-winged, usually dark above and white below. Often to be seen in flocks swimming buoyantly. When disturbed they dive or fly with a rapid whirring flight straight and low over the sea. Obtain food by diving from surface.

Once one has grasped the general characteristics of the Families, it is usually not difficult to decide within which a bird belongs. But to identify the individual species a selective eye to concentrate upon the particular characteristics and field markings which will serve to identify it.

At sea, when the birds are nearly always seen on the wing and glimpses of upperparts and underparts may be fleeting, a good pair of binoculars of, say, 7×50 magnification and diameter is essential.

Taking notes of seabirds seen is always a good plan. It provides a record, avoids the pitfalls of wishful thinking, and is invaluable for later verification. The following points should be noted, and if possible accompanied by a sketch, with arrows pointing to any principal features of plumage colours, and wing and tail shape:

1. Size and **build.**	Size: very large, large, medium, or small.
	Build: heavy, compact, light or slender.
2. Manner of flight.	Wings: straight or angled.
	Wing beats: slow, rapid, fluttering or gliding on fixed pinions.
	Height: above ship or close to surface.
3. Wings.	Short and broad, or long and narrow.
4. Tail.	Very long, short and round, square or wedge-shaped.
5. Plumage colours.	Head; back and upperwing; underparts and underwing; rump; tail; bill and legs.
6. Behaviour and **voice.**	Behaviour; solitary or in flocks, active or sluggish.
	Voice: noisy or silent, harsh or pleasing.

SEABIRD SURVIVAL

The number of different seabird species is very small in comparison with landbirds, and yet the total number of seabirds in the world far exceeds that of landbirds. The wide global distribution and close association with the sea favours suitable breeding localities remote in many cases from civilisation or inaccessible from interference. Moreover, the sea provides an inexhaustible food supply under all conditions irrespective of extremes of weather.

Selective diets: Viewing the immense colonies of breeding seabirds, not only of identical species, which pack every ledge on the high cliffs of mainlands or remote islands, one might question the inexhaustibility of the adjacent food supply. Yet an ecological balance is achieved, for each species demands its own particularly selective diet. One species will be seen to be bringing back small sprats to its young caught from near the surface, another species will be pursuing larger fish or marine life among the shallow bottom weed, whilst a third will be working further to seaward watching for shoals of larger fish, either diving from a height or pursuing them at deeper depths. It has been noticed that, where mass breeding colonies of different species of terns nest in close proximity, some species will fly further afield than others to collect food suitable for their young.

Natural hazards: As in all other wildlife a chain of predation is equally applicable to seabirds. Giant petrels, Skuas, Frigate-birds and the larger gulls pirate both eggs and young of more defenceless species. Attack may occasionally come from beneath the sea for both seals and large predatory fish may drag some unsuspecting seabird beneath the surface. The penguins are particularly vulnerable to the Leopard Seal. Such hazards have little effect on ultimate numbers.

Disasters: Local disasters from uncontrollable elements have occurred occasionally. At rare intervals obscure changes in the direction and surface temperature of ocean currects, the warm surface water causing the destruction of both plankton and small fish has caused mass starvation to millions of seabirds. Such a case has occurred off the west coast of South America in the region of Peru on more than one occasion, where a warm tropical current has unexpectedly intruded into the cold Humboldt current. Huge numbers of Peruvian Boobies starved or were unable to feed their offspring. In another form a phenomenon known as 'The Red Tide' occurred off the coast line of South Africa, caused, it was believed, through an unusual outfall of silt from flooded rivers. This created a multiplication of one-celled organisms containing a substance highly poisonous to seabirds. A more recent cause of local disasters has arisen from the great increase in the number of oil tankers now delivering oil to almost every commercial port in the world. Although waste oil on flushing out tanks on departure should not be carried out until ships are far out to sea, this has frequently been disregarded. Floating oil slicks close to coasts have resulted in very large numbers of seabirds, alcids in particular, being contaminated with fatal results. The dangers from floating oily and chemical pollution of the sea through dumping highly toxic waste locally offshore, although very real, fortunately affects only local colonies of seabirds; in view of their vast distribution elsewhere the danger of extinction is small.

SEABIRDS ON THE DANGER LIST. The following list at present quoted in the Red Data Book by the International Union for the Conservation of Nature and the International Council for Bird Preservation shows these species whose future existence may be in danger. Not all are given the same status, some being severely threatened while others have small and vulnerable populations which require to be watched:

Short-tailed Albatross (*Diomedea albatrus*), Audouin's Gull (*Larus audouinii*), Abbott's Booby (*Sula abbotti*), King Shag (*Phalacrocorax c. carunculatus*), Black-capped Petrel (*Pterodroma hasitata*), Ascension Frigate-bird (*Fregata aquila*), Reunion Petrel (*Pterodroma aterrima*), Galapagos Penguin (*Spheniscus mendiculus*), Waved Albatross (*Diomedea irrorata*), Hawaiian Petrel (*Pterodroma phaeopygia*), Flightless Cormorant (*Nannopterum harrisi*), Cahow (*Pterodroma cahow*), Macgillivray's Petrel (*Pterodroma macgillivrayi*).

SEABIRDS ON BOARD

Seabirds, unlike land birds at sea, have no need to use ships as resting places. Usually when they are found on deck they have arrived during the night, either attracted by the ship's lights or, perhaps, blown across the ship in heavy weather and striking some portion of the ship's structure have come to grief.

Shearwaters and petrels and even tropic-birds are quite unable to take wing of their own accord from the deck, shuffling forward awkwardly on their webbed feet which are set far back in the body, and trailing their long wings. Storm-petrels and tropic-birds are the species most often found on ships, followed by Sooty Terns. Tropic-birds often follow ships at night and Sooty Terns have a similar habit though to a lesser extent. They are both known to feed off squid, which tend to rise to the surface at night, and the birds may pick up the ships during dusk and search for squid churned up by the propellers.

Southern Great Skuas have also been known to alight on board when they occur at sea off southern Australia.

There is one family however that quite frequently and deliberately makes use of a ship at sea – the boobies – and particularly the Red-footed Booby. In the tropics boobies will perch usually on the forecastle head from which vantage point they will plummet again and again as flying fish break water from the bow, catching them in the air, landing in the sea to devour them, and returning once again to their perch. They have been known to remain on board for hours.

When ships are in harbour gulls which are constantly foraging for scraps of food become unusually tame and use a ship's structure or any other handy perching place. This is not so at sea; gulls will follow astern or sail above a ship but usually will not perch on board although they may be tempted to alight momentarily or the bulwarks where food has been specially placed.

LAND BIRDS AT SEA

A passenger in a ship at sea may be quite unaware of land birds in flight in the sky above and may not even notice a little bird flying at low level close alongside the ship making desperate efforts to alight on board. But vary large numbers of land birds alight on ships, not only when the ship's route coincides with a particular migration fly path, but also far out in the oceans where their presence may be least expected.

For land birds, particularly on migration, the presence of a ship at sea must be hailed as a haven of rest, for a great many birds that take shelter are lost or storm-driven and exhausted, and so often appear remarkably tame. Frequently they feel no compulsion to leave, and find themselves being given assisted passages far from their intended destinations. A racing pigeon found on board a ship 400 miles west of Spain and, from its ring number, due to go home to Manchester should have known better – for it was perfectly free to fly away. It stayed on board through the Panama Canal and finally took off towards the Galapagos Islands. Months later its owner was informed!

Three Indian Crows remained with a ship from the moment it left Colombo until its destination in Geelong Harbour, in Victoria, Australia.

One could quote many other such cases and others where land birds varying from White Storks, Egrets, Bitterns, Ospreys and exotic birds have come on board far out to sea, but perhaps the relatively common occurrence of the Peregrine Falcon deserves mention. Peregrines have alighted on ships well out in the ocean – certainly in the Atlantic, Pacific and Indian Oceans, Mediterranean and Red Seas – and made themselves entirely at home perching nearly always high up on the fore truck or platform below the emergency steaming light.

The routes on which the greatest number and variety are likely to occur are primarily those passing through the Mediterranean; the Red Sea; the sea route from the British Isles to Cape Town while passing the bulge of northwest Africa; and off the east coast of North America and Canada.

CARE AND FEEDING

Birds which arrive on board ships at sea and allow themselves to be collected in the hand are usually in an exhausted state, often wet and bedraggled, and all primarily in need of rest, warmth and shelter.

In Ocean Weather Ships on station at sea, where a considerable number and variety of small landbirds seek shelter at intervals, the most convenient arrangement is to construct a commodious cage some 36 inches long, 20 inches high and 14 inches in depth, the floor, ends and back of plywood, the roof of hardboard, the front of vertical wire rods, i.e. barred ½" apart. A vertical barred front is preferable to wire netting as birds fluttering against bars do not injure their faces so easily. If an entrance flap is fitted in the roof it can be large enough to collect birds from all quarters of the cage. A muslin front cover should be arranged which will let in light and yet give air and a feeling of seclusion and keep the birds quiet. The cage should be placed in a secure warm place, and judgment must be used as to the types of birds which can be placed together. At this stage a little water should be provided in a receptacle which will not easily tip up.

As an ad hoc arrangement any open topped large cardboard box perforated plentifully with air holes and covered with muslin will do.

When birds are seen to have 'perked up' the moment has come to provide food. At NO times should oceanic seabirds be placed in a bath of water.

It is rarely possible to provide the natural diet which most species would feed upon in normal freedom. The following suggestions aim to cover a possible 'best' where feed can be stocked in advance, as in Ocean Weather Ships. A good general point in the case of the smaller insectivorous and seed eating landbirds is to remember that they may not recognise inert food, but that their attention may be stimulated by mixing among the feed a number of nice wriggling mealworms or maggots.

Seed-eating small landbirds. Millet on the stalk is always an attraction. In addition canary seed, white millet, and hemp seed can be obtained as mixtures sold by dealers as 'Aviary Mixture', 'Finch Mixture', 'Swoop' etc. Large seed eating birds such as Jays, less likely to come on board, can be tempted with grain. Pigeons will also take readily to uncooked rice.

Insectivorous birds. Mealworms are valuable. Suitable proprietary foods are 'Activite', 'Stimulite', 'Prosecto' or 'Sluis'. Soaked chopped currants and dried or fresh fruit chopped small. 'Starter Crumbs' used for rearing poultry chicks, finely chopped hard-boiled egg or finely grated cheese are valuable alternatives.

Ducks, geese, herons, egrets. Soaked bread, cereals, chopped green vegetable for ducks and geese; finely minced raw meat without fat or tissue and hard-boiled egg for herons, egrets.

Waders, hawks, owls, large thrushes. Finely minced raw meat without fat or tissue, for hawks and owls small squares of raw meat.

Seabirds. Chopped fresh raw fish, finely chopped minced raw meat. Seabirds frequently need feeding forcibly at the outset.

In the absence of special foods. For small landbirds soft breadcrumbs and finely chopped hard-boiled egg or finely grated cheese. For larger seed-eating landbirds – softly-boiled rice or porridge oats can be tried.

Feed should be put in the cages or boxes making sure there is sufficient light and not too much at once. Where birds are too big to cage their radius of action should be restricted so that food is always in view.

Water must always be available.

Mealworms require warmth to keep them alive and should be kept in a tin with holes pierced in the lid at a temperature of say 60°F. They should also be provided with some food, i.e. porridge oats, and occasionally fresh pieces of apple skin, skin will make them fatter. The skin should be removed before it goes mouldy. Maggots can be kept alive for some time but they must be kept in a cool temperature to prevent them pupating.

Mealworms can be bred under the following conditions: Put about 3 inches of barley meal mixed with maize meal in a shallow wooden box covered securely with gauze or muslin for ventilation. Put sheets of crumpled newspaper amongst the meal in layers. Put ½ inch slices of carrot on top of bran and add fresh slices occasionally.

¼lb of mealworms is sufficient to start a colony which takes a little time to get started. Keep in a warm place, 85°F is optimum temperature. Extreme cold will kill colony. Mealworms should not be used as feed until adult beetles have developed and are breeding.

TREATMENT OF OILED SEABIRDS ON BOARD SHIP

An increasing number of seabirds contaminated with oil are arriving on board ships at sea. Ships are not in a position to undertake lengthy rehabilitation but the following action and treatment has proved successful in several cases.

Attempts to clean should not start immediately. At first the bird should be kept *warm* and *quiet* securely wrapped in a cloth with its head and legs only protruding to prevent it preening and thus swallowing more oil, and placed in a suitable cardboard box with ventilation. The feet should be treated with a little ointment or hand cream to prevent cracking.

After the bird has rested an attempt should be made first at suitable feeding or force feeding. Thereafter wash the affected parts in a warm solution of commercial washing-up liquid, ⅛th pint of detergent to 1 gallon of hand hot water at about 105°F holding the affected parts submerged, separating the feathers. A second similar wash is needed usually. Finally rinse in clean hand hot water. Dry by mopping with a clean cloth or in front of a warm 'air duct' and place at once in a *really warm place* in its covered box, e.g. under a hot towel rail, to rest.

Allow the bird to preen and to continue feeding as it gains strength and mobility. Do not launch it into the air until it shows clearly through wing flapping that it is ready and eager to fly away.

THE BIRDS

An Emperor Penguin rookery, with a McCormick's Skua looking for unprotected eggs or dead chicks.

PENGUINS Spheniscidae

Penguins occur solely in the southern hemisphere, breeding and ranging from the Antarctic continent throughout the sub-antarctic islands from Cape Horn to New Zealand, extending to the southern coasts of S. America, S. Africa, Australia and New Zealand. Only the Emperor Penguin and Adelie Penguin breed on the south polar continent itself. The Galapagos Penguin takes advantage of the northern limit of the cold Humboldt Current to breed on the Galapagos Is., ranging only a few degrees south of the Equator.

Apart from the breeding and moulting period at their rookeries penguins spend their entire time at sea, dispersing in some cases northwards during the southern winter.

They are seldom seen on the sea routes. When they are observed, usually at no great distance from coasts, they are not easy to identify except by close observation of the pattern of their head, neck and bill, for they swim low in the water.

Penguins travel at great speed underwater using their flippers to propel them and their feet stretched out behind as rudders. They are sometimes seen progressing in a series of leaps clear of the water in the manner of porpoises. They feed principally on fish.

ADULT PENGUINS
Swimming

Emperor, p.7

King, p.7

Gentoo, p.7

Chin-strap, p.8

Adelie, p.7

Jackass, p.11
other *Spheniscus*
similar

Rock-hopper, p.9

Macaroni, p

JUVENILE PENGUINS
Swimming

Emperor, p.7

King, p.7

Gentoo, p.7

Adelie, p.7

Royal, p.9

Jackass, p.11 other
Spheniscus are similar

Nesting and young

These species nest in colonies on or near the shore, on islands or coasts. They may take *c*. 4–7 years to reach maturity before breeding. The largest species have no nest; some species have open nests on bare ground lined with nearby material such as plant fragments or stones; while others nest among rocks, in crevices and hollows, or in burrows, and nests are composed of a variety of debris carried into these. The species using more open sites often nest very close together. The eggs of the largest species are pear-shaped but those of smaller species are more rounded. The eggs have an irregular white, chalk-like outer layer on a greenish-white shell, and often become very dirty during incubation. The clutch varies from 1 in the larger species to 2–3 in the smaller penguins, but *Eudyptes* species usually lay two, generally discarding the first egg and only incubating one. The Emperor and King Penguins incubate with the egg resting on top of the feet and covered by a fold of feathered skin from the belly. The other species incubate in a more normal manner. The Little or Blue Penguin is double-brooded.

Incubation in smaller species is from 33–40 days. Both adults incubate the periods of alternate sitting varying with the species from 1 to 2½ weeks. The chicks have two successive coats of thick grey or brown down. They are brooded by the adults for 2–3 weeks. After this those nesting in more open colonies gather together in large numbers where they are visited by the parents for feeding. Those nesting in burrows tend to remain there until fledged. The young are fed by regurgitation, taking the food from inside the mouth of the adult. They become very large and fat before the final growth of feathers, appearing larger than the parents. The fledging periods usually varies from 7–10 weeks.

The King and Emperor Penguins have highly specialised breeding cycles. The growth period of the young necessitates a cycle including the winter months. In the King Penguin eggs may be laid from late November to April (late spring to early autumn in the southern hemisphere), and two cycles may be fitted into a three-year period. Incubation is shared by both birds sitting for periods of *c*. 2 weeks, and lasts for 53–55 days. The young are fed sparingly during the winter months and lose considerable weight, regaining this in the spring, but having remained with the adults for 10–13 months before leaving. The Emperor Penguin eggs are laid in the autumn (April onwards in the southern hemisphere). The female leaves and the male incubates alone for *c*. 64 days (during winter darkness), and then begins feeding the newly-hatched young with a crop secretion. The female then returns and feeds the chick for 2–3 weeks. Then both adults feed it and the chick grows rapidly. After *c*. 4 months the chick feathers and leaves, although only partly grown, continuing to grow in its first year.

General Distribution of Penguins on Continental Coasts

B = breeds.   *S* = straggler.   *W* = in southern winter months.

ANTARCTIC MAINLAND Emperor Penguin. Adelie Penguin.
AUSTRALIA Little or Blue Penguin, southern coasts, *B*. Fiordland Crested Penguin *S*, *W*.
NEW ZEALAND Little or Blue Penguin *B*. Erect-crested or Big-crested Penguin *W*. Fiordland Crested Penguin *B*. White-flippered Penguin *B*. Yellow-eyed Penguin *B*. Snares Crested Penguin *S* (breeds on Snares Is.). Royal Penguin *S*.

SOUTH AMERICA Humboldt Penguin, west coast, *B*. Magellan Penguin, southern east and west coasts *B*. Rock-hopper Penguin, southern east coast *W*.

SOUTH AFRICA Jackass Penguin, southern east and west coasts, *B*. Rock-hopper Penguin *S*, *W*.

For the purpose of defining height, penguins have been indicated as follows: Large: over 36 ins, 91 cm. Medium: 24–36 ins, 61–91 cm. Small: 20 ins, 51 cm and below.

KING PENGUIN *Aptenodytes patagonica* **Pages 4, 5 and Pl. 1**
Large, 36–38 ins, 91–96 cm. A handsome penguin rather smaller than Emperor Penguin. Top of head, cheeks and throat black; remainder of upperparts bluish-grey. Foreneck edged on each side by an orange band extending into a lozenge-shaped orange patch around the sides of the back of the head. An orange patch on foreneck, below which underparts white with narrow black line down each side of breast. Bill long, black with an orange-reddish slash at base of lower mandible. Legs black. Immatures similar but patches on foreneck yellow, and bill entirely black.
Stance very erect. Incubates egg in similar manner to Emperor Penguin.
RANGE: Southern oceans breeding on Staten I. South Georgia, Falkland Is, Marion, Crozet, Kerguelen, Heard, and Macquarie Is. Map 1.

EMPEROR PENGUIN *Aptenodytes forsteri* **Pages 4, 5 and Pl. 1**
Large, 48 ins, 122 cm. The largest penguin, and with the much smaller Adelie Penguin the only penguin species which breed on the antarctic continent. Top of head, cheeks, chin and throat black; remainder of upperparts bluish-grey. A wide orange-yellow semi-circular band sweeps around the sides of the upper neck merging into the white foreneck, and a black band borders the front of the shoulder ending in a point at the lower neck. Underparts and under-surface of flipper white. Bill long, bluish-black, curving downwards towards tip, showing a red slash along base of lower mandible. Legs black. Immature similar but band on sides of neck white.
Unique among penguins in incubating its one egg during period of total antarctic winter darkness. Stands upright with egg balanced on feet and covered by pouch of skin.
RANGE: Antarctic continent and seas to edge of pack ice. Map 2.

GENTOO PENGUIN *Pygoscelis papua* **Pages 4, 5 and Pl. 1**
Medium, 30 ins, 76 cm. Head, neck and throat brownish-black. A conspicuous white band extends over the back of the head from eye to eye. Remainder of upperparts slate-grey; underparts white. Flipper edged with white, underside white, black at tip. Bill orange or red, upper edge of upper mandible black. Legs orange. Immature similar but some grey mottling on throat. Easily distinguished at a distance by white band on head. Swims with head and back above water.
RANGE: Islands adjacent to Antarctica, breeding also at S. Shetlands, S. Orkneys, S. Georgia, Falkland, Staten, Bouvet, Marion, Crozet, Kerguelen, Heard and Macquarie Is. Map 3.

ADELIE PENGUIN *Pygoscelis adeliae* **Pages 4, 5 and Pl. 1**
Medium, 30 ins, 76 cm. Top of head, cheeks and throat black, the black extending to a point on foreneck, eyelids white. Upperparts bluish-black. Underparts conspicuously white. The stubby bill brick red; legs pinkish-white; tail noticeably long.

Immature similar but throat white; eyelids black; bill black.

A most engaging and inquisitive penguin. Stance upright; walks with waddling gait, frequently tobogganning over snow on its breast; swims very low in water with back submerged; 'porpoises' out of water at times.

RANGE Antarctic seas to outer edge of pack ice. Breeds on coast of Antarctica, and adjacent sub-antarctica islands, S. Shetlands, S. Orkneys, S. Sandwich Is. and Bouvet I. Map 4.

CHIN-STRAP or BEARDED PENGUIN   *Pygoscelis antarctica*
Page 4 and Pl 1

Medium, 30 ins, 76 cm. Crown and forehead black, remainder of upperparts bluish-grey. Sides of head, throat, neck and underparts white. A black line like a chin-strap extends round the throat from ear to ear. Under-surface of flipper white, outer margin black. Bill black, legs pinkish-white. Immatures similar.

Facial marking and chin strap unlike any other penguin.

RANGE: Antarctic seas and adjacent islands, breeding also at S. Shetlands, S. Orkneys, S. Sandwich Is., S. Georgia, Bouvet and Heard Is.   Map 5.

FIORDLAND CRESTED PENGUIN   *Eudyptes pachyrhynchus*   Pl. 2

Medium, 28 ins, 71 cm. Forehead and crown bluish-black, cheeks, chin and throat dark slate-grey, white streaks showing on cheeks. Pale line of yellow feathers extends from nostril, above the eye, along sides of crown, the posterior feathers neither elongated nor drooping. Underparts white; iris bright reddish-brown; bill reddish-brown; legs pale flesh-colour, soles black. Immatures similar but chin and throat whitish, and features of crest only partially developed.

RANGE: Breeds on southern and south-western coasts of South Island, New Zealand. Occurs occasionally on coasts of Tasmania and Southern Australia.   Map 6.

SNARES CRESTED PENGUIN   *Eudyptes robustus*   Pl. 2

Medium, 29 ins, 73 cm. Similar to the Fiordland Crested Penguin but more robust, darker in colour, especially about the chin, throat and cheeks which are almost black, feathers being dark based. The yellow superciliary crest is brighter and narrower with a more bushy end. Bill large with pink not grey skin at the corner; light reddish-brown. Legs flesh-colour. Immatures similar but chin and throat whitish, and feathers of crest only partially developed.

RANGE: Breeds only at Snares Is., New Zealand, and wanders to nearby parts of South Island.   Map 7.

ERECT-CRESTED or BIG-CRESTED PENGUIN   *Eudyptes sclateri*   Pl. 2

Medium, 28 ins, 71 cm. Whole head, chin, throat and upperparts bluish-black; underparts white. A bright yellow crest extends on each side from the base of the bill, above the eye to the back of the crown. When erected, this curves up sharply from the gape culminating as a bristle at the back of the crown. Iris red; bill light brown; legs pale flesh-coloured with black soles.

Immatures are similar but the chin and throat are mottled and the yellow crest is barely visible.

RANGE: Breeds on Bounty Is., Antipodes, Campbell and Auckland Is. Visits Cook Strait in southern winter. Stragglers reach Tasmania and Southern Australia.   Map 8.

ROCK-HOPPER PENGUIN *Eudyptes crestatus* **Page 4 and Pl. 2**
Medium, 25 ins, 63 cm. Head, sides of face, chin and throat blackish-slate, blacker on crown with slightly elongated feathers. Remainder of upperparts bluish-grey; underparts pure white. A narrow line of golden-yellow feathers extends from behind the nostril feathers, above the eye and along the sides of the crown terminating in greatly elongated plumes. Iris red; bill dull orange-red; legs flesh-colour, soles black.

Immatures are similar but show an ashy-white chin, and a faint whitish-yellow eyebrow with no elongated plumes.

RANGE: Breeds at Tierra del Fuego, Falkland Is., Tristan da Cunha, Gough, Prince Edward, Marion, Crozet, St Paul, Amsterdam Is., Kerguelen, Heard Is. and Bounty, Antipodes, Aukland, Campbell, Snares and Macquarie Is. off New Zealand. Stragglers sometimes occur off the southern tip of Africa and western and southern coasts of Australia. Map 9.

ROYAL PENGUIN *Eudyptes schlegeli* **Page 5 and Pl. 2**
Medium, 26–30 ins, 66–76 cm. Upperparts light bluish-grey; sides of head and neck, chin, throat and underparts white. Some species have the sides of the face grey but there may be considerable variation. An orange crest of elongated plumes extends from the centre and sides of the forehead backwards and downwards on either side behind the eye. Eyes bright geranium-red; bill pale reddish-brown; legs flesh-coloured, soles black. Immatures similar to adult but lack the golden plumes.

Adults differ from other crested penguins in their white or partially grey cheeks and throats.

RANGE: Breeds on Macquarie I. A straggler to New Zealand coasts. Not mapped.

light phase | dark phase

ROYAL PENGUIN. There is considerable variation in the pattern of facial and head plumage. Most have chin, throat and side of head white; others are more or less greyish and some even dark slate grey, almost like a Macaroni Penguin.

MACARONI PENGUIN *Eudyptes chrysolophus* **Page 4 and Pl. 2**
Medium, 26–30 ins, 66–76 cm. Head, chin and throat black, remainder of upperparts dark bluish-grey. Underparts white. Across the forehead and along the sides of the crown a series of long golden feathers occur having black pointed tips. The longest golden plumes extend above and behind the eye. Flipper bluish-grey above, inner margin with white edge, underneath white with black outer margin. Bill black with reddish tip, pink at base. Legs pinkish. Immatures similar but plumes only partially developed and yellow.

Plumes in the Rock-hopper Penguin are pale yellow and do not meet across the forehead.
RANGE: Islands adjacent to Antarctica, and breeds also at S. Shetlands, S. Orkneys, S. Sandwich Is., S. Georgia, Falkland Is., Bouvet, Prince Edward, Marion, Kerguelen and Heard Is.   Map 10.

YELLOW-EYED PENGUIN   *Megadyptes antipodes*   **Pl. 2**
Medium, 30 ins, 76 cm. Upperparts slate-grey. Forehead and crown pale golden showing black shaft stripes; cheeks and chin pale golden; throat and sides of neck brown; remainder of underparts white. A pale yellow band of short feathers extends from behind the eye backwards encircling the. crown. Iris yellow; bill flesh-coloured, dull brown on culmen and at tip of mandibles; legs pale flesh-coloured.
Immatures are similar but yellow band is confined to the sides of the head only.
RANGE: Breeds on east coast of South Island, New Zealand, and at Stewart I., Auckland and Campbell Is., and occurs occasionally in the Cook Strait.   Map 11.

LITTLE or BLUE PENGUIN   *Eudyptula minor*   **Pl. 2**
Small, 16 ins, 40 cm. Crown, hindneck and upperparts deep slate-blue; sides of face below eyes grey; remainder of face, chin, throat and underparts white. Iris silver-grey; bill short and stout, black; legs pale flesh-coloured, soles black. Immatures similar but upperparts brighter blue.
RANGE: Breeds all round coast of South Island, New Zealand, Tasmania and southern and south-western coasts of Australia.   Map 12.

WHITE-FLIPPERED PENGUIN   *Eudyptula albosignata*   **Pl. 2**
Small, 16 ins, 42 cm. Crown, hindneck and upperparts pale slate-grey; sides of face below eyes, chin, throat and underparts white. Iris silver-grey; bill black; legs pale flesh-coloured, black on soles. Immatures similar.
Very similar and cannot be distinguished from Little Penguin in the water. On land a broad white margin on the upper side of both edges of the flippers, and in males a central white patch also serves to distinguish it.
RANGE: Breeds on Banks Peninsula on east coast of New Zealand and occurs in the Cook Strait.   Map 13.

normal   flavistic   albino

All penguins could show flavistic or albino phases like these Jackass Penguins. Where more than one species occurs, identification of these rare colour mutations is very difficult, except by size and bill shapes.

JACKASS PENGUIN *Spheniscus demersus*   **Pages 4, 5, 10 and Pl. 1**
Medium, 25–27 ins, 63–68 cm. Forehead, crown, sides of face, chin, throat and remainder of upperparts black; underparts white. A white band extends from the base of the upper mandible, above the eye, curving downwards dividing the black crown from the black sides of face and joining the white underparts. A very narrow black horseshoe band crosses the breast and extends along the sides to the flanks. Bill stout and rather long, black with a grey transverse bar. Legs black, mottled with grey, soles black. Immatures have black upperparts and plain white underparts.
    The only penguin common to the southern coasts of South Africa.
RANGE: From Angola on west coast to Natal on east coast. Breeds on islands off the S. African coast.   Map 14.

HUMBOLDT PENGUIN *Spheniscus humboldti*   **Pl. 1**
Medium, 27 ins, 68 cm. Forehead, crown, sides of head and throat black, upperparts slate-grey. Chin and underparts white. A narrow white band extends from the base of the bill around the sides of the crown on each side continuing round the black throat.
    A single black horseshoe band surrounds the breast extending down the sides to the tail. Bill stout, blackish, flesh-coloured at base; legs blackish, soles black.
    Immatures show no horseshoe band. The chin, throat and sides of head are grey; sides and front of neck dark brown.
    Considerably larger than Galapagos Penguin, has one horseshoe band only and ranges much further to the south.
RANGE: West coast of S. America from Peru to about 35°S. where it overlaps with Magellan Penguin.   Map 15.

MAGELLAN PENGUIN *Spheniscus magellanicus*   **Pl. 1**
Medium, 28 ins, 71 cm. Crown, sides of face and throat black; chin white. Remainder of upperparts slate-grey. A white band extends from the base of the bill above the eye, curving downwards dividing the black crown from sides of face and running under the black throat. A black band extends around the white foreneck, and an additional black horseshoe band crosses the breast and extends down the sides to the flanks. Bill blackish; legs mottled blackish, soles black.
    Immatures are similar but the throat and the upper band on foreneck dark grey.
    Overlaps at its extreme northern range on west coast of S. America with Humboldt Penguin which shows only a single horseshoe band.
RANGE: Breeds on coasts and islands on west coast of Chile and Juan Fernandez, on Staten I., Tierra del Fuego, Falkland Is., and on east coast north to Point Tombo, 44°S., 65°20′W.   Map 16.

GALAPAGOS PENGUIN *Spheniscus mendiculus*   **Pl. 1**
Small, 20 ins, 50 cm. Forehead, crown, sides of head and throat black, upperparts slate-grey. Chin and underparts white. A narrow white band extends from the base of the bill around the sides of the crown on each side, continuing round the black throat. A black band surrounds the white underparts beneath the foreneck, and an additional black horseshoe band surrounds the breast extending down the sides. Bill has a black upper mandible and yellow lower mandible with black tip. Legs black with white mottling, soles black.
    Breeds only on the Galapagos Is. and rarely seen at any distance from the islands. Cannot be confused with any other penguin.   Not mapped.

Black-browed Albatrosses

ALBATROSSES   Diomedeidae

Albatrosses are easily recognised in flight by their large size, very long narrow wings and distinctive flight. The smaller albatrosses, those having dark backs and upperwings, are often referred to by seafarers as "Mollymawks". Of the thirteen species, nine are confined to the southern oceans, three to the N. Pacific and one to the tropics.

In the most usual flight pattern they plane on flexed pinions with barely a wing beat, gaining height into the wind while losing some air speed, then turning across wind, swooping downwards towards the sea to leeward, thus gaining speed, before banking sharply again into the wind. This they repeat for hours on end. In high winds their wings may be raked back steeply from the carpal joint. They will alight readily on the sea, and find it necessary to run along the surface into the wind before becoming airborne. Their webbed feet are carried open in flight on each side of the tail.

A distinctive feature is the nature of the stout hooked bill, consisting of a number of horny plates, the nostril openings being placed on each side of the middle plate of the upper mandible in short tubes.

In adults the colour pattern of upper- and underwing and the particular colour of their bills provides the best clue to their identity, but the variable colour of immature plumage can be confusing.

In the open sea albatrosses feed from the surface largely on squid and krill, also eating fish, usually only dipping the head and bill beneath the surface. They are equally ready to eat blubber and floating refuse. Probably for this reason they will follow ships for long distances by day, alighting at the stern with wings raised and joining with Giant Petrels, Cape Pigeons and other species in a scramble for scraps thrown overboard from the galley.

Nesting and young

These nest on islands where sites provide good facilities for take-off. In general the incubation, fledging and maturation periods are longer in the larger species. Maturation is slow and birds may not breed until 6–10 years old. Nest sites may be bare hollows in tropical species but are usually largish cones of mud and vegetable matter with a hollow in the top. A single large egg is laid, white or finely marked with red at the larger end. Incubation varies from 60–70 days in smaller species to c. 80 days in larger ones. The male takes the first period after the female has laid the egg. Periods of alternate sitting may be 1½–3 weeks long. The chick has two successive coats of pale grey or whitish down, and is brooded by a parent for the first 3–5 weeks after which it is visited and fed at intervals, with apparently no desertion period, chicks having been seen to be fed at intervals until the time of departure. The chicks are fed on regurgitated food, placing the bill inside the adult's and at right angles to it. Fledging varies from 4–4½ months in smaller species to 9 months in the Wandering Albatross. In the latter the total cycle is 11 months, and successful breeders breed only once in two years.

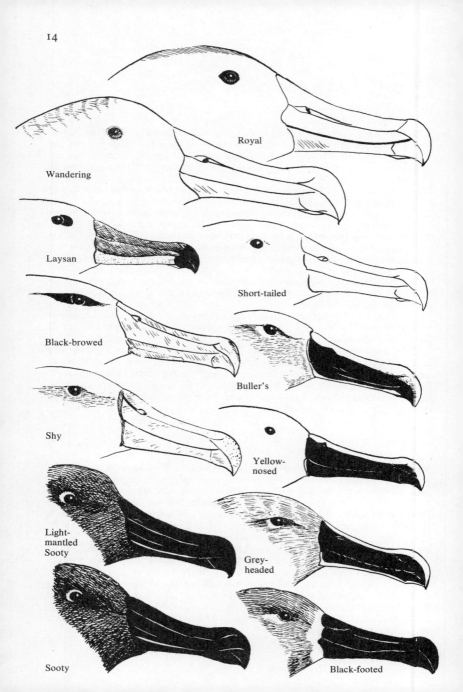

Royal

Wandering

Laysan

Short-tailed

Black-browed

Buller's

Shy

Yellow-nosed

Light-mantled Sooty

Grey-headed

Sooty

Black-footed

BILLS OF ALBATROSSES

After the wing pattern, the colour of albatross bills are a very important character for the identification of species.

Royal Albatross, *Diomedea epomophora*, p.17
Bill faintly pink, cutting edges of both mandibles black.

Wandering Albatross, *Diomedea exulans*, p.16
Bill flesh-coloured.

Laysan Albatross, *Diomedea immutabilis*, p.18
Bill greyish; base of the mandible yellow.

Short-tailed Albatross, *Diomedea albatrus*, p.17
Bill flesh-coloured.

Black-browed Albatross, *Diomedea melanophris*, p.18
Bill yellow with a pink tip.

Shy Albatross, *Diomedea cauta*, p.19
Bill grey, with distinct orange tip; bluish lateral plates run up in front of eye; dark horseshoe stripe behind nostril.

Buller's Albatross, *Diomedea bulleri*, p.19
Bill greyish black, with a yellow stripe along the upper and mandibles. Upper plate widens noticeably at base.

Yellow-nosed Albatross, *Diomedea chlororhynchos*, p.19
Bill black, with a bright yellow line along the ridge of the upper mandible; bright orange tip.

Grey-headed Albatross, *Diomedea chrysostoma*, p.20
Bill blackish; yellow stripe along upper and lower mandibles, ending with bright pink tip.

Light-mantled Sooty Albatross, *Phoebetria palpebrata*, p.21
Bill black with pale blue line along the side.

Sooty Albatross, *Phoebetria fusca*, p. 20
Bill black, with a yellow line along lower mandible.

Black-footed Albatross, *Diomedea nigriceps*, p.17
Bill dark brown.

WANDERING ALBATROSS *Diomedea exulans*   **Page 14 and Pl. 3**
Outsize, 44–48 ins, 117 cm. Wing-span 114–130 ins, 324 cm. The Wandering
Albatross takes many years to adopt full adult plumage and is more often seen in
one of its intermediate phases. The full adult is pure white below, except for a
narrow black border along the trailing edge of the wing and the black primary wing
tips. Back is pure white in extreme southern breeding birds, in others shows a few
dark vermiculations. Upper wing surfaces white with a little dark speckling.
Females sometimes carry a dark crown patch on their white heads. Eyes are dark
brown; bill massive, pale flesh-coloured; legs pale flesh-coloured.
   In the youngest immatures only the side of the face, throat and part of the
underwing are white, the remainder of the body, wings and tail brown. At a later
stage the underparts become progressively whiter, the last brown appearing as a
mottled brown band across the chest. On the upperparts the mantle is the first to
become mottled white, the brown receding from neck to tail. The upper wings do
not begin to turn white until the body is more or less clear of mottling. At this stage a
white patch appears on each upper wing as the white plumage spreads across the
wings. Finally the brown tail is replaced by white. The bill, whitish in young birds
becomes flesh-coloured as do the legs. The whole development to full adult plumage will cover probably not less than five years.
   Note: In flight the bill is usually angled slightly downwards, and at a distance the
heavy bill, peaked crown and humped back are characteristic.
RANGE: Throughout the southern oceans between approximately 60°S. and 25°S.,
but tends to disperse further north in the southern winter and has been met with at
15°S. Breeds at S. Georgia, Tristan da Cunha, Gough, Marion and Crozet Is.,
Amsterdam and St. Paul Is., Kerguelen I., Campbell, Antipodes and Auckland Is.
and Macquarie I.   Map 17.

WANDERING ALBATROSS. Typical courting display at breeding colonies accompanied by
hoarse cries and groaning prior to mating.

ROYAL ALBATROSS *Diomedea epomophora*   **Page 14 and Pl. 3**
(A) outsize, 48 ins, 122 cm. Wing-span 120 ins, 305 cm. Adult; (B) mostly white,
primaries and secondaries black, thin dark margin to trailing edge of underwing;
(C) bill faintly pink, cutting edges of both mandibles black, observable at sea at
close range; (D) legs bluish-white; (E) immatures similar to adults.
RANGE: Largely localised to seas around New Zealand, although a few reach the
coastal waters off the south of S. America, and stragglers off southern Australia.
RACES:
ROYAL ALBATROSS *Diomedea e. epomophora*   **Page 14 and Pl. 3**
Breeds on Campbell and Auckland Is.; (B) Traces of grey on some scapulars and
wing-coverts, pure white in most southerly ranging birds.   Map 18.
ROYAL ALBATROSS (Northern Race) *Diomedea e. sanfordi*   **Pl. 3**
Breeds on Chatham I. and Otago Peninsula; (B) upperwings show variable dark
flecking, sometimes entirely dark blackish-brown.   Map 18.

WAVED ALBATROSS *Diomedea irrorata*   **Pl. 4**
Very large, 35 ins, 89 cm. Wing-span 82 ins, 208 cm. In adults the head and neck are
white, nape noticeably tinged with buff, upper back and rump dusky. The back,
wings and tail are greyish-brown, and the underparts and underwings dusky-white.
The bill is yellow and legs bluish-white. Young birds have an overall brownish
plumage.
   Note: The Waved Albatross is the only albatross existing entirely within the
tropics.
RANGE: Breeds on the Galapagos Is. and winters over the Humboldt Current off
Ecuador and Peru.   Map 19.

SHORT-TAILED ALBATROSS *Diomedea albatrus*   **Page 14 and Pl. 3**
Outsize, 37 ins, 94 cm. Wing-span 84 ins, 213 cm. Adult in fully developed plumage
is white except for totally black upperwings and a black band on tail. The back
between the wings is white. The white head and nape are diffused with yellow. The
bill is pink and proportionally large; around its base a thin conspicuous black line
extending back along edge of mouth to gape. Legs flesh-colour. Fully fledged
juveniles are completely black, replaced progressively as they grow older by white,
beginning with bill, face and legs. Birds become breeding adults before the fully
developed black-and-white pattern is reached.
   In their earlier dark stage they may resemble the Black-footed Albatross, but
their pale bills and legs distinguish them.
RANGE: Confined to the North Pacific, possibly spreading throughout the Western
quarter. A very rare species breeding only on Torishima I. in the Isa Is. Recent
reports indicated a total breeding population of about 57 pairs.   Map 20.

BLACK-FOOTED ALBATROSS *Diomedea nigripes*   **Page 14 and Pl. 6**
Large, 28 ins, 71 cm. Wing-span 80 ins, 203 cm. Overall sooty-brown plumage,
slightly paler on forehead and cheeks, and with a white area around the base of the
dark brown bill. Legs black. Adults are easily identifiable.
   Young birds usually have a more extensive white area around the forepart of the
head and whitish upper tail-coverts. Young birds of the race Short-tailed Albatross
Diomedea albatrus are similar but rather darker and can be distinguished by their
pink bills and flesh-coloured legs, and lack of white on face or rump.
   The Black-footed Albatross is an inveterate ship follower and is usually to be
seen gliding back and forth across the wake looking for garbage. When alighting on

the sea it usually keeps its wings spread unless remaining on the water for some time. It is bolder than the Laysan Albatross which may be seen in company but which tends to hold off further from a ship.

RANGE: Across the entire breadth of the N. Pacific from approximately 20°N. to 55°N. and commonly seen between 30°N. and 45°N. in summer on completion of its breeding season. Breeds on the leeward Hawaiian Is.   Map 21.

LAYSAN ALBATROSS *Diomedea immutabilis*   Page 14 and Pl. 4

Large, 32 ins, 81 cm. Wing-span 80 ins, 203 cm. In adults the head, neck, rump, upper tail-coverts and underparts are white. A dark spot shows in front of the eye. The back and upperwings are dark sooty-brown, and the white tail carries a dark terminal band. Underwings have broad dark margins with dark areas encroaching into the white central lining from the leading edge. The bill is greyish with the base of the mandible yellow. Legs flesh-coloured.

Young birds are similar.

The Laysan Albatross may often be seen following ships in the N. Pacific and is the only white albatross with sooty-brown upperwings and back in the N. Pacific.

RANGE: Across the entire breadth of the N. Pacific from approximately 30°N. to 45°N., extending to 55°N. in the northern summer after the breeding season. Breeds on the leeward Hawaiian Is.   Map 22.

BLACK-BROWED ALBATROSS *Diomedea melanophris* Page 14 and Pl. 5

Very large, 32–34 ins, 81–86 cm. Wing-span 90 ins, 229 cm. Head, neck, rump, upper tail-coverts and underbody white. Upperparts and upper wing surfaces brownish-black, back and tail slightly greyer-black. Central white underwing linings are edged by broad smudgy blackish margins, wider in front. The yellow bill is stout and has a pink tip. Legs pinkish, webs pale blue. At close quarters a dark streak shows above and behind the eye tending to give a 'frowning' appearance. Young birds have dusky-grey heads and necks, and grey merging gradually into the white of the underbody, greyish-black bills, and the undersurface of the wings mainly dark. In many sub-adults the bill appears yellow with a dark tip.

Its thick 'neckless' and 'hump-backed' appearance, yellow bill and much broader dark underwing margins distinguishes it from the more slender and black-billed

BLACK-BROWED ALBATROSS. In calm weather heavy flapping and violent leg action is used to become airborne. The beating of their feet can be heard at a considerable distance.

Yellow-nosed Albatross. Immature Black-browed Albatrosses are difficult to distinguish from immature Grey-headed Albatrosses (see Grey-headed Albatrosses, pp. 14 and 20).
RANGE: S. Pacific, S. Atlantic and S. Indian Oceans and Australian and New Zealand seas from approx. 55°S. to 30°S. but dispersing even further than northern limit during the southern winter in areas of cold currents. Breeds on Staten I. and islands off Cape Horn, the Falkland Is., S. Georgia, Kerguelen and Heard Is., Campbell, Antipodes and Macquarie Is. Map 23.

BULLER'S ALBATROSS *Diomedea bulleri* **Page 14 and Pl. 4**
Very large, 34 ins, 86 cm. Wing-span 84 ins, 213 cm. Buller's Albatross is the rarest of the southern ocean albatrosses. In adult plumage the cheeks and hindneck are grey (reported from sea as appearing a delicate pale blue-grey), the forehead white. A dark patch shows in front of the eye. Back and upperwings are sooty-brown, rump, upper tail-coverts and underparts white. The central portion of the underwing is white, the leading edge carrying a dark margin, the trailing edge a fine dark margin. Bill greyish-black with a yellow band along both the upper and lower mandibles. The upper plate of the bill widens noticeably at its base. Legs bluish-white. Tail sooty-brown.
Adult Buller's and Grey-headed Albatrosses may easily be confused unless the particular differences in plumage are studied.
RANGE: Like the Royal Albatross it is to be seen chiefly in the seas closely surrounding New Zealand, but has also been reported eastwards off the southern coast of Chile. Rarely strays north of 40°N. Breeds on Chatham Is., Solander and Snares Is. Map 24.

SHY or WHITE-CAPPED ALBATROSS *Diomedea cauta* **Page 14 and Pl. 4**
Outsize, 35–39 ins, 89–99 cm. Wing-span 96 ins, 243 cm. Considerably larger than other southern ocean 'Mollymawks'. In adults the forehead white, and, in birds seen in southern seas around Australia and New Zealand, the crown and neck are white. Head, nape and cheeks grey. Upperwings and tail greyish-brown, back pale greyish. Remainder of body white. The whole underwing is white except for very narrow dark margins and a dark tip. The eye shows a greyish-black eye socket. Bill grey with distinct orange tip, deep at base, with bluish lateral plates running up in front of the eye and a dark horseshoe stripe behind the nostrils. An orange stripe shows behind the base of lower mandible. Legs bluish-flesh-coloured. Immatures similar but have dark grey bills. Breeds on Albatross Rock in Bass Strait, off Tasmania and Auckland I. off New Zealand. Map 25.
The flight is similar to the Wandering Albatross with a tendency to turn and bank more sharply. The Shy Albatross usually keep well clear of ships.
RANGE: Southern oceans ranging as far north as 25°S. Breeds on islands in the Bass Strait, off the southern coast of Tasmania and on the Auckland Is. Occurs at sea off both sides of S. Africa. Map 25.

YELLOW-NOSED ALBATROSS *Diomedea chlororhynchos* **Page 14 and Pl. 5**
Very large, 29–34 ins, 74–86 cm. Wing-span 80 ins, 20 cm. A noticeably neater and more slender bird than the Black-browed Albatross, lacking the thick 'neckless' and 'hump-backed' appearance of the latter.
Head and neck white, sides and back of head slightly pale grey. Dark feathers around the eye appear as a triangular patch. The back is sooty-black, the upper wings and tail dark brownish-black, as in Black-browed Albatross. The underwing

has much more white than either the Black-browed or Grey-headed, edged with a clearly defined thin black margin in which the leading edge is broader than the trailing edge. The black underwing tip is formed by a sudden widening of the black margin along the trailing edge. The bill is more slender than that of the previous species, is black with a bright yellow line along the ridge of the upper mandible, and terminates in a bright orange tip. Legs flesh-colour.

Immatures are similar with pure white heads and entirely black bills.

RANGE: S. Atlantic and Indian Oceans eastwards to Australia and New Zealand seas between approximately 50°S. and 25°S., extending further north in the southern winter. Breeds on Tristan da Cunha and Gough Is. and Amsterdam and St. Paul Is.

Is often the first species of Albatross to be observed by ships on southerly sea routes to S. Africa, Australia and S. America appearing sometimes within the Tropic of Capricorn (23½°S.). Map 26.

GREY-HEADED ALBATROSS *Diomedea chrysostoma* Page 14 and Pl. 5

Large, 28–32 ins, 71–81 cm. Wing-span 80 ins, 203 cm. In adult plumage the whole head and neck are dusky-grey, or slate-grey. A distinct half circle of white feathers surrounds the back of the eye. Upperwings sooty-brown; back and tail dark grey, rump, upper tail-coverts and underparts white. The central portion of the underwing is white with dark tips and margins on both leading and trailing edges, wider from the carpal joint inwards on the leading edge. The bill is blackish with a yellow stripe along the upper and lower mandibles ending with a bright pink tip, a feature visible at some distance in good light. Immature birds resemble adults but are somewhat browner above, with slaty-grey heads, the underwings with considerably broader dark margins and bills greyish-black.

The early immature plumages of the Grey-headed and Black-browed Albatrosses are very similar. In the Grey-headed Albatross the whole head and neck looks brownish-grey and is sharply divided from the white on throat and breast, quite distinct from the manner in which the grey blends gradually into the white in the young Black-browed Albatross. At a later stage the head of the Black-browed Albatross becomes white and bill more yellow, while the head of the Grey-headed Albatross always remains grey and the bill dark.

RANGE: Remains in high southern latitudes throughout the year, dispersing throughout the southern oceans between 60°S. and 40°S. Reaches the seas off southern Australia in winter. Breeds at Cape Horn, Falkland Is., S. Georgia, Prince Edward and Crozet Is., Kerguelen, Campbell, Antipodes and Macquarie Is. Map 27.

SOOTY ALBATROSS *Phoebetria fusca* Page 14 and Pl. 6

Large, 32 ins, 81 cm. Wing-span 78 ins, 198 cm. Sooty-brown overall, the wings and head being darker, the back and underparts slightly paler. As in the Light-mantled Sooty Albatross a white ring of short feathers almost encircles the eye and the long tail is wedge-shaped. The bill is black with a yellow line along the lower mandible. The legs are pale flesh-coloured. Young birds are brown overall and indistinguishable from young Light-mantled Sooty Albatrosses.

The flight is similar to that of the Light-mantled Sooty Albatross and excels that of the larger albatrosses in grace and variation. This is the bird into which the ancient seafarers believed that the souls of men drowned overboard passed and that intended in 'The Rime of the Ancient Mariner'.

RANGE: Eastern S. Atlantic eastwards through S. Indian Ocean between 50°S. and 30°S. Ranges further north than the Light-mantled Sooty Albatross. Breeds at Tristan da Cunha and Gough Is., St. Paul and Amsterdam Is.   Map 28.

LIGHT-MANTLED SOOTY ALBATROSS *Phoebetria palpebrata*
Page 14 and Pl. 6

Large, 28 ins, 71 cm. Wing-span 82 ins, 208 cm. The two dark mollymawks, the Light-mantled Sooty Albatross and the Sooty Albatross of the southern oceans are somewhat similar.

In the Light-mantled Sooty Albatross the head is dark greyish-brown, the back and underparts ash-grey, and the wings greyish-brown with blacker primaries. A conspicuous white ring encircles the eye, broken in front. The noticeably long wedge-shaped tail appears black, the bill also is black and shows a pale blue line along its side. The legs are pale flesh-coloured. Young birds of both species are browner overall and indistinguishable at sea.

The two species are the most graceful of all the albatrosses in flight having a quality of manoeuvre unequalled by the larger albatrosses.

RANGE: Disperses throughout the southern oceans between 55°S. and 35°S., breeding on islands in the higher latitudes and dispersing towards its northern limits in the southern winter. Ranges further south than the Sooty Albatross. Breeds at S. Georgia, Bouvet, Kerguelen and Heard Is., Campbell, Auckland, Antipodes and Macquarie Is.   Map 29.

Nest and nestling of the Sooty Albatross. Albatrosses lay their single large egg in a bare hollow on the ground or a nest built of earth and vegetable matter. The *Phoebetria* species build nicely cup-shaped nests in vegetation on rocky islands. The chick has a goat-like greyish down.

Manx Shearwaters returning to their nesting burrows at night.

PETRELS and SHEARWATERS   Procellariidae

The principal distinguishing feature of this family of oceanic seabirds is in the character of the bill which is slightly hooked at the tip and with two nostrils opening together at the end of a double tube on the upper mandible. For this reason they are sometimes referred to as 'tube-noses'.

Except when breeding they spend their whole life at sea adapting themselves to the severest storms, constantly on the wing gliding, banking, shearwatering, or swooping in high arcs making use of the up currents of wind along the weather side of the troughs of the swell, and rising above the breaking crests of the comers. Indeed it appears that they must be able to exist without true sleep for long periods. Their food consists chiefly of crustacea, organic plankton, squids, and fish, diving below the surface as necessary, and in some cases floating scraps which come their way.

Viewed as they so often are at some distance from a ship the particular characteristics of their flight assists in differentiating between them.

Nesting and young

A few species nest on open ground or on ledges, but most nest in burrows or natural crevices and cavities in rocks. The breeding sites are usually in colonies, often large, on islands, rocky shores, cliff-tops and screes, usually on the coast but in some instances well inland on mountain slopes, sometimes necessitating a flight over forest. The burrow may be dug by the birds themselves. Plant material from around a burrow mouth may be gradually dragged down to form a nest pad. The single white egg is large for the size of the bird. Incubation varies from c. 40–60 days, according to species, and both birds sit for alternate periods of 2–12 days. The eggs and young can survive periods of neglect and chilling, presumably an adaptation to the long gaps between change-over of incubation and the infrequent visits of the parents. Young in burrows are only brooded for the first 2–3 days, and then only visited at intervals for feeding, but species nesting in open sites may guard the young for the first fortnight. The young have two successive thick coats of greyish or brownish down. They are fed by regurgitation, placing their bills crosswise in those of the adults. In many species they can defend themselves by spitting quantities of oil. They become very large and fat but lose this while the feathers are growing. The adults may continue to visit the young until they leave the nest. Fledging takes 45–55 days in the smaller species, and up to 100–135 days in the largest.

SOUTHERN GIANT PETREL *Macronectes giganteus*   **Pl. 7**
Outsize, 33–36 ins, 84–92 cm. Wing span 84 ins, 213 cm. The Giant Petrel is as large
as a small albatross, males being larger and with heavier bills than females. The
more normal plumage is a dusky grey-brown, much paler on the head, neck and
throat. As feather plumage wears, a more mottled appearance is frequently apparent. A noticeable feature is its enormous plated bill, usually greenish-yellow, and its
elongated nasal tube. Its small pale eyes are shrouded by a ridge of feathers, giving
the bird an unpleasant frown. Legs vary from brown to sooty-black. Young birds
are uniformly rich chocolate-brown with darker eyes, but otherwise similar to
adults. Its wings are narrower than those of albatrosses, and its flight appears
ungainly in comparison, flapping awkwardly or gliding in a stiff-winged attitude
with humped back and head held low. It frequently follows ships in search of refuse.
Amongst the more southerly breeding colonies birds with predominantly white or
almost pure white plumage occur, and may be seen occasionally in the higher
latitudes.
RANGE: Throughout the southern oceans from the Antarctic to the Tropic of
Capricorn and even further north. Breeds on the antarctic continent, on many
sub-antarctic islands, S. Shetlands, S. Orkneys, S. Sandwich Is., S. Georgia.
Falkland Is., Bouvet and Heard Is. and Macquarie Is. Nests socially, eggs in late
October.   Map 30.

Giant Petrels scavenging on a dead seal washed onto the beach.

NORTHERN GIANT PETREL *Macronectes halli*   **Pl. 5, 7**
Outsize, 33–36 ins, 84–92 cm. Wing-span 84 ins, 213 cm. The northern species has a
darker brown body and head, pale face and freckled cheeks and a darker
yellowish-brown bill with dark marks at tip. Young birds however show a less dark
plumage than those of the southern species. In flight its characteristics are similar to
the southern species. There is no white phase.
RANGE: Breeds on islands chiefly north of the Antarctic Convergence on Gough,
Marion and Crozet Is., Kerguelen Is., Chatham, Stewart, Snares, Auckland,
Campbell and Macquarie Is. Some overlapping occurs. Nests singly unlike the
social habits of the southern species and earlier in the year. Eggs from late August.

   Both species overlap at sea, more particularly immatures of the southern species
which disperse northwards, but to an observer at sea the differences will not be
apparent except in the case of a white bird of the southern species.   Map 31.

NORTHERN FULMAR *Fulmarus glacialis* **Pl. 11**
Medium size, 19–20 ins, 48–51 cm. Wing span 42 ins, 107 cm. At a distance its pearl-grey upperparts, white head, neck and underparts in its light phase give it a resemblance to a gull. At closer quarters its thick neck, stout yellowish slightly hooked tubenose bill, dusky spot in front of its dark eye, slate-grey primaries and pale patch near the tip of each wing are distinctive. Its legs are pale flesh-coloured or bluish. In its northern range some 'dark' or 'blue' forms occur with the head and underparts bluish-grey. In flight it planes continuously on stiffly held wings, making use of every variation in wind currents to bank and soar with a characteristic mastery of flight.
RANGE: N. Atlantic and N. Pacific Oceans and adjacent arctic seas. Map 32.

SOUTHERN FULMAR or SILVER-GREY PETREL **Pl. 11**
Fulmarus glacialoides
Medium, 18 ins, 46 cm. Wing-span 42 ins, 107 cm. The forehead, cheeks and underparts are white. The upperparts and tail are pearly-grey slightly paler on the crown and neck. A dark spot shows before the eye. The primary flight feathers are dark, a white patch showing on the upperwings in flight. The tubenose bill is horn-coloured, bluish on the nostril, tip dark; legs pale flesh-coloured. In flight it planes continuously on stiffly held wings making use of every variation in wind currents to bank and soar with a characteristic mastery of flight.

Closely related to the Fulmar Petrel of the northern hemisphere with a paler pearly-grey appearance. It has no dark phase.
RANGE: Antarctic seas and southern oceans rarely north of 40°S. Breeds as far south as the antarctic continent and on S. Orkney and S. Shetland Is., Bouvet and Kerguelen Is. Map 33.

CAPE PIGEON or PINTADO PETREL *Daption capensis* **Pl. 11**
Small–medium, 14 ins, 36 cm. Wing-span 35 ins, 89 cm. A medium built petrel with broad wings and short round tail. Quite unmistakable with the dark brown and white chequered pattern of its upperwing surfaces showing two large white patches on each wing, and the sooty-brown head, chin, sides of neck and back. The upper tail-coverts are white. Beneath the chin the underparts are pure white save for dark brown margins to its underwings. Bill short and brown; legs dark brown. In flight it proceeds with periods of stiff-winged flapping and shorter glides usually at 'deck level'.

Known to seafarers as the 'Cape Pigeon' it habitually follows ships in flocks and is seen more regularly in the southern oceans than any other species of petrel.
RANGE: Throughout the southern oceans from the antarctic ranging north to the Tropic of Capricorn. Breeds on the antarctic continent and adjacent sub-antarctic islands, S. Shetlands, S. Orkneys, S. Sandwich Is., S. Georgia, Bouvet, Crozet, Kerguelen, Heard, New Zealand adjacent islands and Macquarie I. Map 34.

SNOW PETREL *Pagadroma nivea* **Pl. 11**
Small–medium, 14–16 ins, 36–41 cm. This beautiful pure white petrel with its black bill and dark grey legs is unmistakable.

Snow Petrels rarely range beyond the pack ice.
RANGE: Antarctic seas. Breeds in antarctic continent and also on S. Shetlands, S. Orkneys, S. Sandwich Is., and Bouvet I. Map 35.

ANTARCTIC PETREL *Thalassoica antarctica* **P . 11**
Medium, 17 ins, 43 cm. Wing-span 36 ins, 92 cm. Head, upper neck and back brown, sides of neck and throat slightly paler. Upperwings brown showing a broad white outer area caused by shafts and inner webs of primaries, all secondaries and greater wing-coverts being white. Leading primaries show brown tips. Upper tail-coverts and tail white, tail feathers tipped brown. Underparts and underwing-coverts white. Bill black; legs yellowish.
The brown upperparts and white area on wings and tail are unmistakable.
RANGE: Breeds on antarctic continent and rarely ranges more than 100 miles to seaward of the pack ice. Map 36.

BLUE PETREL *Halobaena caerulea* **Page 42 and P . 11**
Small, 11 ins, 28 cm. Wing-span 19 ins, 48 cm. A small stocky petrel with moderately long wings and a short square tail. The crown, nape and shoulders appear dark against the blue-grey of the upperparts and tail. The forehead is generally white with some freckling. The leading primaries are brownish-black and a distinct dark 'W' pattern is formed by a darker band from the carpal joint across the wing-coverts. The secondaries and scapulars show white tips. The throat and whole of the underparts and underwings are white. Bill short black with a bluish-grey line along the lower mandible. Legs blue with flesh-coloured webs. The central tail feathers are white tipped and two outer tail feathers white forming a white terminal band.
Very similar to the prions in plumage but distinguished by the squareness of its tail and its white terminal band.
RANGE: Antarctic seas rarely north of 40°S. Breeds in the Falkland Is., Marion and Crozet Is., Kerguelen and Macquarie Is. Map 37.

PRIONS

Prions were known to seagoing whalers and sealers as 'Whale-birds', 'Ice-birds' or 'Fire-birds', the latter title derived from their habit of being attracted to and flying into fires at night at the whaling stations while they came and went to and from their breeding burrows in the dark. All are very small petrels varying between 10–11 ins, 254–280 mm in length, wing span 16–18 ins, 407–457 mm, and are of such similar plumage that it is virtually impossible to distinguish between them at sea. The particular feature which determines each species is in the considerable variation in the breadth and proportion of their bills. One overall description follows:
Small, 10 ins, 25 cm. Upperparts delicate blue-grey slightly darker on the crown. Sides of face grey with a black patch behind and below the eye. Edge of shoulders, scapulars and outer primaries black, forming a distinct 'W' pattern across the upperwings. Underparts and underwings white, bluish on flanks. Upper tail-coverts and tail grey, the tail feathers with broad black tips showing as a black terminal band. Tail wedge-shaped. Bill bluish-grey; legs blue. Flight very fast and erratic, birds frequently in flocks, banking and zig-zagging low over the sea, appearing and disappearing as they show their white underparts then grey-blue backs which tone in with the colour of the sea.

BROAD-BILLED PRION *Pachyptila vittata* **Page 27**
Bill length 1.5 ins, 38 mm, breadth at base 0.7–0.8 ins, 18–21 mm. Bill steel-grey above, bluish yellow below.

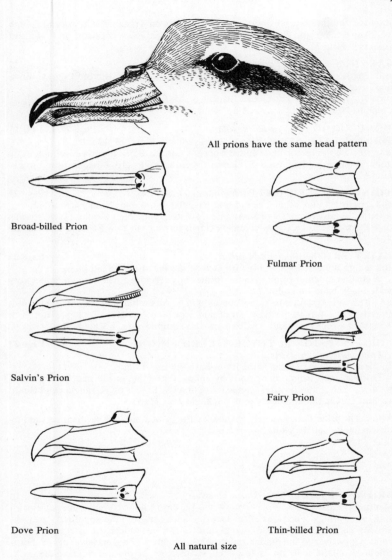

All prions have the same head pattern

Broad-billed Prion

Fulmar Prion

Salvin's Prion

Fairy Prion

Dove Prion

Thin-billed Prion

All natural size

Prion bills, *Pachyptila* species (p.28). The upper figures show the bill from the side; the lower figures the bill from above.

RANGE: Southern oceans north to 30°S. Breeds on Tristan da Cunha and Gough Is., Amsterdam and St. Paul Is. and on South I., New Zealand and adjacent islands.   Map 38.

SALVIN'S PRION *Pachyptila salvini*   Page 27
Bill length and breadth at base slightly less than *P. vittata*. Bill bluish-grey above and below.
RANGE: Southern Indian Ocean. Breeds on Marion and Crozet Is. and extends its range to New Zealand seas.   Map 39.

DOVE PRION *Pachyptila desolata*   Page 27 and Pl. 11
Bill length 1.5 ins, 38 mm, breadth at base 0.5–0.6 ins, 13–15 mm.
RANGE: Sub-antarctic and southern oceans north to 35°S. Breeds in sub-antarctic zone, in Antarctic Peninsula, S. Georgia, Kerguelen, Heard, Macquarie and Auckland Is.   Map 40.

THIN-BILLED PRION *Pachyptila belcheri*   Page 27
Bill length 1.5 ins, 38 mm, breadth at base 0.3 ins, 8 mm. Very narrow bill.
RANGE: Southern coasts of S. America, Australia and New Zealand seas. Breeds on Falkland Is. and Kerguelen I. and extends its range to New Zealand seas.   Map 41.

FAIRY PRION *Pachyptila turtur*   Page 27
Bill length 0.9 ins, 23 mm, breadth at base 0.4 ins, 10 mm. Bill blue.
    A smaller stockier prion than the former species with a paler crown, and a very wide black band on end of tail.
RANGE: Sub-antarctic to 35°S., common in S. Australian and New Zealand seas. Breeds on islands in the Bass Strait and on islands off New Zealand from Poor Knights Is. to Snares and on Chatham and Antipodes Is.   Map 42.

FULMAR PRION or THICK-BILLED PRION   Page 27
    Pachyptila crassirostris
Bill length 0.9 ins, 23 mm, breadth at base 0.6 ins, 15 mm.
    Distinguished from other prions by enlarged swelling of bill plates.
RANGE: Sub-antarctic rarely range north of 40°S. Breeds on Kerguelen and Heard Is. and on Chatham, Bounty and Auckland Is.   Map 43.

Note: The Blue Petrel closely resembles the prions but can be distinguished by observing its square white-tipped tail.

BROWN PETREL *Procellaria cinereus*   Pl. 10
Medium, 19 ins, 48 cm. Wing-span 48 ins, 122 cm. A large heavily built petrel with long broad wings. The sides of the face and neck are grey; the upperparts greyish-brown, darker on the head, wings and tail. The underparts are white. The underwing-coverts and under tail-coverts are grey. The massive bill is horn-coloured on the nail, tip, side plates and bottom of the lower mandible, with blackish nostril and upper ridge. Legs are bluish and tail medium-round. In flight it alternates between rapid flaps, long glides and some shearwatering.
    With newly moulted feathers in May when breeding season starts it appears

considerably greyer, and browner when plumage has become worn. Known by seafarers as the 'Pediunker' or 'Cape Dove' it frequently follows ships.

RANGE: Southern oceans rarely north of 30°S. Breeds at Tristan da Cunha, Gough, Marion, Kerguelen, Campbell, Antipodes and Macquarie Is. Map 44.

WHITE-CHINNED PETREL *Procellaria aequinoctialis* Pl. 7

Medium large, 21 ins, 53 cm. Wing-span 53 ins, 135 cm. A large heavily built petrel with long broad wings and a medium round tail. It is seen most usually in an overall black to sooty-brown plumage offset by a distinctive white chin. The white at the chin is however variable; in the S. Atlantic birds may sometimes be seen with the white extending over the face giving a spectacled appearance; in the seas around New Zealand the white on the chin is frequently almost lacking and may not be visible at sea. Its bill is long and massive, yellowish or horn-coloured with dark nostrils and black ridge on the culmen, a noticeable feature at some distance. In flight it proceeds with loose flaps and glides, is a persistent follower of ships, and one of the commonest petrels throughout the southern oceans.

Known by seafarers as the 'Cape Hen' or 'Shoemaker'.

RANGE: Southern oceans ranging from the edge of the pack ice to 30°S. Breeds on Falkland Is., S. Georgia, Tristan da Cunha, Marion and Crozet Is., Kerguelen, Macquarie, Campbell, Auckland and Antipodes Is. Map 45.

PARKINSON'S PETREL *Procellaria parkinsoni* Pl. 7

Medium, 18 ins, 46 cm. Stoutly built with long narrow wings. Overall plumage dark blackish-brown. Bill yellowish horn-coloured with a dark nostril and line along ridge of culmen, and a dark tip. Tail medium round. In flight in moderate winds it tends to swoop and soar. It has been identified rarely at sea and is easily confused with the larger White-chinned Petrel and cannot be distinguished from the Westland Petrel.

RANGE: Disperses eastwards and northwards from its breeding grounds during the contra nuptial periods. Breeds in mountain tops in both North and South Is. of New Zealand. Eggs in December. Map 46.

WESTLAND PETREL *Procellaria westlandica* Pl. 7

Medium, 20 ins, 51 cm. Slightly larger but otherwise identical with Parkinson's Petrel. Eggs however in May.

RANGE: Disperses into the Tasman Sea from breeding grounds inland on the W. coast of South Island, New Zealand. Map 47.

WHITE-FACED or STREAKED SHEARWATER Pl. 8
Calonectris leucomelas

Medium, 19 ins, 48 cm. Wing-span 48 ins, 122 cm. Upperparts generally brown with pale speckling on back and upper wings. Front and sides of head and neck whitish, showing dark streaks. Primaries blackish. Underparts and under surface of wings white with darker streaked underwing margins. Bill horn-coloured. Legs flesh-coloured. Tail brown. Flies lightly with long easy wing-beats and glides, wrists bent.

A rather large shearwater easily distinguished by its white streaked face and white underparts. Very large flocks occur off Japan and in the China Sea in summer months.

RANGE: N.W. Pacific Ocean, dispersing southwards in winter to areas off the Philippines and N. Borneo. Breeds on the Pescador Is., and islands off north of Japan. Map 48.

CORY'S SHEARWATER   *Calonectris diomedea*   **Pl. 9**
Medium, 18–22 ins, 46–56 cm. Wing-span 44 ins, 112 cm. A rather large shearwater
with broad wings and heavy body. Its upperparts are medium-brown with pale
flecking on the back and wing-coverts and rather darker head, wings and tail. In
some lights the upperparts appear lightish-brown. The underparts are pure white;
most of the underwing whitish, slightly darker on the edges. A narrow-curved white
band of feathers is sometimes noticeable above the base of the tail. The bill is stout
and yellow and can be observed at some distance. Legs yellowish. Its flight is
unhurried and effortless, gliding for long periods low over the sea, occasionally
making easy shallow wingbeats. While planing and shearwatering in this way its
wings often seem to project slightly forward and droop, the tips lower than the
belly.
   Rather similar in appearance to the Great Shearwater but the throat and sides of
the neck are greyish, and it lacks the distinctive dark capped appearance of the
Great Shearwater.
RANGE: N. to S. Atlantic Oceans and Mediterranean Sea, dispersing southwards
during northern autumn and winter to W. coast of southern Africa. Breeds on
Azores, Madeira, Salvage, Canary and Cape Verde Is., coast of Portugal and in the
Mediterranean, recently on Filfla Rock, Malta.   Map 49.

PINK-FOOTED SHEARWATER   *Puffinus creatopus*   **Pl. 8**
Medium, 20 ins, 51 cm. Wing-span 43 ins, 109 cm. A heavily built shearwater with
long narrow wings, similar in build and flight pattern to the Pale-footed Shearwater
from which it can be distinguished by its whitish underparts and mottled-white
underwings (both underparts and underwings are brown in the Pale-footed Shearwater).
   The crown and sides of neck are dark grey, upperparts dark greyish-brown,
rump black. The throat, breast and flanks are mottled-grey, remainder of underparts white. The bill is long, massive and pale pink with a black tip. Legs pink and
tail short and round.
   Distinguished from the pale phase of the Wedge-tailed Shearwater by its larger
size, round as opposed to long wedge-shaped tail and slower deliberate and less
graceful flight.
RANGE: Eastern S. Pacific, migrating north of the Equator during the southern
winter. Breeds on the Juan Fernandez Is. and Mocha I.   Map 50.

PALE-FOOTED SHEARWATER   *Puffinus carneipes*   **Pl. 8**
Medium, 20 ins, 51 cm. Wing-span 43 ins, 109 cm. A large heavily built uniform
chocolate-brown shearwater with long narrow wings and a short round tail. Its most
conspicuous feature is its long straw-coloured bill ending in a brown tip. Legs
yellowish-flesh coloured. Its flight is deliberate consisting normally of a few powerful wingbeats interspersed with short glides low over the sea.
   It is liable to be confused with the dark phase of the Wedge-tailed Shearwater
which however has a long wedge-shaped tail, long slender grey bill and a lighter
more graceful flight.
RANGE: S. Indian and S. Pacific Oceans. Migrates north of the Equator to Arabian
Sea and central Pacific during southern winter. Breeds on the S. coast of Western
Australia, North Island of New Zealand and Lord Howe I.   Map 51.

GREAT SHEARWATER *Puffinus gravis* **Pl. 9**
Medium, 18–21 ins, 46–53 cm. Wing-span 45 ins, 111 cm. The Great Shearwater is in many respects very similar to Cory's Shearwater with brown upperparts, darker on wings and tail and with a noticeably darker crown and white cheeks. The neck is white nearly all round. The underparts are white flecked with darker feathers in the centre of the abdomen. The longer upper tail-coverts are tipped white forming a white band across the rump. The underwing is not as white as in the case of Cory's Shearwater, and shows brown streaking. The bill is long, slender and dark and legs flesh-coloured. In flight it glides on stiff pinions beating its wings rather more rapidly than Cory's.
A distinguishing feature is its 'dark capped' appearance, the white of the neck contrasting with its dark crown.
RANGE: S. and N. Atlantic Oceans, undertaking transequatorial migration during southern winter. Breeds on the Falkland Is., Tristan da Cunha and Gough Is.   Map 52.

WEDGE-TAILED SHEARWATER *Puffinus pacificus* **Pl. 7**
Medium, 15.5 ins, 39 cm. Wing-span 38 ins, 97 cm. This is a variable species occurring in both pale and dark phases. Lightly built it has long broadish wings, a long slender bill and noticeably long wedge-shaped tail. In the dark phase it is a uniform dark chocolate-brown overall plumage, long slender grey bill, and flesh-coloured legs. In the pale phase it is slightly paler above, has white underparts and white underwings showing dark margins, dark under tail-coverts and some-times a pale flesh-coloured bill. It usually flies low over the sea with little upward movement frequently banking from side to side holding its long bill horizontal and tending to throw its head upwards during shallow wingbeats. When shearwatering and banking in calm weather it has been seen to touch the water with its lower wing leaving a trace behind it. In stronger winds it tends to bank more steeply in easy graceful flight.
In the dark phase it is liable to be confused with the Pale-footed Shearwater where both occur together, but its long wedge-shaped tail, slender grey bill and swifter and more graceful flight should serve to distinguish it.
RANGE: Ranges widely over the Indian and Pacific Oceans. Breeds throughout range.   Map 53.

GREY-BACKED SHEARWATER *Puffinus bulleri* **Pl. 8**
Medium, 16.5 ins, 42 cm. Wing-span 42 ins, 107 cm. The outstanding feature of this lightly built long-winged shearwater is the contrast between the completely white underparts and underwings and the sooty-black and grey pattern of its upperparts. The back of the head and neck, lesser wing-coverts, primaries and tail are dark, the back, greater wing-coverts and upper tail-coverts grey, showing a dark '**W**' upper wing pattern in flight. The bill is long, bluish in colour, legs flesh-coloured and tail long and wedge-shaped. In fresh winds it swoops and soars on stiffly held wings, but in light wings it glides between wingbeats, its body appearing to dip and rise with each wingbeat cycle.
RANGE: S. Pacific Ocean, migrating northwards towards the Equator from its breeding quarters on Poor Knights Is. off the North Island of New Zealand during non-breeding season.   Map 54.

SOOTY SHEARWATER *Puffinus griseus*   **Pl. 8**
Medium, 16–20 ins, 41–51 cm. Wing-span 43 ins, 109 cm. A rather heavily built
shearwater with long narrow wings, uniformly sooty-brown upperparts and
greyish-brown underparts, paler under the chin. The central portion of the underwing lining is very distinctly pale, almost silvery, and considerably paler than in the
smaller Short-tailed Shearwater. The bill is blackish, long and slender, legs bluish
and tail short and round. In calm weather in flight it proceeds with a few quick
wingbeats followed by short glides with wings bent at the wrists. In moderate to
high winds it is capable of much soaring and shearwatering on stiff wings.
    This is the 'Mutton Bird' of New Zealand. It may easily be confused with the
Short-tailed Shearwater where both occur in the Pacific Ocean for its characteristics are similar. Its much larger size, the silvery lining of its underwing, and, where
this is observable, its pale chin, help to distinguish it.
RANGE: S. Atlantic and S. Pacific Oceans migrating north of the Equator in the
southern winter. Breeds in New Zealand and adjacent sub-antarctic islands, on
islands off Tasmania and south-eastern Australia, Falkland Is., and islands off the
W. coasts of Chile.   Map 55.

SHORT-TAILED SHEARWATER *Puffinus tenuirostris*   **Pl. 8**
Small–medium, 13 ins, 33 cm. Wing-span 38 ins, 97 cm. A medium built shearwater
with long narrow wings, sooty-brown upperparts, greyish underparts and a greyish
central lining to the underwings. Due to its short round tail its body looks extremely
short behind the wings. The bill is medium long and dark and legs bluish-grey. In
calm weather in flight it proceeds with flaps and glides. In moderate to high winds its
flight is fast and effortless with much soaring and shearwatering interspersed with
rapid stiff wingbeats.
    The Short-tailed Shearwater is known as the 'Mutton Bird' in Tasmania and the
islands in the Bass Strait. During the breeding season the sea is sometimes churned
white with plunging birds. See also Sooty Shearwater.
RANGE: S. Pacific Ocean, migrating north of the Equator in the southern winter.
Breeds on islands in the Bass Strait and on the coasts of New South Wales, Victoria
and S. Australia.   Map 56.

CHRISTMAS SHEARWATER *Puffinus nativitatis*   **Pl. 7**
Small–medium, 14 ins, 36 cm. Wing-span 32 ins, 82 cm. A medium sized lightly built
shearwater of overall chocolate-brown colour with long broadish wings, a long dark
slender bill, brown legs and short rounded tail. A white edge to the wing-coverts and
secondaries has been reported in flight but is unconfirmed. In flight it glides easily
with rather stiff wingbeats close over the surface.
    It resembles the dark phase of the Wedge-tailed Shearwater but is smaller, more
chestnut in colour, with only half the length of tail, and has dark legs as opposed to
flesh-coloured legs, and a faster wing-beat.
RANGE: Tropical Pacific Ocean with a limited range away from land. Breeds
throughout range. Recently found breeding on Easter I.   Map 57.

MANX SHEARWATER *Puffinus puffinus*
Small–medium, 12–15 ins, 31–38 cm. Dark upperparts, white underparts (except
P.p. opisthomelas and *P.p. mauretanicus*). Dark crown extends below level of eye.
Bill long, slender, leaden-black. Legs pinkish flesh-coloured. Wings long and
narrow. In flight it planes (except *P.p. gavia*) on rigid wings close above the sea,

tilting from side to side, showing first white, then black, with three or four rapid wing-beats at intervals.

RANGE: Atlantic, Pacific, Mediterranean.

RACES:

MANX SHEARWATER *Puffinus p. puffinus* **Pl. 9**
Atlantic, Mediterranean. Black upperparts. Legs pinkish, webs blue. Breeds in British Is., Azores, Madeira and Salvage Is.   Map 58.

LEVANTINE SHEARWATER *Puffinus p. yelkouan* **Pl. 9**
E. Mediterranean, extending into Sea of Marmora. Recently on Filfla Rock, Malta. Dark upperparts rather browner. Breeds in Aegean Is.   Map 59.

BALEARIC SHEARWATER *Puffinus p. mauretanicus* **Pl. 9**
Balearic Is., extending into N. Atlantic in autumn. Brownish-black upperparts and pale brown underparts. Breeds in Balearic Is.   Map 60.

RACES IN N. PACIFIC:

TOWNSEND'S SHEARWATER *Puffinus p. auricularis* **Not illustrated**
E. Pacific. Breed on Rivella, Gizedo and Clipperton Is. Like *P.p. puffinus* but with black legs and under tail-coverts.   Map 61.

NEWELL'S SHEARWATER *Puffinus p. newelli* **Not illustrated**
Breeds on Kanai Is. and possibly the Hawaiian islands. Common within 200 miles of them May–October. Two small white patches on the dark back, though too hard to distinguish at sea.   Map 62.

BLACK-VENTED SHEARWATER *Puffinus p. opisthomelas* **Pl. 9**
E. Pacific. Breeds on coast of Lower California. Upperparts brownish-black. Under tail-coverts and flanks dark. Tail long.   Map 63.

RACES IN S. PACIFIC:

FLUTTERING SHEARWATER *Puffinus p. gavia* **Pl. 10**
New Zealand coastal waters, extending N.W. to Australia. Breeds on islands off North Island of New Zealand. Smaller than other races (12–14 ins, 31–36 cm) with shorter (30 ins, 76 cm) and broader wings, upperparts brown. Underwings have narrow dark margins. Sides of head and neck mottled. Legs flesh-coloured. Flight fluttering except in strong winds, with short glides close to the surface. Frequently gathers in flocks on the water, diving and feeding.   Map 64.

HUTTON'S SHEARWATER *Puffinus p. huttoni* **Pl. 10**
Cook Strait and E. Coast of New Zealand, extending to S. Australia. Like *P.p. gavia* but uniformly darker brown and breeding season two months later. Map 65.

LITTLE SHEARWATER *Puffinus assimilis* **Pl. 9**
(A) Small, 10.5–12 ins, 26–30 cm, wing-span 21 ins, 53 cm; (B) Upperparts slaty-black; (C) Underparts, sides of cheeks, neck, under tail-coverts white; (D) Underwings white; (E) Bill, legs bluish-black, the latter observable against white under tail-coverts; (F) Tail short; (G) Flight: very rapid wing-beats, short glides on stiff wings.

BREEDS (Map 66):

S. Atlantic – Tristan da Cunha and Gough Is.

S.W. Pacific – Lord Howe, Norfolk, Kermadec and Austral Is.

Australia – islands off S.W. Australia.

New Zealand – off N.E. coast of Auckland Province and Bay of Plenty. Individual races off Australia and New Zealand cannot be identified as such at sea.

N. *Atlantic* – *P.a. baroli*: Madeira, Azores, Salvage and Canary Is. (C).
Shows more white in front of eye.
P.a. boydi: Cape Verdi Is. (C). Under tail-coverts.

AUDUBON'S SHEARWATER *Puffinus l'herminieri*

(A) Small, 12 ins, 31 cm. Wing-span 27 ins, 69 cm; (B) Sturdily built, wings rather short, narrow; (C) Upperparts dark brown; (D) Underparts white, dark shoulder patch; (E) Underwings white, under tail-coverts black; (F) Bill long, slender, black, legs whitish flesh-colour; (G) Tail rather long, rounded; (H) Flight: six or seven rapid wing beats followed by short glides close over the sea. Swims and dives freely.

Much smaller and browner than Manx Shearwater *Puffinus puffinus*, with shorter wings and longer tail. The smaller Little Shearwater *Puffinus assimilis* has black upperparts, white under tail-coverts and bluish legs; a point to look for.
RANGE: Tropical W. Atlantic, Indian and Pacific Oceans.
RACE IN ATLANTIC, INDIAN AND PACIFIC OCEANS:

AUDUBON'S SHEARWATER *Puffinus l'h. l'herminieri*   **Pl. 9**
Tropical W. Atlantic, Caribbean, breeds throughout W. Indies, Bahamas and islands off Central America and Venezuela, and on islands in Indian and Pacific Oceans. Map 67.

RACE IN ARABIAN SEA AND PERSIAN GULF:

PERSIAN SHEARWATER *Puffinus l'h persicus*   **Fl. 10**
Southern quarter of Red Sea, Gulf of Aden, N. Arabian Sea, Gulf of Oman, Persian Gulf. (A) 12–13 ins, 31–33 cm; (C) Sooty-brown; (D) Central portion of abdomen white, upper parts of sides and flanks brown; (E) Central portion of underwing white, merging into wide brown margins, axillaries brown, under tail-coverts brown; (F) Bill dusky, legs flesh-colour; (G) Tail short, rounded. Map 68.

HEINROTH'S SHEARWATER *Puffinus heinrothi*   **Pl. 9**

Very small, 7.5 ins, 19 cm. This species is known only from specimens from the coast of New Britain.

Its general plumage is similar to the Short-tailed Shearwater, brownish-black above, underparts slightly paler, throat and chin grey, and showing pale underwing-coverts. Bill greyish-black, relatively long and slender. Legs flesh-coloured.

Due to its very small size it might be confused with Bulwer's Petrel, but its long slender bill and shorter tail should be looked for.
RANGE: Unknown. Not mapped.

GREAT-WINGED or GREY-FACED PETREL   **Fl. 10**
Pterodroma macroptera

Medium, 15–16 ins, 38–41 cm. Wing-span 42 ins, 107 cm. A rather heavy long winged petrel of overall dark brown plumage with a grey patch around the base of the bill and throat, sometimes extending above the bill to the forehead. Its dark wings are exceptionally long and narrow. Its bill is short and black and legs black. In flight in calm weather it flaps and glides, but in moderate winds it swoops and soars in fast high towering arcs well above the horizon, the wings looking like great scythes.

It pays no attention to ships. New Zealand breeding birds show more grey on the forehead, face and throat than those seen in the S. Atlantic and S. Indian Oceans.
RANGE: Southern oceans between 50°S. and 30°S. Breeds on islands in the southern S. Atlantic and S. Indian Oceans, the S. coast of Western Australia and North Island of New Zealand. Map 69.

WHITE-HEADED PETREL *Pterodroma lessoni* Pl. 11
Medium, 18 ins, 46 cm. Wing-span 36 ins, 92 cm. A medium built rather large petrel with long narrow wings and a medium round tail. The crown, hind neck and upper tail-coverts are pale grey, the back greyish and upperwings sooty-brown. The front of the head, face, throat, underparts and base of tail are white, a dark patch showing around the eye. The underwings are grey. Bill short and black; legs flesh-coloured. Its flight is fast with much banking and swooping.

Easily recognised by its rather large size, large amount of white on the head and pale hind neck and pale tail.
RANGE: Antarctic seas ranging to the edge of the pack ice. New Zealand waters and north to about 34°S. Breeds in Kerguelen I. and in Auckland, Antipodes and Macquarie Is. Map 70.

SCHLEGEL'S PETREL *Pterodroma incerta* Pl. 10
Medium, 17.5–18 ins, 45–46 cm. A stoutly built petrel with long narrow wings and a medium round tail. The whole head, neck and upperparts are brown, rather paler on the hindneck. The throat and foreneck are brown sharply divided from the white of the lower neck, breast and abdomen, which in turn contrast with the dark brown underwings and under tail-coverts. Bill black; legs yellowish.

It has been seen following ships and is easily distinguished.
RANGE: S. Atlantic Ocean. Breeds in Tristan da Cunha. Map 71.

SOLANDER'S PETREL *Pterodroma solandri* Pl. 12
Medium size, 16 ins, 41 cm. Wing-span 37 ins, 94 cm. A heavily built petrel with slaty-grey upperparts contrasting with a darker brown head, wings and tail. The forehead and throat are white, a dark patch noticeable in front of the eye. The underparts and underwings are greyish-brown, some white feathers showing as a white oval patch towards the centre of the underwing. Bill short and black; legs flesh-coloured. Flight normally consists of long glides and upswinging banking turns.

The grey appearance of the back and the white oval patches on the underwings help to distinguish it.
RANGE: Sub-tropical S. Pacific Ocean dispersing northwards across the Equator during the southern winter. Breeds on Lord Howe I. Map 72.

MURPHY'S PETREL *Pterodroma ultima* Pl. 12
Medium, 15 ins, 38 cm. Wing-span 38 ins, 97 cm. A medium built petrel with narrow wings and medium round tail. At sea it appears as an overall greyish-brown petrel with a short black bill and flesh-coloured legs. At close quarters the crown and nape appear darker, and the back, scapulars and upperwing coverts greyish-brown.

The throat is mottled with white and a dark patch shows before and under the eye. The feathers of the forehead and lores appear greyish. Bill short and black; legs flesh-coloured. Flight in moderate winds fast, swooping, banking and soaring.

Somewhat similar to Solander's Petrel, but is smaller and shows no white underwing patch.
RANGE: Central sub-tropical Pacific Ocean. Breeds in Tuamotu, Austral Is., Lucie I. and Oeno I. Map 73.

PEALE'S PETREL or MOTTLED PETREL　　　Pl. 12
Pterodroma inexpectata
Small–medium, 14 ins, 36 cm. Wing-span 30 ins, 76 cm. A fairly small medium build petrel with long narrow wings and a medium round tail. The crown, nape, upperparts and upper surface of tail are grey, the scapulars and wings darker, and a 'W' pattern is observable across the upperwings. The forehead, throat, breast and under tail-coverts are white. A conspicuous dark patch surrounds the eye showing against the whitish sides of the face. The forward portions of the underparts are white, but a distinct grey patch shows on the after portion of the underbelly. The axillaries are black, the centre of the underwing is white with thick black edging on the forward edge, finer on the trailing edge, and a noticeable dark band cuts across the white central lining from the carpel joint to the abdomen. Bill short and black; legs flesh-coloured. Flight fast, swooping and soaring in high arcs, wrists bent, well above the horizon.
　　Known as the 'Rainbird' in New Zealand. At sea in flight its most distinctive feature is its underwing pattern.
RANGE: Breeds on Stewart and Snares Is., migrating northwards from New Zealand waters widely into the western North Pacific to 55°N, extending eastwards towards the west coast of North America. Map 74.

KERGUELEN PETREL　*Pterodroma brevirostris*　　Pl. 11
Small–medium, 13 ins, 33 cm. Wing-span 26 ins, 66 cm. An almost uniformly dark slate-grey petrel with slight mottling on forehead and face, and in some cases on flanks. Slightly darker grey on wings and tail. Bill black, narrow and compressed; legs purplish flesh-coloured.
　　Its overall grey appearance distinguishes it from other petrels.
RANGE: S. Atlantic and S. Indian Oceans from 60°S. to about 40°S. Occasionally reaches the pack ice. Ranges east to New Zealand occasionally. Breeds on Gough, Kerguelen and Marion Is. Map 75.

SOFT-PLUMAGED PETREL　*Pterodroma mollis*　　Pl. 10
Small–medium, 13.5–14 ins, 34–36 cm. Wing-span 26 ins, 66 cm. The back of the head and back are slate-grey, the tail dark grey and the upperwings brown. The face and throat are white, a dark patch showing below the eye. The underparts are greyish-white and a darker band occurs across the chest. The under surface of wings dark brown; bill short and black; legs flesh-coloured. Its flight is fast with rapid wingbeats and much zig-zagging while planing on angled wings close over the sea.
RANGE: Atlantic and S. Indian Oceans. Breeds in Madeira, Cape Verde and Tristan da Cunha in the Atlantic, and in Kerguelen and St. Paul Is. in the southern Indian Ocean. Map 76.

TAHITI PETREL　*Pterodroma rostrata*
(A) Small–medium, 14 ins, 36 cm. Wing-span 33 ins, 84 cm. Stockily built with moderately long wings and tail; (C) Head, neck, upperparts dark brown; (D) Upper breast dark brown with a sharp dividing line between dark breast and remainder of

white underbody and under tail-coverts; (E) Underwings dark brown; (F) Bill massive, short, black, legs flesh-colour, feet black; (G) Flight: banks, arcs and glides seldom above horizon, interspersed with deep wing-beats. Distinguished from Phoenix Petrel *Pterodroma alba* by its heavier build, darker brown plumage and lack of any white on chin and throat.

RANGE: Tropical and sub-tropical central and western Pacific south of the Equator. Breeds on Marquesas Is., Society Is., New Caledonia and possibly Solomon Is.

RACES:

TAHITI PETREL *Pterodroma r. rostrata* **Pl. 12**

Not reported breeding on Solomon Is. Map 77.

BECK'S PETREL *Pterodroma r. becki*

Little known, only two specimens recorded N. of Solomon Is. (A) Smaller with shorter wings and tail; (D) Flanks and white under tail-coverts show some brown streaking. Not mapped.

REUNION PETREL *Pterodroma aterrima* Pl. 12

Small–medium, 14 ins, 36 cm. The present existence of this Indian Ocean Gad-fly Petrel remains uncertain. In appearance it is a stockily built black petrel with a short massive black bill, moderately long wing and rather long slightly pointed tail. Legs dark reddish; inner third of inner part of toe pink, outer toe and webs black with sharp dividing line. Its flight may be expected to be fast with swooping and arcing above the horizon.

In the Indian Ocean it might be confused with the dark phase of the Trinidade Petrel *Pterodroma arminjoniana* which is also likely to be somewhat rare and has much the same area of distribution.

RANGE: In the Indian Ocean it may still breed in the Mascarene Is., probably Reunion where petrels are said to breed in inland cliffs. Not mapped.

PHOENIX PETREL *Pterodroma alba* Pl. 12

Medium, 15 ins, 38 cm. Wing-span 33 ins, 84 cm. A medium built petrel with long narrow wings and medium round tail. The whole head, neck and upperparts are dark sooty-black. The throat, lower breast, abdomen and under tail-coverts are white. A distinguishing feature is a broad dark band across the chest, always present. Axillaries are white and the under surface of wings all dark. Bill short, stout and black; legs flesh-coloured or yellowish. In flight tends to glide and bank in steep arcs, its long sickle-shaped wings bent at the wrists, between loose wing-beats.

The Herald, Kermadec, Tahiti and Collared Petrels in the Pacific Ocean, the Soft-plumaged Petrel in the S. Atlantic and S. Indian Oceans frequently have similar dark breast bands. Of these only the Tahiti and Soft-plumaged Petrel has a completely dark underwing however the latter does not range into the Pacific Ocean. The Phoenix Petrel is best recognised by its sickle-shaped wings, very dark head and black underwings.

RANGE: Ranges widely throughout sub-tropical and tropical belt of the Pacific Ocean. Map 78.

KERMADEC PETREL *Pterodroma neglecta* Pl. 12

Medium, 15.5 ins, 89 cm. Wing-span 36 ins, 92 cm. A lightly built petrel with long narrow wings and a medium round tail. Head usually freckled whitish-brown. Upperparts brown, upperwings and tail blackish-brown. The underbody varies considerably; sometimes white with brownish feathers on breast and flanks, at other times entirely brown. The underwing is always brown, showing a white area near the tip of the underwing due to the white shafts of the primaries. Bill black. Legs black or yellow. Flight unhurried with deep wingbeats alternating with steep banked arcs and glides, wings bent at the wrists.

Can be confused with the smaller Herald Petrel, but is a somewhat paler brown above, and can be distinguished by its entirely brown underwings which show a distinct white patch near the tip.

RANGE: Sub-tropical and tropical zone of the Pacific Ocean. Breeds on Lord Howe and Kermadec Is., Austral and Tuamotu Is., Ducie and Oeni Is., and in the Juan Fernandez Group off the west coast of S. America.   Map 79.

TRINIDADE PETREL *Pterodroma arminjoniana*

Small—medium, 16 ins, 41 cm. Wing-span 38 ins, 97 cm. Lightly built with long narrow wings. Occurs in variable plumage.

DARK PHASE: (A) Dark brownish overall; (B) Underwing mottled-brown showing a white area towards tip; (C) bill short, black; (D) tail medium length, rounded.

PALE AND INTERMEDIATE PHASE: (A) Brownish-grey or brown upperparts, face and chin paler; (B) Underbody either white or more often white with dark breast band and flanks, or whole breast and flanks brown, abdomen mottled-white, underwing as in dark phase; (C) bill short, black, legs black or pinkish; (D) Flight: graceful swoops and banks close over the sea with wings bent at the wrists.

RANGE: Indian, S. Atlantic and Pacific Oceans.

RACE IN INDIAN AND S. ATLANTIC OCEANS:

TRINIDADE PETREL   *Pterodroma a. arminjoniana*   Pl. 10
Reported breeding on Round I., Mauritius, and possibly Reunion I. in the Indian Ocean, and at Trinidad and Martin Vas Is. in the S. Atlantic. Little is known of its oceanic range.   Map 80.

RACE IN PACIFIC;

HERALD PETREL   *Pterodroma a. heraldica*   Pl. 10
Breeds on Easter I., Ducie, Oeno, Henderson, Tuamotu, Chesterfield, Tonga and Marquesas Is., and disperses northwards into N. Central Pacific. (B) Both phases, underwing mainly dark with a thin irregular white centre line.   Map 81.

WHITE-NECKED PETREL *Pterodroma externa*   Pl. 11

Medium, 17 ins, 43 cm. Wing-span 38 ins, 97 cm. A rather large but lightly built petrel with long narrow wings and short wedge-shaped tail. The crown and nape are brownish-black, and a greyish-white collar around the neck separates the nape from the grey back and rump. The upperwings are medium-grey with darker 'W' pattern across wings and back. Tail black. The forehead and face are white, the area around the eye dark grey. The underparts and under-surface of wings are white with dark margin between bend of wing and leading primary. Bill short, heavy and black, legs yellowish. Its flight is fast with much banking and swooping on wings bent at the wrist often rising high above the horizon.

Distinguished from the White-headed Petrel by its very dark crown, whitish collar and white underwings. Those breeding at Juan Fernandez Is. tend to have greyish neck collars but turn whitish with feather wear, sometimes known as Juan Fernandez Petrels.

RANGE: Pacific Ocean from western sector of S. Pacific and from west coast of Chile, ranging northwards into central Pacific during southern winter. Breeds in the Kermadec Is. and in Mas Alfuera I. in the Juan Fernandez group.   Map 82.

BLACK-CAPPED PETREL *Pterodroma hasitata*
(A) Medium, 16 ins, 41 cm; (B) Upperparts sooty-brown, crown darker blackish-brown; (C) Forehead white, a whitish collar surrounds the nape; (D) Upper tail-coverts and base of tail white; (E) Underbody, under tail-coverts white, sides of breast greyish-brown; (F) Central linings to underwings white, with broad dark leading margins, axillaries white; (G) Bill short, stout, black, legs flesh-colour, webs black; (H) Flight: series of rapid wingbeats and arcs on angled wings. Distinguished by its white collar and white rump patch (the rather similar Bermuda Petrel *Pterodroma cahow* has dark nape and rump, the Great Shearwater *Puffinus gravis* has a long slender bill).
RANGE: Within the Caribbean and wanders northward occasionally off Florida and S. Carolina.
RACES:
  BLACK-CAPPED PETREL *Pterodroma h. hasitata* **Pl. 10**
  Breeds in Hispaniola. Map 82.
  JAMAICA PETREL *Pterodroma h. caribbaea* **Pl. 10**
  Possibly now extinct, once bred in Jamaica. (C), (D), (E), (F) all dark sooty-brown, but shows an indistinct pale rump. Not mapped.

BERMUDA PETREL *Pterodroma cahow* **Pl. 10**
Small–medium, 14–15 ins, 36–38 cm. Wing-span 36 ins, 92 cm. A dark capped petrel with sooty-grey crown, upperparts and tail. Upper tail-coverts sooty-grey. Forehead, lower sides of face, underbody and under tail-coverts white. Axillaries white. Central linings to underwings white with broad dark margins. Sides of breast dusky. Bill short, stout, black. Legs pink, webs dark. In flight it swoops and glides in arcs low over the water on long angled wings followed by a short series of rapid wing-beats.
  Very similar to the Black-capped Petrel which occurs in the Caribbean but is larger and heavier in build and lacks white above rump and white on nape.
RANGE: Breeds on Bermuda and appears to range at no great distance from the islands. Not mapped.

HAWAIIAN PETREL *Pterodroma phaeopygia* **Pl. 12**
Medium, 17 ins, 43 cm. Wing-span 36 ins, 92 cm. A medium built petrel with long narrow wings and short wedge-shaped tail. Its upperparts are dark greyish-brown with black upperwings and tail; its forehead white, the cheeks and area around the eye black. Its underparts and the central portion of its underwing white with broad dark edges. Bill short and black; legs pink. In flight it swoops and soars in steeply banked arcs, its wings bent at the wrists.
  It is liable to be confused with the larger White-necked Petrel and is best distinguished from it by its very dark brown coloration above, and thick dark underwing margins.
RANGE: Sub-tropical and tropical waters of the Pacific Ocean. Breeds on Hawaiian and Galapagos Is. Map 83.

BARAU'S PETREL *Pterodroma baraui* **Pl. 10**
Medium, 15 ins, 38 cm. A rather lightly built petrel with long narrow wings and a noticeably short round tail. The forehead and cheeks below the eye are white and the whole underbody and under tail-coverts white. The crown and nape are brownish-black, contrasting with the greyish back; upperwings sooty-brown, rump and upper tail coverts sooty-brown. The central underwing linings are white with

dark leading and trailing margins combining in a dark underwing tip. Bill short, black. Legs yellowish, webs yellow at base with broad black tips. Flight fast, banking and swooping.

A recently discovered species closely associated with a group of tropical petrels of the type of the Black-capped Petrel and Cahow but occurring in a different ocean. RANGE: Found breeding on Reunion I., Indian Ocean, and probably ranges eastwards along the sub-tropical convergence. Map 85.

BONIN PETREL *Pterodroma hypoleuca* Pl. 12

Small–medium, 12–13 ins, 31–33 cm. Wing-span 27 ins, 69 cm. A lightly built petrel with long narrow wings and a short round tail. The forehead and cheeks are white, the remainder of the upperparts mid-grey, darker on crown and nape. The upper surface of the wings is sooty-grey with lighter coverts so that an inconspicuous 'W' pattern is discernable in flight. The underparts and under tail-coverts are white. The central portion of the underwing is white with a thick black band to the leading edge and dusky-grey band to the trailing edge. Underwing axillaries usually white. Bill stout and black; legs flesh-coloured with dark tip to toes; tail sooty-black. Flight in light airs consists of flaps and glides, dipping and rolling; in moderate winds fast, swooping, soaring and banking.

Bonin Petrel is difficult to distinguish from other petrels of the 'Cookilaria' group of genus *Pterodroma*, Cook's, Gould's, Collared, Black-winged and Stejneger's, but is larger with a stouter bill and more flesh-coloured legs than the latter species. RANGE: Western N. Pacific. Breeds on the leeward Hawaiian Is., Bonin and Volcano Is. Observed regularly between 25°N. and 35°N. between breeding area and Japan. Map 86.

BLACK-WINGED PETREL *Pterodroma nigripennis* Pl. 12

Small–medium, 12 ins, 31 cm. Wing-span 26 ins, 66 cm. Small, lightly built with long narrow wings and short round tail. Crown, hind neck, back and upper tail-coverts grey. Upper wings slaty-black. Forehead mottled, dark patch around eye, cheeks and underparts, including underwing-coverts white; a dark patch shows on sides of cheeks. Underwings have thick prominent dark margins, white axillaries. A prominent dark 'W' band shows across upperwings. Bill short, stout and black; legs flesh-coloured. Flight fast and erratic in steep arcs, wings bent at the wrists, with some rapid deep wingbeats.

Very similar to Gould's, Cook's and Stejneger's Petrels and difficult to separate species at sea. Distinguished from Chatham Petrel which has *black* axillaries. RANGE: Breeds in Kermadec and Three Kings Is. off N. coasts of New Zealand and migrates to N. Central Pacific from May to September ranging there between 5°N. and 30°N. Map 87.

CHATHAM ISLAND PETREL *Pterodroma axillaris*

Small–medium, 12 ins, 31 cm. A small lightly built petrel. Crown, nape, back and upper tail coverts medium-grey, wings dark slaty-black. A dark 'W' band across upperwings. Forehead, underparts and underwing white. Axillaries black. Bill short, stout, black. Legs flesh-coloured, webs with dark outer ends. Flight fast, swooping and arcing.

The black axillaries which can be observed at sea with birds on the wing at close quarters distinguishes it from the Black-winged Petrel which has white axillaries. RANGE: Breeds on Chatham Is. Range at sea uncertain, probably over the cool waters of the S. Pacific. Not mapped.

'*Hypoleuca*' and '*Cookilaria*' petrels in flight showing underwings.
   1 Bonin Petrel, *Pterodroma hypoleuca*, p.40. Broad dark band on leading edge, dusky grey
       trailing edge.
   2 Gould's Petrel, *Pterodroma leucoptera*, p.43
   3 Collared Petrel, *Pterodroma leucoptera brevipes*, p.43
   4 Stejneger's Petrel, *Pterodroma longirostris*, p.42
   5 Black-winged Petrel, *Pterodroma nigripennis*, p.40
   6 Chatham Island Petrel, *Pterodroma axillaris*, p.40. Medium dark band, black axillaries.
   7 Cook's Petrel, *Pterodroma cooki*, p.42

Petrels with **W** wing pattern
1 Cook's Petrel, *Pterodroma cooki*, and allies have this pattern fairly conspicuously; see Plate 12 and below.
2 Prions, *Pachyptila* species, always show the W wing pattern clearly; see Plate 11 and pages 26–8.
3 Blue Petrel, *Halobaena caerulea*: W pattern and dark cap, pale tail. See Plate 11 and page 25. Some *Pterodroma* species also have dark cap and back; see Plates 10–12 and pages 34–43.

COOK'S PETREL *Pterodroma cooki*   Pl. 12

Small, 11 ins, 28 cm. Wing-span 26 ins, 66 cm. A small lightly built petrel with long narrow wings and short round tail. Crown, nape, sides of neck and breast light grey, tinged brown. Dark area before the eye. Forehead white or finely freckled grey and white. Back, rump and upper tail-coverts pale grey. Upper wing-coverts slightly darker grey, a very distinct '**W**' pattern showing across the wings. Primaries dark with white inner webs. The underparts, axillaries and underwings are white, the underwings showing thin dark edges. Bill short and black; legs pale blue; end of webs black. Tail very dark grey, outer feathers white. Flight in light airs languid and rolling; in moderate winds fast and erratic with steep banks and arcs showing alternatively the white underparts and upper wing pattern.

Distinguished from Gould's Petrel by its paler upperparts and clear '**W**' pattern on back.
RANGE: S. Pacific Ocean from New Zealand to west coast of S. America migrating northwards into N. Pacific during southern winter. Breeds on Little Barrier I. and Stewart I., New Zealand, and Juan Fernandez I. off S. America.   Map 88.

STEJNEGER'S PETREL *Pterodroma longirostris*

(A) Small, 10 ins, 25 cm. Wing-span 28 ins, 71 cm; (B) Slightly built, long narrow wings; (C) Forehead white, head and nape dark grey; (D) Back, wing-coverts, upper tail-coverts light grey; (E) Wing quills slaty-black; (F) distinct '**W**' pattern across wings and back; (G) Underparts, under tail-coverts white, underwing white

with narrow dark margin to leading edge; (H) Bill short, black, legs blue; outer toes black, webs white; (K) Tail short, blackish-grey, outer tail feathers grey, rounded; (L) Flight fast, buoyant, rapid wing-beats and steep upward banks, wings bent.
RANGE: S. Pacific dispersing into N. Central Pacific during non breeding season.
RACES:

STEJNEGER'S PETREL *Pterodroma l. longirostris* **Pl. 12**
Breeds only in Mas Afuera I. in the Juan Fernandez group west of Chile, dispersing northwards and westwards and crossing the Equator during non breeding season. Map 89.

PYCROFT'S PETREL *Pterodroma l. pycrofti* **Not illustrated**
Breeds in Poor Knights Is. and Hen and Chicken Is. off North Island of New Zealand. Full range uncertain, probably disperses northwards and eastwards during non breeding season. (A) 11 ins, 28 cm; (B) Wings slightly shorter; (H) Bill slightly shorter; (K) Tail longer. Map 90.

GOULD'S PETREL *Pterodroma leucoptera*

(A) Small, 12 ins, 31 cm. Wing-span 28 ins, 71 cm. Slightly built with long narrow wings and short rounded tail; (B) Forehead white with some speckling, face white, dark area before eye; (C) Crown, nape, sides of neck sooty-black; (D) Upperwing-coverts medium-grey, an indistinct '**W**' pattern showing across wing-coverts and back, primaries black, inner webs white at base; (E) Back, rump, dark grey, tail slaty-black; (F) Underparts vary, shoulders grey, underbody sometimes white, more often with dusky patch on breast and flanks; (G) Underwings white with thin dark margin on leading edge; (H) Bill short, black, legs bluish; (K) Flight: rapid wing-beats and steep banks and arcs, wings bent at wrists.
RANGE: Western Pacific in sub-tropical and tropical waters.
RACES:

GOULD'S PETREL *Pterodroma l. leucoptera* **Pl. 12**
From eastern Australia, eastwards into sub-tropical Pacific. Breeds on Cabbage Tree I. Map 91.

COLLARED PETREL *Pterodroma l. brevipes* **Pl. 12**
Sub-tropical and tropical western Pacific. Breeds on New Caledonia, New Hebrides and Fiji. (D) Slaty-grey; in good light the area forward of '**W**' appears paler accentuating the '**W**' pattern; (F) Dusky band across breast, occasionally entire underbody dusky; (G) Dark wedge along forewing from body to carpal joint, thin dark trailing edge. Map 92.

JOUANIN'S PETREL *Bulweria fallax* **Pl. 9**

Small–medium, 14 ins, 36 cm. Jouanin's Petrel is a larger Indian Ocean representative of Bulwer's Petrel of the Atlantic and Pacific Oceans.

A lightly built small–medium petrel uniformly brownish-black overall, sometimes showing paler upper wing-coverts, with a noticeably short thick black bill and flesh-coloured legs with darker edges to the tarsus and toes. Its wings are long and slender, its tail long and wedge-shaped. Its flight is very fast and mobile, swooping and rising high over the horizon on the upswing, and it tends to point its short stout bill downwards during flight.

In the Arabian Sea it is most likely to be confused with a dark phase of the Wedge-tailed Shearwater, which however can always be distinguished by its long slender bill, and heavier slower flight.
RANGE: Arabian Sea and Gulf of Aden. Map 93.

BULWER'S PETREL *Bulweria bulwerii*   **Pl. 9**
Small, 10.5–11 ins, 27–28 cm. Wing-span 24 ins, 61 cm. A small sooty-brown petrel with slightly paler underparts. A pale band on the upperwings can usually be discerned. The dark wings are long, narrow and slender, and a distinguishing feature is its rather long wedge-shaped tail. Bill black. Legs flesh-coloured. In moderate winds it flies in shallow swooping arcs and glides low over the water with occasional rapid wing-beats. In light winds it employs easy deep irregular wing-beats.

It is only slightly larger than the dark storm-petrels but its flight is stronger and of a different character. Its long tail helps in identification.
RANGE: N. Atlantic and N. Pacific Oceans. Breeds on the eastern N. Atlantic Is., leeward Hawaiian Is., Bonin and Volcano Is., Phoenix and Marquesas Is. and on the coast of China. Frequently seen west of the Hawaiian Is. towards Japan and in the China Sea.   Map 94.

Bulwer's Petrel   Macgillivray's Petrel   Storm Petrel

The Macgillivray's Petrel illustrated here is possibly not a full species: it is only known from a single specimen. Identification at sea would be very difficult.

MACGILLIVRAY'S PETREL *Bulweria macgillivrayi*
Small, 11.5 ins, 29 cm. Plumage uniformly sooty-black overall with a relatively long wedge-shaped tail and stout black bill. Lacks paler band on upperwings.

At present only known from a single specimen from the Fiji Is. Very similar but larger than Bulwer's Petrel with a larger bill.
RANGE: Tropical zone of Pacific Ocean but extent of range unknown.   Not mapped.

STORM-PETRELS Hydrobatidae

Storm-petrels or 'Mother Carey's Chickens' as they are known to seafarers are the smallest of oceanic seabirds, sometimes compared in size to large stocky swallows, and their flight to that of butterflies. The majority have overall sooty-black or sooty-brown plumage showing white patches above the rump; others are sooty-black altogether and yet others have white or partially white underparts. Their flight is generally weaker, more erratic and fluttering than true petrels, and they may be seen weaving across the wake of ships dropping their legs to touch the water and hopping or skipping as they search for minute crustaceans or other food particles. Their bills are short and black, the tube-nosed nostrils forming a single orifice. Legs which are black vary considerably in length.

WILSON'S PETREL. Storm petrels are very small seabirds. They all look similar: watch for the wing pattern, rump colour, and the shape of the tail.

Nesting and young

These nest on rocky shores and islands; nesting in crevices, cavities, burrows and sometimes in stone walls, either natural or excavated by the birds themselves. Sometimes small amounts of nest material may be pulled into burrows. Breeding usually occurs in colonies, and the birds may not breed until 2–3 years old. The eggs and young can withstand periods of neglect, eggs have been recorded as left for up to 11 days, and this usually only delays incubation and development. The single white egg is incubated for 38–40 days, or occasionally up to 50 days, by both birds, taking alternate periods of several days. Young are brooded for the first week and fed daily at first but later at several day intervals The young have thick grey or brownish down, in two successive coats. They become very large and fat, heavier and apparently larger than the adults; but lose this when they feather, although they may be fed to within a day of leaving. The fledging period is from 56–70 days.

WILSON'S STORM-PETREL *Oceanites oceanicus*   PL. 13
Very small, 7–7.5 ins, 18–19 cm. Wing-span 16 ins, 41 cm. Upperparts sooty-black, a palish brown band showing across the greater wing-coverts, and sometimes a pale line noticeable across the upperwings at the base of the secondary wing feathers. A clear patch of white feathers shows above the rump, formed by the upper tail-coverts, the upper and lower limits appearing slightly curved; some white feathers extend to the lower flanks on either side. Underparts sooty-brown. The tail is black and square, but appears rounded at the tips. A distinguishing feature in flight at close quarters is the sight of the feet just protruding beyond the tail, for it possesses exceptionally long legs. When examined in the hand the webs of the feet will be seen to be yellow. Bill black. Flight normally consists of short glides interspersed with loose wingbeats with a tendency to tilt and roll from side to side. When searching for food it hops and flutters paddling along the surface with its long legs touching the water. Wilson's Storm-petrels regularly follow ships.
   Particularly in the N. Atlantic where the British Storm-petrel, Madeiran Storm-petrel, Leach's Storm-petrel and Wilson's Storm-petrels may occur in the same area, identification at sea is very difficult. Both the British and Wilson's are likely to follow ships, the British being the smaller, the Madeiran and Leach's have freer flight and Leach's appears browner and larger with the most dashing flight.
RANGE: Breeds on the antarctic continent in Adelie Land, Haswell I., islands off Graham Land, adjacent sub-antarctic islands, S. Shetlands, S. Orkneys, S. Sandwich Is., S. Georgia, Falkland Is., Kerguelen, Heard and Bouvet Is. Migrates far north of the Equator in Atlantic, Indian and Pacific Oceans.   Map 95.

ELLIOT'S STORM-PETREL *Oceanites gracilis*   P. 13
Tiny, 5.8 ins, 148 mm. An extremely small dark storm-petrel, sooty black above with browner upperwing-coverts, and a white patch above the rump extending around the sides. The central portion of the underparts is white, remainder sooty-black; underwings black. Bill black; legs black, middle of webs yellow. Tail square, slightly indented and glossy black. Flight weak, fluttering, legs frequently pattering on the water.
   Its plumage is very similar to Wilson's Storm-petrel, but it is much smaller, its flight weaker. Its range is liable to clash with Wilson's Storm-petrel.
RANGE: Pacific coast of S. America from the Galapagos Is. southwards to Chile. Breeds in the Galapagos Is.   Map 96.

GREY-BACKED STORM-PETREL *Garrodia nereis*   Pl. 14
Very small, 6.5–7 ins, 165–178 mm. A very small species. The head, neck and breast are sooty-grey. The back is ashy-grey, the rump, upper tail-coverts and tail a paler grey. The upperwings, with the exception of the secondary wing-coverts which are also pale grey, are brownish-black, and the grey portions having white edges give a scaly grey appearance to the bird. Below the breast the underparts including the inner underwing linings and under tail-coverts are white. A noticeable feature is the black terminal band on the tail. Bill and legs black.
   Its greyish appearance, lack of any white patch above the rump and black tail band help to distinguish it.
RANGE Southern oceans ranging north to 35°S. Breeds in Falkland Is., S. Georgia, Gough I., Kerguelen I. and Chatham, Antipodes and Auckland Is.   Map 97.

WHITE-FACED STORM-PETREL *Pelagodroma marina* **Pl. 13**
Small, 8 ins, 20 cm. Wing-span 17 ins, 43 cm. Easily recognised by its distinctive plumage pattern. The crown and nape are greyish-brown, darker on the crown, the back of the neck and upper part of the back grey. The upperwings are brown, primaries black. Further aft again the rump and upper tail-coverts are ashy-grey contrasting with the short black square tail. The most distinctive features are the white forehead and face showing a dusky patch beneath the eye and the completely white underparts and underwing-coverts. Bill and legs black; legs long, webs yellow. Its flight is fast and erratic, darting from side to side, sometimes hopping over the water with legs dangling. It does not follow ships.

Birds breeding in the Kermadec Is. have white rumps and upper tail-coverts.
RANGE: N. and S. Atlantic Ocean, western S. Pacific and tropical Pacific and Indian Oceans, ranging north of the Equator to the Arabian Sea in the southern winter. Breeds in the N. Atlantic Is., Tristan da Cunha and Gough Is., S.W. and southern coasts of Australia. New Zealand, Chatham, Auckland and Kermadec Is. Map 98.

WHITE-BELLIED STORM-PETREL *Fregetta grallaria* **Pl. 13**
Small, 7.5–8.5 ins, 19–22 cm. Wing-span 19 ins, 48 cm. The head, neck and upperparts are sooty-black, greyish-black on the back. Wings and tail black. The upper tail coverts are white, showing a rather indistinct white patch above the rump. Abdomen is white, the flanks sometimes dusky. The under tail-coverts and inner underwing-coverts are white. Bills and legs black. Tail square. Its flight is weak; it is usually seen fluttering and hopping, both feet touching the water together, and is inclined to follow in the wake of ships.

See Black-bellied Storm-petrel (p. 47).
RANGE: Southern oceans from about 35°S., ranging northwards to the tropics, apparently crossing the Equator in the Indian Ocean during the southern winter. Breeds in Tristan da Cunha and Gough Is., Lord Howe I. Austral Is. and Mas a Tierra I. in the Juan Fernandez group. On Lord Howe I. a dark phase occurs having a dark underbody. Map 99.

White-bellied   Black-bellied
These two species are best identified by the different shapes of their 'noses'.

BLACK-BELLIED STORM-PETREL *Fregetta tropica* **Pl. 13**
Small, 8 ins, 20 cm. Wing-span 19 ins, 48 cm. The head and upperparts are sooty-black, rather paler on the median wing-coverts. The upper tail-coverts are white forming a white patch above the rump. The distinctive features are the white flanks and sides of the abdomen and a longitudinal dark band in the centre. The axillaries are white and a whitish central area of the underwing shows indistinctly. Bill and legs are black. The flight appears distinctly erratic, the bird usually swinging from side to side and zig-zagging exposing its white underside.

The Black-bellied Storm-petrel and the White-bellied Storm-petrel are exceedingly difficult to differentiate between at sea, and indeed the Black-bellied species may show no dark central feathers under the belly on occasions. Both species are in the habit of following ships.

RANGE: Southern oceans from the sub-antarctic ranging northwards and apparently crossing the Equator during the southern winter in the Indian Ocean. Breeds in sub-antarctic islands, S. Shetlands, S. Orkneys, S. Sandwich Is., S. Georgia, Crozet Is., Kerguelen Is., and in Auckland, Bounty and Antipodes Is. Reported breeding on Amsterdam I. Map 100.

WHITE-THROATED STORM-PETREL　*Nesofregetta fuliginosa*　Pl. 13

Small, 8.5 ins, 216 mm. Wing-span 20 ins, 51 cm. Head, neck, upperparts and wings above sooty-black, greater wing-coverts paler. A narrow white patch on rump. Underparts are very variable. Pale birds have white throats and underparts and broad sooty breast bands. Intermediate birds have dark streaking on throat and underbody. In the central Pacific some birds may be melanistic and entirely dark. Underwings are greyish-white, under tail-coverts usually white with dark tips. Legs long, black and noticeably flattened. Tail black, deeply forked. In flight it bounds and skips with fluttering wings in an erratic manner.

The Samoan and Striped Storm-petrels are now considered to be simply melanistic White-throated Storm-petrels.

RANGE: Tropical central and western Pacific Oceans. Breeds on New Hebrides, Fiji, Marquesas, Phoenix and Line Is. Map 101.

BRITISH STORM-PETREL　*Hydrobates pelagicus*　Pl. 13

Very small, 5.5–7.5 ins, 14–19 cm. Wing-span 14 ins, 36 cm. A small dark storm-petrel, with sooty-black upperparts usually showing a narrow pale line across the upper wing-coverts. Underparts sooty-brown. It has a clear patch of white feathers above the rump, the forward and after limits appearing slightly curved towards the tail. A distinguishing feature when its wings are raised is a small patch of white feathers at the base of the underwing. Some white shows in the under tail-coverts. Tail black and square; legs black. Its flight is weak and fluttering with short glides, occasionally pattering over the water. It sometimes follows in the wake of ships.

Smaller than the dark Wilson's and Madeiran Storm-petrels but may easily be confused with them at sea. See note under Wilson's Storm-petrel (p. 46).

RANGE: Eastern N. and S. Atlantic Oceans and Mediterranean sea. Migrates southwards reaching the west coast of southern Africa in winter. Breeds in British Isles, Brittany, Canary Is. and Mediterranean. Recently on Filfla Rock, Malta. Map 102.

LEAST STORM-PETREL　*Halocyptena microsoma*　Pl. 14

Tiny, 5.5–6 ins, 140–152 mm. This tiny storm-petrel is the smallest of the storm-petrels with dark sooty-black upperparts, slightly brownish-grey greater wing-coverts and dark brownish underparts. Its tail is wedge-shaped scarcely visible at sea. Its flight is weak and fluttering.

Its overall dark plumage and tiny size readily distinguish it.

RANGE: Pacific coast of America from Lower California to Equator. Breeds on San Benito Is., Lower California. Map 103.

GALAPAGOS STORM-PETREL　*Oceanodroma tethys*　Pl. 13

Very small, 6.5–7 ins, 165–178 mm. This very small storm-petrel has a sooty-black plumage, slightly browner on the upperwing-coverts, a very slightly forked tail and a white somewhat triangular patch above the rump. Bill black; legs very short and black. Its flight, as in other very small storm-petrels, is weak and fluttering.

The greater fore and aft length to its triangular white patch is a guide in identification.

RANGE: Sea areas around the Galapagos Is. extending at times from Lower California to Peru. Breeds in the Galapagos Is.   Map 104.

MADEIRAN STORM-PETREL   *Oceanodroma castro*   Pl. 13

Very small, 7–8 ins, 178–203 mm. Wing-span 18 ins, 46 cm. A dark storm-petrel with sooty-black upperparts, the wing-coverts somewhat browner and sooty-brown underparts. It has a clear cut square white patch above the rump, the upper and lower limits appearing straight and parallel. A few white feathers occur on the flanks and under tail-coverts. A slight cleft in the tail cannot be called forked and is not observable at sea. Its flight is more direct and fast than in many storm-petrels with more constant wingbeats, and it takes no notice of ships.

It looks larger than Wilson's and certainly larger than the British Storm-petrel but is most elusive and difficult to identify. Leach's Storm-petrel looks browner and has a distinctive buoyant free flight.

RANGE: Eastern N. Atlantic and eastern and western N. Pacific Oceans. Breeds in the N. Atlantic Is., Ascension and St. Helena. Galapagos and Hawaiian Is. and in Japan.   Map 105.

LEACH'S STORM-PETREL   *Oceanodroma leucorhoa*   Pl. 13

Small, 8–9 ins, 20–23 cm. Wing-span 19 ins, 48 cm. A medium sized storm-petrel, blackish-brown above with a rather broad prominent paler band across the upperwing-coverts, which varies with feather wear. Underparts sooty-brown. A white patch above the rump is oval in shape, indistinctly divided down the centre by a few dark feathers, not always visible at sea. Some white feathers extend to flanks below rump. Wings long, pointed and rather broad at the base. Tail distinctly forked, broadening towards the tips and noticeable at close range.

Flight fast and buoyant, often swooping steeply between short glides and alternate fast-wing-beats. Sometimes follows ships, at other times pays little attention.

In the southern and western tropical Pacific Leach's Storm-petrels occur with dark rumps, and are smaller than Tristram's and Matsudaira's Storm-petrels or Bulwer's Petrel.

RANGE: Ranges widely over Atlantic and Pacific Oceans. Breeds on both sides of the N. Atlantic and on the coasts of both western N. America and Canada and eastern Asia. In the Pacific Ocean occurs regularly in the central tropical zone.   Map 106.

GUADALUPE STORM-PETREL
Oceanodroma macrodactyla

Small, 8.5 ins, 22 cm. Very similar to Leach's Storm-petrel with somewhat blacker upperparts and greyer underparts and underwings. The white upper tail-coverts show broad dusky tips.

Possibly now extinct. Could not be distinguished from Leach's Storm-petrel at sea.

RANGE: May breed on Guadaloupe I. Range at sea unknown.   Not mapped.

SWINHOE'S STORM-PETREL *Oceanodroma monorhis* Pl 14
Very small, 7–7.5 ins, 178–191 mm. Swinhoe's Storm-petrel is virtually identical in plumage to the Tristram's Storm-petrel, but considerably smaller, with shorter wings and a shorter medium-forked tail. Bill and legs black. It has a distinctive flight, bounding and swooping over the water like a tern, and never pattering.

See note under Tristram's Storm-petrel. An additional species of storm-petrel, *Oceanodroma matsudairae*, is reported to occur in the same area as Swinhoe's Storm-petrel, but is so similar that identification between them at sea is probably impossible.
RANGE: South and west of Japan and S. China Sea, penetrating across the N. Indian Ocean. Breeds on Pescador Is. Map 107.

TRISTRAM'S STORM-PETREL *Oceanodroma tristrami* PL 14
Small, 9–10 ins, 23–25 cm. Wing-span 22 ins, 56 cm. A large storm-petrel. Plumage sooty-brown, a pale brown band showing across the upperwing-coverts. Under-wings a shade paler. The black tail is deeply forked. Bill and legs black.

Flight freer than the smaller storm-petrels, gliding and banking more often and occasionally fluttering.

Formerly quoted as Sooty Storm-petrel.
RANGE: Western N. Pacific Ocean from the leeward Hawaiian Is. westwards towards Japan. Frequently seen north of the Hawaiian Is. outside its breeding season. Breeds on the leeward Hawaiian Is. and on Volcano Is. Map 108.

MARKHAM'S STORM-PETREL *Oceanodroma markhami* PL 14
Small, 9–10 ins, 23–25 cm. Wing-span 22 ins, 56 cm. This species is similar to Tristram's Storm-petrel but ranges in the cool waters off the coasts of Peru. It is doubtful if it could be distinguished from Tristram's Storm-petrel but the two range in widely separated zones.

Formerly quoted as Sooty Storm-petrel. Breeding area unknown. Map 109.

Matsudaira's Storm-petrel   Swinhoe's Storm-petrel

MATSUDAIRA'S STORM-PETREL *Oceanodroma matsudairae* Pl. 14
Small, 10 ins, 25 cm. Wing-span 22 ins, 56 cm. A large sooty-brown storm-petrel with forked tail. It may well be confused with Swinhoe's Storm-petrel *Oceanodroma monorhis* which ranges into the same area. By close observation.

apart from its paler wing coverts which are also evident in Swinhoe's Storm-petrel, its white primary feather shafts show as a whitish area towards the ends of the wings.

RANGE: Breeds on Volcano Is. south of Japan, dispersing southwards to the area of the Philippines, and S. China Sea, a few probably spreading across the N. Indian Ocean. Map 110.

ASHY STORM-PETREL *Oceanodroma homochroa* Pl. 14

Very small, 7.5 ins, 190 mm. A very small sooty storm-petrel with short dark legs and a forked tail. The edges of the upperwing coverts and underwing coverts are slightly paler.

Its distribution may coincide with that of the Black Storm-petrel *Loomelania melania* which is noticeably larger with longer legs and more deeply forked tail. The even smaller Least Storm-petrel *Halocyptena microsoma* has a wedge-shaped tail and a more southerly general range.

RANGE: Off the coast of California. Breeds at Farallon and St. Barbara Is. Map 112.

HORNBY'S STORM-PETREL *Oceanodroma hornbyi* Pl. 14

Small, 8–9 ins, 203–229 mm. A distinctively plumaged species. The top of the head is chocolate-brown; forehead and sides of head white; chin, throat, breast and underbody white, with a clear cut brownish-grey band across the breast. The back is greyish-brown with upper tail-coverts darker. The upper wings are dark brown with greyer greater wing-coverts. The underwings are grey. A noticeable feature is the white collar which extends across the back of the neck. Bill and legs black. Tail dark brown and deeply forked. In flight it flutters and hops.

The white collar and dark band across the breast are the best diagnostic features at sea.

RANGE: Throughout the west coast of S. America. Breeds in the Chilean Andes. Map 113.

FORK-TAILED STORM-PETREL *Oceanodroma furcata* Pl. 14

Small, 8 ins, 203 mm. Wing-span 18 ins, 457 mm. Unique amongst storm-petrels in the pale grey of its plumage. The head and upperparts are pearl-grey, upperwing-coverts with paler edges. A black area shows below the eye. The underparts are even paler grey, appearing white on the throat and under tail-coverts. Axillaries and underwings are greyish-black, edged white. Bill black; legs black; tail noticeably forked. In flight it glides and weaves erratically, often fluttering with rapid wing-beats.

RANGE: N. Pacific and Bering Sea from 55°N. to 35°N. Breeds in the Kuril Is., Aleutian Is., southern Alaska southwards to Oregon. Map 114.

BLACK STORM-PETREL *Loomelania melania* Pl. 14

Small, 9 ins, 23 cm. This is one of the largest of all dark storm-petrels. The upperparts are sooty-black with uniform sooty-brown upperwing-coverts. Underparts brownish-black. Tail black and deeply forked; bill black; legs black and long.

It is liable to be confused with the rather smaller Markham's Storm-petrel which however has shorter legs and whose range does not overlap.

RANGE: Eastern N. Pacific Ocean between California and Peru and does not range any distance to the westward. Breeds in islands off Lower California. Map 111.

Diving Petrel coming to its nest site at night, the pouch is filled with food for the chick.

DIVING-PETRELS Pelecanoididae

Diving-petrels are small stubby birds and, with the exception of the Magellan Diving-petrel, are almost identical in plumage pattern and shape. They have short wings, black upperparts and white underparts. Their bills are short, black and hooked, broadening at the base; their legs short, blue, set far back in the body and their tails short and stumpy. Although resembling the Little Auks of the northern hemisphere, diving-petrels are confined to the southern hemisphere and are true tube-nosed petrels. Their nostrils however open upwards side by side from the base of the upper mandible, and between the sides of the lower mandible there is a distensible pouch. Although the Peruvian Diving-petrel is larger than the remainder, and the Magellan Diving-petrel may be distinguished by the white half collar on the sides of its neck, it is probably impossible to distinguish between them at sea. When examined in the hand the shape and size of the bill are diagnostic.

As their name implies, their principal preoccupation is in diving underwater using their wings to propel them, at other times resting on the surface. When disturbed they either dive or flutter along the surface, but once airborne they fly short distances close over the sea with rapidly whirring flight, usually diving on landing.

Diving-petrels usually keep close to the coasts and are very rarely seen on shipping routes except in New Zealand coastal waters. They feed on small fishes, crustaceans and other marins organisms.

Nesting and young

These breed on islands in the cooler parts of the southern hemisphere. They mature faster than other petrels and may breed in their second year. The nest is in a burrow several feet long dug by the birds themselves in open ground or under trees. Some nest material may be pulled into the burrow. There is a single large white egg which is incubated by both birds, alternating nightly, for c. 8 weeks. The chick's first down is sparse compared with that of other petrels, but the second coat is thicker. It is brooded for the first week or two, as compared with 2–3 days in other petrels. The chick is visited and fed daily and leaves the nest at 47–60 days.

PERUVIAN DIVING-PETREL *Pelecanoides garnoti*   Pl. 14

Small, 8.2–9 ins, 209–229 mm. Bill length, 0.7–0.9 ins, 18–23 mm. Breadth at base, 0.35–0.4 ins, 9–10 mm. Similar to Common Diving-petrel but considerably larger. No band on foreneck.

Strictly limited to inshore waters of Humboldt Current.

RANGE: Coasts of Peru and Chile south to 50°S. A more northerly range than any other diving-petrel. Breeds in islands off the coast.   Map 115.

MAGELLAN DIVING-PETREL *Pelecanoides magellani*   Pl. 14

Small, 7.5–8.8 ins, 191–224 mm. Bill length, 0.6–0.7 ins, 15–18 mm. Breadth at base, 0.35–0.4 ins, 9–10 mm. Similar to the Common Diving-petrel but a conspicuous white collar on each side of the neck forms a partial collar, and foreneck is always white.

RANGE: From Cape Horn to about 50°S. Breeds on coasts of Straits of Magellan.   Map 116.

GEORGIAN DIVING-PETREL *Pelecanoides georgicus*

Very small, 7–8.5 ins, 178–216 mm. Bill length, 0.5–0.6 ins, 13–15 mm. Breadth at base 0.35–0.4 ins, 9–10 mm. Similar to Common Diving-petrel, but its bill is wider at the base and tapers more sharply. Legs pale blue, webs black.

Can only be distinguished by the shape of its bill. See drawing opposite

RANGE: Breeds on S. Georgia, Kerguelen and Heard Is., and Auckland Is.   Map 117.

COMMON DIVING-PETREL *Pelecanoides urinatrix*   Pl. 14

Very small, 7–8 ins, 178–203 mm. Bill length, 0.5–0.7 ins, 13–18 mm. Breadth at base, 0.25–0.35 ins, 6–9 mm. Head and upperparts black. Sides of neck and breast grey, foreneck sometimes mottled grey, the remainder of the underparts white, the sides of the flanks greyish. The underwing-coverts are a greyish-white. Bill black, short and hooked, the lower mandible broad and narrowing sharply towards the tip. Legs blue. Tail short and black.

The Common Diving-petrel tends to range further north than the other species except the Peruvian Diving-petrel.

RANGE: Southern oceans from 55°S. to 35°S. Local to breeding islands which stretch from the Falkland Is. eastwards through the S. Atlantic and S. Indian Ocean to S.E. Australia, Tasmania, New Zealand and adjacent islands.   Map 113.

Diving-petrel bills. On the left the upper bill is shown from above; the lower from the underside. Note also the different patterns above the eye and at the collar.

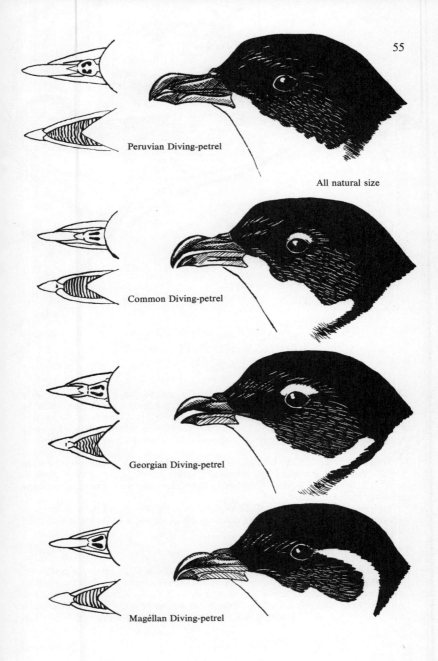

55

Peruvian Diving-petrel

All natural size

Common Diving-petrel

Georgian Diving-petrel

Magéllan Diving-petrel

Red-tailed Tropic-bird on their nesting site.

TROPIC-BIRDS Phaethontidae

These beautiful white seabirds, distinguished in adult plumage by their immensely elongated two central tail feathers or 'streamers', are known as 'Bo'sun Birds' by seafarers, their central tails being likened to 'marlin-spikes'. They range far out into the ocean in the tropical belt and are usually seen flying high with powerful quick wingbeats. They are capable of twisting and turning sharply and plunge steeply to the water for food.

Tropic-birds feed chiefly on squid which rise to the surface at night. It is perhaps for this reason that tropic-birds frequently follow astern in the wake of ships at night, and becoming dazzled by the ship's lights, hit some part of the structure and are later found on board.

Viewed against a background of blue tropical sky it is no easy task to distinguish between the Red-billed and White-tailed species. All tropic-birds swim with their tails cocked.

Nesting and young

These nest on islands of the tropical and subtropical zones. Tropic-birds move with difficulty on land and the nest is usually on a ledge sheltered by an overhang, or in a cavity or crevice in the face of a cliff or steep rock face overlooking the water to allow an easy take-off, occasionally on flatter and more open sites. The nest is a bare hollow, sometimes with a few feathers, and the single egg is pale-shelled, rarely with dark blotches, but usually so heavily marked with very fine freckling of purple-brown as to appear dark in colour. Both birds incubate for 6–6½ weeks. The chick has thick buff or grey down from hatching. It is fed by both parents and leaves the nest at *c*. 12–15 weeks.

RED-BILLED TROPIC-BIRD *Phaethon aethereus* **Pl. 15**
Medium, 24 ins, 61 cm, including tail streamers 38 ins, 96 cm. Wing-span 44 ins, 112 cm. The general appearance is mainly white. Adults have white heads with a striking black band running before, over and through the eye. Whole upperparts are finely barred with black. Leading primaries black, appearing as a black band on outer wing tips. Bill stout, slightly curved downwards and pointed, coral red. The two central white tail feathers are extremely elongated. Legs usually greyish-white, webs of feet black. Immature birds have heavy black barrings over upperparts, the long central tails are absent or much reduced.
The tail possesses 14 tail feathers.
RANGE: Tropical and sub-tropical zones of Atlantic, Indian and Pacific Oceans. Map 119.

RED-TAILED TROPIC-BIRD *Phaethon rubricauda* **Pl. 15**
Medium, 18 in, 46 cm, including tail streamers, 36 ins, 91 cm. Wing-span 44 ins, 112 cm. The plumage of the adult Red-tailed Tropic-bird is a silky white sometimes diffused with a beautiful pink tinge. A broad black crescent passes before and through the eye. The shafts of the white primaries and tail feathers are black and some black feathers sometimes show in the flanks. In adult plumage the most outstanding feature is the addition of two long blood red central tail feathers or streamers, which are shed however in moult. The stout bill is coral red in adults; legs pale blue, feet black.
Young birds are white, lacking the pink flush, have upperparts broadly barred with black markings, and carry no elongated central tail feathers. Bill black changing to yellow and orange.
The flight is more leisurely than in other species, its wingbeats slower, and it is apt to sail between wingbeats. The Red-tailed Tropic-bird has 16 tail feathers.
RANGE: Tropical and sub-tropical Indian and Pacific Oceans; it does not occur in the Atlantic. Highly oceanic. Map 120.

WHITE-TAILED TROPIC-BIRD *Phaethon lepturus lepturus* **Pl. 15**
Medium, 16 ins, 41 cm including tail streamers 32 ins, 81 cm. Wing-span 36 ins, 92 cm. The general appearance is mainly white. Adults have white heads with a striking black band running before and over the eye. The whole upperparts are white except for a black band across the upperwings and black outer wing tips. Bill stout, slightly curved downwards and pointed, yellow. The two central white tail feathers are extremely elongated. Legs usually greyish-white, webs of feet black. Immature birds have black barring over upperparts but not as pronounced as other species. The long central tail feathers are absent or much reduced.
The tail possesses 12 tail feathers.
RANGE: Tropical and sub-tropical zones of Atlantic, Indian and Pacific Oceans. Map 121.
RACE:
  CHRISTMAS TROPIC-BIRD *Phaethon lepturus fulvus* **Pl. 15**
  This sub-species breeds on Christmas I. in the Indian Ocean and occurs only locally. Similar to the White-tailed Tropic-bird but distinguished by the golden tint of its plumage. Not mapped.

Eastern White Pelicans:
a breeding colony with young birds.

PELICANS Pelecanidae

Pelicans with their great size, heavy bodies, broad rounded wings, and huge bill carrying a large distensible pouch are quite unmistakable. Most species frequent inland lagoons and marshes. With the exception of the Chilean Pelican they will not occur on sea routes but may be seen by ships visiting harbours and ports and when passing close to islands. In flight they carry their necks tucked back into their shoulder and may often be seen in small parties flying low over the water in formation in a somewhat undulating flight with steady wingbeats and glides the birds keeping precise time with their leader. When fishing they fly with bills pointing downwards, suddenly checking their flight and plunging awkwardly into the sea with an enormous splash. At other times they will swim in formation until locating fish when they will all submerge in unison.

The maps show only coastal areas where they are most likely to be seen by ships.

58

Nesting and young

They nest in colonies, on sites providing some protection from predators and may
desert *en masse* if badly disturbed. Nests are in coastal mangroves or other trees,
on bare islands, or high rocks, or low islands and ridges in extensive estuarine or
lakeside swamps. Nest material may be absent or large mounds assembled on the
ground. Large twig platforms are built in trees. 2–4 eggs are laid. These are white
with a chalk-like white outer layer of irregular thickness. Both adults incubate for
c. 4 weeks. The young are naked at first and later covered with brown or blackish
down. In colonies on level ground the larger young may assemble in huddled
groups. They are fed by both parents, taking food from their gullets, and they fledge
in *c.* 10 weeks.

WHITE PELICAN *Pelecanus onocrotalus*   **Pl. 16**
Outsize, 55–70 ins, 140–178 cm. Wing-span 100 ins, 254 cm. Almost entirely white
plumage with black primaries and secondaries, a small crest on the back of the

head, and a tuft of yellowish feathers on the breast. Naked skin on face is purplish or yellowish-white; bill grey with pink edges; pouch yellow; legs pink.

Young birds are buff coloured above with brown primaries, and have white underparts.

pouch filled with fish.

pouch empty

Eastern White Pelican (p.59)

Sometimes the white plumage in adults shows a pinkish flush. Distinguished from Pink-backed Pelican by its pink legs.

RANGE: Southern Europe, Africa, and central Asia. In winter to India, Malay Peninsula and adjacent islands. Occurs in Persian Gulf.   Map 122.

PINK-BACKED PELICAN *Pelecanus rufescens*   **Pl. 16**
Outsize, 55–60 ins, 138–152 cm. Wing-span 85 ins, 214 cm. The overall plumage is similar but somewhat greyer than that of the White Pelican, but the back, rump, flanks and under tail-coverts show a distinct pink flush. The crest on the back of the head is more evident, the feathers on the breast are longer shaggy plumes. The tail is grey. Bill yellowish-white with orange tip; pouch flesh-coloured; legs yellowish. Adults in winter plumage and young birds show brown wings and tails.

Distinguished from White Pelican by its grey tail and yellowish legs.

RANGE: Rarely in southern Africa but northwards to Gambia, Ethiopia, Madagascar (Malagasy) and southern Arabia. Liable to overlap with the White Pelican on coasts of Arabia.   Map 123.

GREY PELICAN *Pelecanus philippensis*   **Pl. 16**
Outsize, 50–60 ins, 127–152 cm. Head, neck and upperparts including upperwings grey. Underparts greyish-white, under tail-coverts mottled-brown. A crest of elongated brown feathers, tipped white on the back of the head. Bill pinkish; pouch purple; legs dark brown.

Easily distinguished by its overall grey appearance.

RANGE: Southern Asia from Persia to Ceylon, Malaysia, southern China and Philippines. Breeds on islands in Persian Gulf and inland waters in Ceylon and Burma. Rarely seen on sea coast.   Map 124.

DALMATIAN PELICAN *Pelecanus crispus* **Pl. 16**
Outsize, 60–70 ins, 152–177 cm. Wing-span 100 ins, 254 cm. Upperparts silvery-grey; wing quills blackish-brown, secondaries greyish-brown. Underparts dull greyish-white with large yellow patch on lower throat, absent in winter. Feathers on back of head only slightly elongated and curly. Eye pale yellow; skin of face pink; bill grey; pouch orange. Legs lead-grey. Young birds have brownish-grey upperparts, dirty white underparts and yellowish bill pouches.

Dalmatian Pelican   Eastern White Pelican (p.59)

In flight Dalmatian Pelican shows almost totally white underwing and grey legs compared with dark band of flight feathers and pink legs of Eastern White Pelican.

Easily confused with White Pelican except in flight where White Pelican shows dark underwing pattern of primaries while Dalmation Pelican shows an almost totally white underwing. Lead-grey legs of Dalmation compare with pink legs of White.
RANGE: Breeds on inland lakes and seas in S.E. Europe, Asia Minor, Persia eastwards to China. May be seen by ships in Persian Gulf but rarely seen on sea coast elsewhere.   Map 125.

AUSTRALIAN PELICAN *Pelecanus conspicillatus* **Pl. 17**
Outsize, 60 ins, 152 cm. Wing-span 100 ins, 254 cm. A mainly white pelican with black wing quills, and black band on each side of lower back and above tail, scapulars and portions of upperwing-coverts. The foreneck and underparts are white, the feathers on the foreneck elongated, yellow, and a greyish crest at the back of the head. The large bill is flesh-coloured with blue sides; pouch flesh-coloured; legs slaty-blue; rump patch and tail-band black.
Young birds are similar but the black areas in adult plumage are brown and lack yellow plumes.
The only species of pelican in Australia and New Guinea. Most likely to be seen by ships in the Bass Strait. Breeds on inland lagoons and also off the coasts around Australia and in the Bass Strait and Tasmania.   Map 126.

AMERICAN WHITE PELICAN *Pelecanus erythrorhynchus* **Pl. 17**
Outsize, 55–70 ins, 140–178 cm. Wing-span 110 ins, 269 cm. Plumage generally all

white with primaries and leading secondaries black. Elongated crest on back of head in breeding plumage white or very pale yellow with pale yellow shade on breast and wing-coverts. In winter the crest is replaced by a grey area. Bill, with horny knob, and pouch reddish-orange in summer, yellow in winter, horny knob absent. Naked skin on face orange, in winter yellow. Legs reddish-orange. Young birds are similar to adults in winter plumage.

RANGE: Outside the breeding season it tends to resort to salt water bays. Breeds inland in western N. America and migrates south in winter occurring chiefly off Florida, Cuba and coastal waters of Gulf of Mexico to the Panama Canal. Rarely seen in the W. Indies. Map 127.

BROWN PELICAN
Pelecanus occidentalis　　Pl. 17
Outsize, 40 ins, 110 cm. Wing-span 90 ins, 229 cm. In summer plumage back of head, neck and foreneck chestnut-brown; in winter whole head and neck whitish-yellow.

Head white, dirty yellow on crown, a white line continuing down each side of the brown neck. There is a crest on the back of the head and a tuft of elongated blackish-yellow feathers on the lower foreneck. The primary wing feathers are black, upperwing-coverts and tail grey. The facial skin is blue, the large bill

Brown Pelican diving.

yellowish, pouch dusky and legs greyish-black. Whole underparts dark greyish-brown.

Young birds have brownish upperparts and white underbodies.

The smallest of the pelicans. Seen regularly in bays, harbours and along coastlines.

RANGE: Both coasts of U.S.A. from N. Carolina southwards through the W. Indies to tropical Brazil. On the west coast of U.S.A. from Washington to Peru. Breeds from S. Carolina to the Orinoco, from California to Ecuador, and on the Galapagos Is. Map 128.

CHILEAN PELICAN *Pelecanus thagus* Pl. 17

Outsize, 60 ins, 152 cm. Much larger but otherwise similar to the Brown Pelican, but a pale straw-coloured crest on the back of the head is more developed, and white flecking shows on underparts. Yellow feather tuft on foreneck. The bill is yellow with red sides and tip; pouch black with blue lines and legs slate-coloured.

Young birds are similar to young Brown Pelicans.

RANGE: Abundant in the coastal areas of the Humboldt Current off the coasts of Peru and Chile. Breeds on islands off the coast of Peru. Map 129.

Brown Pelican
Chilean Pelican
Both in non-breeding plumage.
When found together, they
are only distinguishable in the
field by their difference in
size.

Australian Gannets fishing. The dark bird is an immature 1st year.

GANNETS and BOOBIES   Sulidae

Gannets and boobies are by our 'size definition' outsize birds of some 30 ins or more in length with cigar shaped bodies, long narrow wings, stout conical bills and long wedge-shaped tails. Those that live in the temperate latitude belts are gannets, the tropical species being known as boobies.

The flight of all the species is similar. At sea they may be seen flying in steady direct flight, sometimes at sea level, more usually at some 30 ft above the sea employing powerful rather rapid regular wingbeats with occasional glides. When in company they often fly in a ragged single line ahead formation. They obtain their food by rising to 50 ft or more above the sea and, when fish are located, checking their flight before hurtling in a headlong dive with wings partially closed into the sea. Boobies usually dive from lower levels at more slanting angles.

Boobies frequently perch on ships at sea, sometimes using a vantage point on the forecastle structure from which to dive upon flying fish skipping away from the bow wave. They may remain thus for several hours; indeed their name originated in the seafarers' term for them for they appear particularly stupid, often showing no concern on being approached and captured.

Nesting and young

These often nest in large colonies, and in some species the nests are closely packed together. Nesting may be on more level ground of flattish islands or cliff tops, on cliff ledges, on bushes or on trees. As with cormorants the nests may vary from a pile of seaweed and debris on the ground or a ledge, to a substantial stick nest in a tree. The eggs, 1–2 according to species, are pale blue, but with the colour almost entirely concealed by an irregular chalk-like white outer layer. During incubation, performed by both birds, warmth is conveyed to the eggs through the webs of the feet which cover them. Incubation lasts 42–47 days. The young hatch naked and dark-skinned and after about a week grow a thick white down. They are fed by both parents, taking regurgitated food from the adult gullet. They become very large and fat and starve for a week or so before leaving the nest. They fledge in 10–12 weeks in the gannets, but it may be up to 17 weeks in other species, possibly varying with the food supply.

NORTHERN GANNET *Sula bassana*   **Pl. 18**
Outsize, 36 ins, 92 cm. Wing-span 68 ins, 173 cm. Mainly white with primaries only blackish-brown. Tail feathers white. Head and nape pale straw-yellow; naked skin on face and throat bluish-black; bill pale horn-coloured; legs black.

Young birds have upperparts greyish-brown with white speckling; underparts whitish with brown mottling.
RANGE: N. Atlantic Ocean from Iceland southwards off west coasts of Europe and east coast of N. America and Canada reaching Canary Is. and N.W. coast of Africa. Breeds in Iceland, Norway, the Faroes, British Isles, Channel Is., Brittany, Newfoundland and Gulf of St. Lawrence.   Map 130.

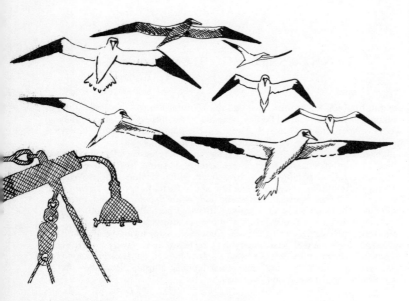

Gannets following a ship.

CAPE GANNET *Sula capensis* P. 18

Outsize, 33–35 ins, 84–89 cm. Mainly white with primaries, secondaries and all twelve tail feathers brown. Crown and nape yellow; naked skin on face and throat black; bill pale bluish; legs brownish-black.

Young birds have greyish-brown upperparts with white speckling and whitish underparts with brown bars.

Known locally as the 'Malagas'.

RANGE: Both coasts of S. Africa from Cape of Good Hope to 20°S. Map 131.

AUSTRALIAN GANNET *Sula serrator* P. 18

Outsize, 36ins, 92 cm. Wing-span 68 ins, 172 cm. Mainly white with primaries and secondaries blackish-brown, and the majority of the central tail feathers blackish-brown, outer tail feathers white. The crown and nape are yellow; naked skin of face and throat slate-blue; bill bluish-grey; legs greyish-black with bright green lines running along top of the toes.

Young birds have upperparts brown with white speckling; underparts mainly white with some brown mottling on the throat and flanks.

RANGE: S. and E. coasts of Australia, the Bass Strait, Tasmania and New Zealand coastal waters. Breeds within the Bass Strait, in Tasmania and in New Zealand. Map 132.

BLUE-FOOTED BOOBY *Sula nebouxii* P. 19

Outsize, 32–36 ins, 83–92 cm. Wing-span 60 ins, 152 cm. Head, neck and upper breast cinnamon-brown, with some white mottling, the back also being mottled white. The wings and tail are brown, the central tail feathers white. Lower breast and underparts white. The naked skin on face and throat slate-blue; bill olive-blue. Its most distinctive feature is its bright blue legs.

Young birds are very similar but their white underbodies show considerable dusky mottling.

In adult plumage it differs from other boobies by the brown and white appearance of its upperparts. Unless its bright blue legs are seen however it is liable to be mistaken for immature birds of the other species.

RANGE: West coast of tropical America. Breeds on islands off the coast of Mexico, Ecuador, northern Peru and the Galapagos Is. Map 133.

PERUVIAN BOOBY *Sula variegata* Pl. 19

Very large, 29 ins, 74 cm. The whole head, neck and upper back are white, the lower back, tail and flanks mottled black and white. Underparts white. Wings brownish-black. Bill blue; legs bluish-black.

Young birds are very similar but show mottled underparts.

Easily distinguished by its white and speckled plumage.

RANGE: West coast of S. America. Abundant off the coasts of Peru and Chile. Breeds on islands off coast of Peru. Map 134.

ABBOTT'S BOOBY *Sula abbotti* Pl. 19

Large, 28 ins, 71 cm. Adult. Head, neck, back and upper tail-coverts white. Black skin and dark orbital ring around brown eye conspicuous. Underbody white with black thigh patches evident when wings are raised. Underwing-coverts white. Upperwing-coverts black with some small indistinct white feathers. Wing quills black, the inner webs of some primaries white, showing in flight. Carpal joint feathers spotted with white extending to leading edge. Tail black with some white mottling. Bill large, deep at base, varies in male yellow or blue-grey tinged with pink, in female yellow or rosy, both sexes showing a broad black tip. Legs leaden-grey.

Immatures similar to adult males with indistinct buff edges to scapulars and upperwing-coverts. Bill greyish, broadly tipped black.

Note: Wings tend to bleach brown and may appear as such when immatures and adults are virtually indistinguishable.

RANGE: Breeds on Christmas I. (Indian Ocean), nesting high up in tall jungle trees in the central plateau inland. Not mapped.

BLUE-FACED BOOBY or MASKED BOOBY *Sula dactylatra* Pl. 18

Outsize, 32–36 ins, 81–92 cm. Wing-span 60 ins, 152 cm. Mainly white, with chocolate-brown primaries and secondaries forming a complete dark margin to the edge of the wing, and a chocolate-brown tail. The naked skin on face and throat is bluish-black giving it a 'masked' appearance from which it is also known as the Masked Booby. The stout bill varies in colour but is usually yellowish; legs usually greyish-blue but vary, sometimes orange.

Young birds in first plumage have the head and neck dark brown, the remainder of upperparts greyish-brown, second year birds having mainly white heads and mottled greyish-brown upperparts.

Distinguished from the adult Red-footed Booby in the light phase by having both primary and secondary flight feathers and the tail dark.

RANGE: Widespread throughout the tropical and sub-tropical belt of the oceans. Breeds throughout its range on islands in the Atlantic, Indian and Pacific Oceans. Map 135.

BROWN BOOBY *Sula leucogaster*   Pl. 19

Very large, 28–30 ins, 71–76 cm. Wing-span 57 ins, 145 cm. The whole head, neck, upperparts and breast are dark chocolate-brown, the remainder of its underbody and under tail-coverts white. Tail dark chocolate-brown. The axillaries and median underwing-coverts show white against the dark outer areas of the underwing.

A clear cut line divides the dark chocolate breast from the white underparts. Stout pointed bill usually bluish-white or greenish-yellow; legs yellow or bluish-green. The naked skin on face and throat varies from greenish-yellow to purple.

Young birds are dusky-brown above including breast, underparts below breast mottled-brown.

Unmistakable in adult plumage from all other boobies, but immature plumage may be confusing.

RANGE: The commonest booby throughout the tropical and sub-tropical belts of the oceans, but does not range far from land. Breeds throughout its range on islands in the Atlantic, Indian and Pacific Oceans.   Map 137.

RED-FOOTED BOOBY *Sula sula*   Pl. 19

Very large, 26–29 ins, 66–74 cm. Wing-span 38 ins, 97 cm. Adult birds may be in three plumage phases.

WHITE PHASE. Plumage mainly white, often with a golden-buff tint. Primaries and secondaries blackish-brown. Tail-coverts and tail white.

INTERMEDIATE PHASE. Head, neck and underparts dull white to pale buff, head and neck sometimes with golden tint. Back and wings chocolate-brown to greyish-brown. Tail-coverts and tail white.

DARK PHASE. Head, neck and underparts ashy-grey or ashy-brown, head and neck often with a golden-brown tint. Tail-coverts and tail white, sometimes pale grey.

Naked skin on face, blue. Gular sac, black. Bill, bright medium-blue, and base of both mandibles pink. A deep blue-black stripe extends below lower mandible towards junction with feathers. Legs and feet, coral-red. Eye ring and skin around eye, rich blue.

Young birds are generally brownish-grey with paler underparts. Facial skin dark blue. Bill blackish.

There is considerable variation in tones of plumage in the intermediate and dark phases and in colour of soft parts, but the red legs are quite distinctive.

RANGE: Tropical Atlantic, Indian and western and central Pacific Oceans, breeding in islands throughout its range including the Galapagos Is.   Map 136.

All Gannets and Boobies nest on the ground or on rock, except for Abbot's Booby and the Red-footed Booby. These two species, in their relatively safe nest sites in trees, lay only a single egg.

Common Cormorant nesting colony in trees. They also nest on cliffs.

CORMORANTS   Phalacrocoracidae

Cormorants are heavy-bodied birds with long sinuous necks, long rounded wings and rather long wedge-shaped tails. Their bills are long, slender and sharply hooked at the tip; their legs and large webbed feet are set well aft in their bodies. In certain parts of the world some of the family are known as shags, a name frequently applied to the whole family by seafarers.

Cormorants are predominantly black in colour, those found in the northern hemisphere almost exclusively so, while in the southern hemisphere many have white underparts and in some cases pied plumage.

They are essentially coastal seabirds, sociable in habits, frequently seen in harbours but rarely on the sea routes. On the surface they swim low in the water, and when feeding gain their food by springing from the surface in a 'jack-knife' dive beneath the water in pursuit of fish, using both wings and legs for propulsion. Indeed when fishing they may often be seen with only their long necks appearing above the surface. When disturbed they usually dive at once.

In flight, usually low over the sea but on long journeys sometimes rising to a considerable height, they proceed with necks fully extended and steadily flapping wings interspersed with short glides, flocks in a 'V' formation. Cormorants are extremely partial to perching on posts, beacons or rocks with wings extended in order to dry their body feathers in the air.

Nesting and young

These usually breed in colonies; on cliffs, rocky shores, islands and islets, and inland lakes and rivers. The nest site may be a ledge or level open site, or a tree in or near water. Material is carried to the site, and the nest is usually a bulky structure of seaweed or sticks according to site, with a finer lining. The clutch is usually of 2–4 eggs; the pale blue shell covered with a white, chalk-like layer of irregular thickness, wholly or partly concealing the underlying colour. Both birds incubate for c. 27–30 days. The young hatch naked, but later grow a coat of short dark down. They take their food from the gullet of the parents. They may leave the nest at 5–6 weeks and move about the colony, sometimes gathering into groups. They become independent in c. 10–12 weeks.

DOUBLE-CRESTED CORMORANT *Phalacrocorax auritus*   **Pl. 21**
Very large, 29–35 ins, 74–89 cm. Wing-span 50 ins, 127 cm. General plumage glossy greenish-black, back, scapulars and upperwing-coverts bronze, feathers edged with black. In breeding plumage a tuft of black or black and white curly feathers shows on each side of the head.

A noticeable feature is the orange colour of the naked skin on the face and throat. Bill slate-grey, yellow at base; legs black. Young birds have greyish-brown upperparts, black rump, whitish breasts and blackish underbodies. Naked skin dull yellow.

A widespread N. and Central American species, considerably larger than the Bigua Cormorant. A number of different races occur.

RANGE: N. and Central America, W. Indies, and Pacific coast of N. America.   Map 138.

BIGUA CORMORANT *Phalacrocorax olivaceus*   **Pl. 21**
Very large, 25–30 ins, 64–76 cm. Wing-span 40 ins, 102 cm. General plumage glossy black. In breeding plumage the face and throat are edged white, and it carries a white tuft of feathers on each side of the head. The bill is brown; naked skin on face and throat a dull yellow and legs black. The tail is noticeably long.
Young birds have brown upperparts and greyish-white underparts.
Smaller than the Double-crested Cormorant with which it is liable to be confused.
RANGE: On both coasts of tropical and sub-tropical America, the W. Indies, extending down the full length of the west coast of S. America. Map 139.

LITTLE BLACK CORMORANT *Phalacrocorax sulcirostris*   **Pl. 23**
Large, 24–25 ins, 61–64 cm. Wing-span 32 ins, 82 cm. Plumage entirely black with dull green gloss, ashy-grey on shoulders and upperwing-coverts. In breeding plumage narrow white plumes occur on the sides of the head and about the eyes, not noticeable at any distance. Pouch dull bluish-purple; bill rather long and dull lead colour; iris green; legs black. Young birds generally duller brownish-black.
Frequents lakes and estuaries but also occurs on the sea coast, birds tending to keep in flocks.
RANGE: Malay Archipelago and E. Indies. Breed in E. Indies, Australia, Tasmania, New Zealand and Norfolk I. Map 140.

COMMON CORMORANT *Phalacrocorax carbo*
(A) Outsize, 36 ins, 92 cm. Wing-span 60 ins, 152 cm; (B) Chin and sides of face white; (C) General plumage glossy bluish-black, upperwing-coverts dull bronze; (D) In breeding plumage some white filo plumes sprinkle head and neck, feathers on back of head elongated but do not form a crest, and a large white patch shows on each flank; in winter these are absent; (E) Naked skin on lores and throat-pouch yellow; (F) Bill long, slender, lead-grey, tip hooked, legs black; (G) Immatures brownish above, underparts whitish.
RANGE: Widespread throughout the world.
RACES:
  COMMON CORMORANT *Phalacrocorax c. carbo*   **Pls. 20 23**
  Breeds in Labrador, Nova Scotia, Greenland, Iceland, Norway, Faroe Is., Shetland Is., British Isles, France, Mediterranean, Spain, Australia and New Zealand. Map 141.
  COMMON CORMORANT (continental race) *Phalacrocorax c. sinensis* **Pl 20**
  Breeds in central and southern Europe, to central Asia, India, Japan and China. (B), (D), dark band from eye circles sides of face and throat; in breeding plumage nape and neck almost entirely white. Map 142.

WHITE-NECKED CORMORANT *Phalacrocorax lucidus*   **Pl 20**
Outsize, 36 ins, 92 cm. Wing-span 60 ins, 152 cm. Top of head, back of neck and upperparts black, upperwings with bronze tint. Face, front of neck and breast white; remainder of underparts black. White patch on flanks in breeding plumage. Bill yellow; legs slate grey.
Immatures have brown upperparts and wings, and whitish underparts. The largest of the S. African cormorants.
RANGE: West, south and east coasts of S. Africa, extending to coasts of E. Africa. Occurs both on coasts and inland on lakes and rivers. Map 143.

INDIAN CORMORANT *Phalacrocorax fuscicollis*   **Pl. 23**
Large, 24–27 ins, 610–686 mm. General plumage metallic bronze-black with pale

brown cheeks and throat. In breeding plumage the male has a tuft of whitish feathers on each side of the head. Naked skin of face and throat pale green. Bill brown. Legs black. Young birds have brownish upperparts and brownish-white underparts.

Overlaps with the Javanese Cormorant in range, but may be distinguished by its paler cheeks, larger size and longer bill and tail.

RANGE: India, Sri Lanka, Burma. Breeds on lagoons and tanks, but also frequents the sea coast. Map 144.

CAPE CORMORANT *Phalacrocorax capensis* Pl. 20

Large, 25 ins, 64 cm. Wing-span 43 ins, 109 cm. General plumage black, foreneck and breast dark brown. Naked skin on face and throat yellow; bill slaty-black; legs black. Tail noticeably short.

Young birds have brownish upperparts and underparts, their forenecks and chests whitish.

The commonest cormorant of S. African coasts. Considerably smaller than both the Bank and white-necked Cormorant of S. Africa and distinguished by its overall dark plumage and yellow throat.

RANGE: Both coasts of S. Africa from southern Angola to Durban. Found only on salt water. Breeds in large numbers on guano islands. Map 145.

SOCOTRA CORMORANT *Phalacrocorax nigrogularis* Pl. 20

Very large, 30 ins, 76 cm. General plumage glossy-black overall, wing-coverts and scapulars tinged with bronze. Naked skin on face and throat black; bill greyish-black, greenish at base of lower mandible; legs black.

Young birds have brownish-black upperparts and paler brown underparts.

Distinguished from the Common Cormorant by lack of any white facial or flank patches.

RANGE: Persian Gulf, coastal on Arabian coasts, southern Red Sea and Socotra. Map 146.

BANK CORMORANT *Phalacrocorax neglectus* Pl. 20

Very large, 27–30 ins, 69–76 cm. Wing-span 52 ins, 132 cm. General plumage dark-glossy overall, slightly browner on the wings, showing white feathers in the form of a patch above the rump. In breeding plumage the feathers on the forehead are elongated to form a crest. The bill, naked skin on face and pouch are black; legs black.

Young birds are brownish-black overall.

Distinguished from White-necked Cormorant by its black as opposed to white breast, and from Cape Cormorant by its larger size and black as opposed to yellow pouch. More 'woolly' in appearance than other African cormorants.

RANGE: South and west coasts of S. Africa. Map 147.

JAPANESE CORMORANT *Phalacrocorax capillatus* Pl. 20

Very large, 32 ins, 81 cm. Wing-span 54 ins, 137 cm. Very similar to the Common Cormorant which also occurs in Japan. It differs only in the naked skin on the face being more orange in colour, and in breeding plumage by the head and neck being covered with white filo plumes, and throat feathers extend forward to lower mandible.

Young birds are similar to young Common Cormorants.

RANGE: Coasts of N.E. Asia, China and Japan. Breeds in Korea, Japan and Sakhalin I.   Map 148.

BRANDT'S CORMORANT *Phalacrocorax penicillatus*   **Pl. 21**
Very large, 30 ins, 76 cm. General plumage glossy greenish-black. The throat is fawn coloured. In breeding plumage fine white hair-like plumes are scattered over the neck and upper back, these feathers extending to a point on the throat. Tufts of white feathers show behind the ears. Naked skin on face and throat blue; bill grey; legs black.

Young birds have brown upperparts, paler underparts.

The commonest cormorant on the Pacific coast of the U.S.A. Considerably larger than the Pelagic Cormorant and never showing any white patch on the flanks.

RANGE: Pacific coast of N. America as far south as Lower California.   Map 149.

SHAG or GREEN CORMORANT *Phalacrocorax aristotelis*   **Pl. 21**
Very large, 26–30 ins, 66–76 cm. Wing-span 48 ins, 122 cm. General plumage glossy greenish-black overall. In breeding plumage the feathers on the crown are elongated forming a very noticeable crest curving forwards, and some white filoplumes occur here and there about the neck. The naked skin around the bill is yellow on the throat black with yellow spots. Bill and legs are both black.

Young birds are brownish above and below.

Its more slender build, and lack of any white on the body serve to distinguish it from the Common Cormorant.

RANGE: Coastal along the western seaboard of Europe and northern Africa and throughout the Mediterranean.   Map 150.

PELAGIC CORMORANT *Phalacrocorax pelagicus*   **Pl. 21**
Very large, 28 ins, 71 cm. Wing-span 40 ins, 102 cm. General plumage glossy greenish-black overall. In breeding plumage tufts of bronze feathers on the crown and nape form two crests and a large white patch occurs on each flank. Naked skin on face dark greyish, throat and pouch coral-red. Bill very slender, blackish-brown; legs black.

Its small head, thin neck and bill and more agile rapid flight distinguish it from Brandt's Cormorant which never shows white flank patches and has a fawn coloured throat.

RANGE: Coastal on both eastern and western seaboards of N. Pacific from Alaska south to Mexico, from Siberia south to Japan and China in winter. A common species on the coast of British Columbia.   Map 151.

RED-FACED CORMORANT *Phalacrocorax urile*   **Pl. 21**
Very large, 28–30 ins, 71–76 cm. General plumage glossy greenish-black. In breeding plumage two tufts of bronze feathers show, one on the crown and another on the nape, and a white patch of feathers occurs on each flank. The forehead is bare and the naked skin on both forehead and face red, on throat blue with red wrinkles at the base. Bill blue; legs black.

Young birds are dark brown overall.

Distinguished by colour of skin on face. It differs from the Common and Japanese Cormorants by its black as opposed to white chin and throat. Larger but very similar to Pelagic Cormorant.

RANGE: Breeds on the coasts of Kamchatka, N.E. Siberia, Bering Sea, Aleutian Is., Kuril Is., south in winter to Hokkaido, rarely seen further south in Japan.   Map 152.

MAGELLAN CORMORANT *Phalacrocorax magellanicus* **Pl. 22**
Large, 26 ins, 66 cm. Wing-span 36 ins, 92 cm. Head and neck black in summer; in winter chin, throat and foreneck white. Upperparts greenish-black; flanks and under tail-coverts black; remainder of underparts white. In breeding plumage long white plumes occur on head and neck and some white feathers on lower back and flanks. Naked skin on face and throat red; bill black; legs flesh-coloured.
  Differs from Blue-eyed Cormorant in its red face and black neck in breeding plumage.
RANGE: Breeds on coasts and islands north to Chiloe I. on west coast of S. America, and to Point Tombo, 44°S., 65°20′W., on east coast, and Falkland Is. Map 153.

GUANAY CORMORANT *Phalacrocorax bougainvillei* **Pl. 22**
Very large, 30 ins, 76 cm. Head, neck and upper parts glossy greenish-black, the chin and underparts below the neck white. In breeding plumage the dark feathers on the head are elongated forming a crest, and a patch of white plumes shows above the eye. Naked skin on face red; bill horn-coloured with a red wattle at the base; legs pink.
  Young birds are very similar but the foreneck is whitish.
  Distinguished by its white throat and underparts and distinctive red face. Unlike many coastal cormorants it is often seen flying at a considerable height to locate shoals of fish from the air, diving from a height to capture them.
RANGE: Throughout the entire length of the west coast of S. America from Peru southwards where it occurs in enormous numbers. Extends northward in small numbers on east coast to Point Tombo, 44°S., 65°20′W. Breeds on coasts and islands. Map 154.

PIED CORMORANT *Phalacrocorax varius* **Pl. 22**
Very large, 28–32 ins, 71–81 cm. Top of head, hind-neck, upperparts and tail glossy greenish-black. Wing quills bronze-grey with greenish gloss, feathers bordered with black. Sides of face, front and sides of neck and underparts white. Iris sea-green. Naked skin in front of eye yellow, blue on face and pink on pouch. Bill dark horn colour, legs black. Dark eye shows below, separate from black crown.
  Young birds are browner above, the pale underparts mottled-brown.
  The commonest cormorant on Australian coasts.
RANGE: Coasts of Australia, and New Zealand. Map 155.

BLACK-FACED CORMORANT *Phalacrocorax fuscescens* **Pl. 22**
Very large, 28–30 ins, 71–76 cm. Top of head, hind-neck, upperparts, underwing-coverts and tail glossy blue-black. The sides of the face, throat, sides of neck and underparts white, terminating in blue-black thighs. Naked skin around eye and pouch black. Bill dark grey; legs black. Iris bright green. Young birds have brown upperparts and white underparts.
  Very similar to Pied Cormorant but differs in having blue-black thighs and a mat of short white feathers on neck, rump and thighs.
RANGE: South coast of Australia and Tasmania. Map 156.

ROUGH-FACED CORMORANT *Phalacrocorax carunculatus*
(A) Very large, 30 ins, 76 cm. (B) No crest; whole head, back, sides of neck metallic bluish-green. (C) Upperwing coverts glossy green showing a white alar bar on inner median wing-coverts, usually a white patch on outer scapulars and a white patch on back, but extent of these varies. (D) Wings, tail, blackish-brown. (E) Underbody

white, thighs bluish-green. (F) Eye-ring bright blue. (G) Naked skin on face and throat reddish-brown, patch of yellow caruncles above base of bill. (H) Bill brown, legs pink. (K) Immatures dull brown above, underparts white.

RANGE: At no distance from coasts breeding on the principal islands in the New Zealand seas.

RACES:

ROUGH-FACED CORMORANT   *Phalacrocorax c. carunculatus*   Pl. 22
Islands and outlying rocks in the Cook Strait, New Zealand.   Map 157.

CAMPBELL ISLAND CORMORANT   *Phalacrocorax c. campbelli*   Pl. 22
Breeds only on Campbell I. and adjacent small islands. (A) Smaller, 25 ins. 64 cm; (B) and (C) Uniformly darker shade, white alar bar and white patches always absent; (E) Black throat band 3 ins wide; (F) Eye-ring purple; (G) Naked skin dark red; (K) Foreneck mottled brown. Breeds on Campbell I. and its adjacent islands.   Not mapped.

KERGUELEN CORMORANT   *Phalacrocorax verrucosus*

Large, 27 ins, 69 cm. Head, cheeks, sides of neck and upperparts metallic greenish-black. Throat, foreneck and underparts white, feathers of throat extending forwards to base of lower mandible. A crest occurs on the head in breeding plumage. Yellow caruncles at base of bill. Legs pink. Young birds are brown overall, underparts slightly paler and show a white throat. Very similar to Rough-faced and King Cormorants which breed in different areas.

RANGE: Breeds on Kerguelen Is.   Map 158.

RED-LEGGED CORMORANT   *Phalacrocorax gaimardi*   Pl. 21

Very large, 28 ins, 71 cm. Wing-span 35 ins, 89 cm. Head and neck dark grey with an elongated white patch on each side of the neck. Upperparts dark grey, wing coverts silvery-grey. Underparts pale grey. Naked skin on face red; bill bright yellow, orange-red at base; legs coral-red.

Young birds have upperparts dark brown showing white patches on the sides of the neck; wing-coverts and underparts brownish-white mottling.

Easily identified by the white patches on sides of neck and very noticeable bright red legs which can be seen as the bird dives under water.

Blue-eyed Cormorant   King Cormorant   Kerguelen Cormorant
All in breeding plumage.

King Cormorants nesting.

RANGE: Throughout the entire length of the west coast of S. America from Peru southwards. A small breeding colony is also known at Puerto Deseado, 48°S., on east coast.   Map 159.

SPOTTED CORMORANT *Phalacrocorax punctatus*

Handsome diversified plumage. (A) Very large, 29 ins, 74 cm. Breeding plumage: (B) Stripe from bill over crown, top of head to nape, and crests on forehead, back of neck, greyish-black; (C) Back of neck, lower back, rump glossy greenish-blue; (D) Sides of neck, throat black; (E) White curving band from above eye to shoulder dividing sides of neck from throat to shoulder; (F) Upperwings, scapulars, wing-coverts pale grey, black spots at ends of feathers; (G) Underparts silver-grey, thighs and under tail-coverts greenish-black; (H) Naked skin on face bluish-green, on pouch bright blue; (K) Bill pale brown-colour, gular pouch bright blue, legs bright orange-yellow; (L) Non breeding, white areas mottled; (M) Immatures dark grey above, whitish-grey underparts, legs brownish-pink.

RANGE: Coasts of New Zealand and Chatham Is., confined to salt water close to coasts.

RACES:

> SPOTTED CORMORANT *Phalacrocorax p. punctatus*   **Pl. 22**
> Uncommon in North Island, New Zealand, breeds at two localities; breeds abundantly in South Island.   Map 160.
>
> PITT ISLAND CORMORANT *Phalacrocorax p. featherstoni*   **Pl. 22**
> Breeds only at Chatham I. (A) Smaller, 25 ins, 64 cm; (B), (C), (D) Black with bluish tint; (E) White neck band absent; (F) Deep grey with greenish gloss, triangular black spots at end of feathers; (G) Dark silvery-grey; (H) Purple; (K) Legs orange; (M) Immatures brownish above, pale brown below. *Note:* Scapulars and upperwing-coverts resemble adults at (F).   Not mapped.

BLUE-EYED CORMORANT *Phalacrocorax atriceps*   **Pl. 22**

Very large, 27–29 ins, 69–74 cm. Wing-span 44 ins, 112 cm. Top of head, back of neck and upperparts glossy-black. Throat, cheeks, foreneck and underparts white. In breeding plumage a fine tuft of plumes forms a crest above each eye, a white bar extends across the upperwings and a white patch shows on the back. Bill brownish

breeding

imm.

winter

breeding

winter

King Cormorant

Blue-eyed Cormorant

King Cormorant never show a white patch on the back; the dark area around the head extends lower on the cheeks than in Blue-eyed Cormorant (p.77).

with yellow excrescence at base of upper mandible. Ring around eyes bright blue; naked skin of face blue; legs flesh-coloured, webs black.

Distinguished from Magellan Cormorant by its blue naked skin of face (in Magellan Cormorant this is red). In breeding plumage also the neck of the Magellan Cormorant becomes entirely black.

RANGE: From islands adjacent to Antarctica northwards. Breeds on S. Shetlands, S. Orkneys, S. Sandwich Is., S. Georgia, off Cape Horn and Patagonia and at Heard I.   Map 161.

KING CORMORANT *Phalacrocorax albiventer*   **Page 76 and above**
Very large, 27–29 ins, 69–74 cm. Wing-span 40 ins, 102 cm. Similar in plumage to Blue-eyed Cormorant except that the glossy-black plumage on sides of head extends much lower on the cheeks below the line of the bill. At no time is there a white patch on the back.
RANGE: Breeds in the Falkland Is., on east coast of Patagonia, north to Point Tombo, Argentina, 44°S., 65°20'W., Crozet Is. and Macquarie I.   Map 162.

LITTLE PIED CORMORANT *Phalacrocorax melanoleucus*   **Pls. 22, 23**
Medium–large, 22–24 ins, 56–61 cm. Wing-span 29 ins, 74 cm. Compared with other cormorants the Little Pied Cormorant is considerably smaller and occurs in variable plumage.

In the light phase the top of the head, hind neck, upperparts and tail are glossy-black. A white line shows over the eye, and the sides of the face, throat, front and sides of neck and underparts are white. The underwing-coverts and under tail-coverts are black. The tail is unusually long in proportion. Naked skin on face and throat yellow; bill black above, yellow below; legs black. In breeding plumage the feathers on the crown are elongated forming a small crest.

In the dark phase in New Zealand, usually known as the Little Shag or White-throated Shag, only the sides of the face, chin and throat are white, the remainder of the underparts and whole of the upperparts glossy-black.

Young birds are dull brownish overall, showing a conspicuous yellow bill and face, the light phase race often dusky-white below.

RANGE: The dark phase predominates in New Zealand coastal waters. The light phase ranges widely throughout the E. Indies, islands in the western central Pacific Ocean, Australia and Tasmania. Breeds mainly in freshwater areas inland. Map 163.

REED CORMORANT *Halietor africanus* Pl. 23

Medium–large, 23 ins, 58 cm. Wing-span 35 ins, 89 cm. Breeding plumage is glossy-black with greyish scapulars and upperwing-coverts. A tuft of black feathers occurs on the forehead and a few white plumes on face and neck. The winter plumage is a dull brown with a greyish-white throat. Naked skin of face and gular pouch red. Legs black; tail noticeably long. Young birds have brown upperparts and yellowish-white underparts.

Mainly frequents rivers and lagoons, swimming very low in the water.

RANGE: Distributed widely throughout Africa, breeding and resorting largely to inland rivers and lakes. In southern Africa coastal birds are found only on west coast from Walvis Bay to Cape Agulhas where they breed also. Map 164.

JAVANESE CORMORANT *Halietor niger* Pl. 23

Medium–large, 22 ins, 56 cm. Plumage glossy-black, scapulars and upperwing coverts greyish, feathers with black edges. In winter throat is white. In breeding season feathers on nape are elongated with a few scattered white plumes on head and neck. Naked skin on face black. Bill purplish-brown. Legs black. Young birds have dark brown upperparts and whitish throats.

The Javanese Cormorant overlaps in range with the Indian Cormorant, but can be distinguished by its greyer wing-coverts, smaller size and shorter bill.

RANGE: From India through Sri Lanka, Burma, Java and Borneo. Map 165.

PIGMY CORMORANT *Halietor pygmaeus* Pl. 23

Medium size, 19–23 ins, 48–58 cm. General plumage glossy greenish black. Head and neck reddish-brown, scapulars and upperwing-coverts grey, feathers with black margins. A triangular patch on the head and a line through the eyes white. In breeding plumage a short crest occurs on the back of the head, and the neck, underparts and upper tail-coverts show small white spots. Bill brownish. Naked skin of face flesh-coloured. Feet dusky. Young birds have blackish-grey upperparts, whitish throats and abdomen, flanks and under tail-coverts black. Bills yellowish.

Its small size, reddish-brown head and neck and white markings readily distinguish it.

RANGE: Central and S.E. Europe, northern Africa, S.W. and central Asia. Breeds largely on lakes and rivers inland, and is unlikely to be seen on the sea coast. Map 166.

FLIGHTLESS CORMORANT *Nannopterum harrisi* Pl. 20

Outsize, 36–39 ins, 91–99 cm. Plumage generally brownish-black, paler on breast. Scapulars and upperwing-coverts dark grey, feathers with dark edges. A few plumes occur on head and neck. The wings are greatly reduced in size with few flight feathers, its breast bone is without a keel and it has lost all power of flight. Naked skin on face slate-coloured, on gular pouch flesh-coloured. The legs are black and a stiff flap of skin occurs on the tarsus.

RANGE: Confined to the Galapagos Is. Not mapped.

Frigate-birds
Male courting display.

FRIGATE-BIRDS Fregatidae

As a family these large mainly black sinister-looking pirates of the tropical belt, known to seafarers as 'Man-o'-War Hawks', cannot fail to be recognised.

They spend much of their time soaring high in the air, their long wings motionless, their long slender sharply hooked bills, and extremely long deeply forked tails silhouetted against the blue sky. As they wheel or fight among themselves in the air their forked tails will be seen to open and close 'scissor fashion' to retain balance. At other times they fly with deep deliberate wingbeats. Never landing on the water they obtain their varied diet by snatching up surface marine food or scraps. They never miss a chance however of harrying neighbouring seabirds by vicious chases and, if need be, pecks from their hooked bills, forcing them to disgorge their catch and snatching it up before it reaches the water. During breeding seasons they range over nesting colonies snatching up chicks in low swoops without touching the ground.

Adult males are all black with bright red throat patches which they inflate into large balloons during display. Females have partly white underparts varying in each species, and immatures have white heads. The adult female Ascension Frigate-bird however has a completely dark underbody, and the male Christmas Frigate-bird a white abdomen.

Frigate-birds are seen frequently at a considerable distance from land.

Nesting and young

These nest on oceanic islands. The nests are built on top of low bushes, or in trees, or on the ground where vegetation is absent. They nest in colonies close to those of other breeding seabirds which they can harry for food and rob of chicks. The nests are untidy platforms of sticks, feathers and other debris, built by both birds, which incubate a single white egg for *c.* 7 weeks. The chick is naked at first and later covered in grey down. It may fly at 4–5 months but appears to have a much longer period of complete or partial dependence on the adults for food after fledging.

ASCENSION FRIGATE-BIRD *Fregata aquila* **Pl. 24**
Outsize, 38 ins, 97 cm. Wing-span 85 ins, 165 cm. The adult male has black overall plumage with a glossy-green sheen on the back, red pouch and red legs. The female is similar but shows a dark brown breast.

Young birds have white heads and brownish-black plumage.

The female is the only species of female frigate-bird with totally dark underbody. A very rare form with white breast and abdomen may still occur.

RANGE: Disperses around Ascension I. where it breeds. Not mapped.

CHRISTMAS FRIGATE-BIRD *Fregata andrewsi* **Pl. 24**
Outsize, 35–40 ins, 89–100 cm. The adult male has black glossy-green upperparts, the foreneck and breast black, the abdomen white. Pouch bright red; bill black; legs black, feet with yellow soles. The female has head, neck and upperparts black. Throat black, breast and abdomen white. Bill reddish; legs white.

Young birds have brownish-black upperparts with a pale wing bar; head and neck rufous; abdomen white showing a dark band across the chest.

Immature Frigate-birds.

The male is the only species of male frigate-bird with a white abdomen.
RANGE: Local to Christmas I. in Indian Ocean and surrounding sea. Not mapped.

MAGNIFICENT FRIGATE-BIRD *Fregata magnificens* Pl. 24

Outsize, 38–40 ins, 97–100 cm. Wing-span 95 ins, 241 cm. The adult male is similar to the adult Great Frigate-bird but its upperwings lack the brown band across the wing-coverts. Its bill is usually bluish and legs black. The adult female differs from the female Great Frigate-bird in having a whitish collar at the back of the neck, a black throat and foreneck forming a contrast with the white underparts, the abdomen and flanks black. Its bill is horn-coloured and legs red. Young birds are similar to young Great Frigate-birds but lack the rusty colouring.

The male cannot be distinguished at sea from the adult male Ascension Frigate-bird. The female can be distinguished from the female Great Frigate-bird by its black throat.
RANGE: In the Atlantic breeds throughout the W. Indies, Central America, Fernando Noronha I., Brazilian coastal islands and Cape Verde I. Also ranges into Gulf of Panama and Galapagos Is. Map 167.

GREAT FRIGATE-BIRD *Fregata minor* Pl. 24

Outsize, 34–40 ins, 86–100 cm. Wing-span 90 ins, 229 cm. The adult male has generally black upperparts with a greenish sheen and a brown band across the median wing-coverts. Underparts brownish-black. Beneath its long slender black hooked bill it carries a large bright red distensible pouch. Its legs are usually black, sometimes pinkish. The female has similarly coloured upperparts with a brown collar at the back of the neck. Its throat and foreneck are greyish, the lower neck, breast and sides white, the rest of the abdomen and flanks black. Its bill is usually horn-coloured but varies, and legs reddish or bluish.

Young birds have brownish upperparts, the head, neck and underparts whitish rusty-coloured.

The adult female is the only species with a whitish throat immediately adjoining its white underparts.
RANGE: In the S. Atlantic breeds on Trinidad and Martin Vas Is. Ranges widely over the tropical Indian and Pacific Oceans, including Galapagos Is. Map 168.

LESSER FRIGATE-BIRD *Fregata ariel* Pl. 24

Very large, 31 ins, 79 cm. Wing-span 90 ins, 229 cm. Adults have generally black upperparts with a deep blue purplish sheen on the back; underparts browner.

Adult males have grey bills, bright red pouches, a noticeable white patch on either side of the dark abdomen under the wings and reddish-brown or black legs. Adult females have a chestnut collar on the hindneck, not easily seen, and a brownish patch on the upperwing-coverts. The throats of the females are black, the breasts white and a white patch shows on each side of their dark abdomens. Their bills are bluish, skin on the throat and legs red.

Young birds have brownish-black upperparts, the head, neck, breast and abdomen white with rusty streaks. Their heads are sometimes rufous.

Adults of both sexes differ from other frigate-birds by the white patch on each side under the wings. They are considerably smaller than Great Frigate-birds.
RANGE: In the Atlantic breeds on Trinidad and Martin Vas Is. Ranges widely over islands in the tropical Indian Ocean and W. Pacific. Breeds also on small islands in N. Queensland, and N.W. Australia. Map 169.

Phalaropes swim buoyantly, bobbing like corks on the water.

PHALAROPES Phalaropodidae

Phalaropes are a unique family of small dainty waders 'clothed and booted specially to enable them to live for the greater part of their entire lives apart from the breeding season on the open ocean.

To this end their under plumage is thick, they possess underdown like ducks, and their toes are fitted with broad webbed fringes to assist them in swimming.

They feed at sea on plankton, congregating to 'winter' in certain favoured sea areas where surface plankton is rich.

They are extremely slender little birds, somewhat resembling sandpipers, swim buoyantly and usually collect in flocks at sea. When disturbed flocks fly with rapid jerky wingbeats for short distances to settle once again. When feeding they paddle and twirl in circles as they peck hurriedly for surface plankton.

On the sea routes they are, rather naturally, almost always seen in their pale winter plumage, vastly different from the brighter splashes of orange or red in breeding plumage, and are thus extremely difficult to identify positively by species.

Nesting and young

These tend to nest in loose sociable groups on tundra or grassy waterside sites. The sex roles are reversed, the larger, brighter females displaying and courting, the males incubating and tending the young alone. The females are probably polyandrous. The nest is a hollow on the ground, lined with vegetation to form a cup nest; and usually concealed in vegetation where possible. There is a clutch of 4 eggs, pyriform and cryptically coloured in olive-green with dark markings. The male incubates for *c*. 3 weeks. The young are downy and striped; feeding themselves, but brooded and guarded by the male. They become independent in *c*. 3 weeks.

GREY PHALAROPE *Phalaropus fulicarius* Pl. 25

Very small, 7.5–9 ins, 191–229 mm. Wing-span 15 ins, 38 cm. A somewhat sturdier little bird than the Red-necked Phalarope with a shorter more thick-set bill. *Winter plumage*: head, neck and underparts white, a dusky patch extending from below the eye backwards across the cheeks. The back of the head and hindneck are slaty-grey, the remainder of the upperparts lightish blue-grey, darker on wings and tail, with only pale streaking and a white wing bar conspicuous in flight. Bill relatively short, heavy and broad in comparison with that of the Red-necked Phalarope; bill yellow, tip black; legs horn-coloured. *Breeding plumage*: females have rich red throats, necks and underparts, white cheeks, crown and chin darkish and upperparts more richly streaked with buff and black. White wing bar. Underwings and sides of rump white. Bill yellow with black tip; legs yellowish. Males are less showy than females.
RANGE: See Map 170.

WILSON'S PHALAROPE *Steganopus tricolor* Pl. 25

Small, 8.5–10 ins, 216–254 mm. Wing-span 14 ins, 36 cm. Larger than the other two species with a slender neck and long slender black bill. *Winter plumage*: upperparts pale grey, wing quills darker grey. The upper tail-coverts, sides of the back, rump and underparts are white, and a broad white stripe shows above the eye. Bill black, long and slender; legs black. No white wing bar. *Breeding plumage*: the crown and middle of the back are bluish-grey, the wings and lower back greyish-brown, upper tail-coverts white and tail grey. The sides of the face are white and a black stripe extends through the eye to the side of the neck, continuing as a chestnut stripe along the side of the back. The throat and abdomen are white, the foreneck and breast pale rufous. Bills and legs black.

In winter plumage Wilson's Phalarope looks considerably whiter than the other two species, and shows no white wing bar in flight.
RANGE: See map 171.

RED-NECKED PHALAROPE *Lobipes lobatus* Pl. 25

Very small, 6.5–8 ins, 165–203 mm. Wing-span 14 ins, 36 cm. A rather smaller and daintier bird than the Grey Phalarope with a very slim neck and longer straight needle-like bill. *Winter plumage*: similar to Grey Phalarope but both back and wings darker and the back more conspicuously streaked. White wing bar is more conspicuous in flight. *Breeding plumage*: the crown and cheeks are slate-grey, and a white spot shows above the eye. The chin and throat are white and a rufous band stretches down the sides and front of the neck, the underparts thereafter being white. The upperparts and wings are slate-grey, the back with buff streaking. Bill and legs bluish-grey.

In winter plumage the shorter and broader yellow bill with a dark tip and the white forehead in the Grey Phalarope helps to distinguish it from the Red-necked Phalarope.
RANGE: See map 172.

Yellow-billed Sheathbills and Gentoo Penguin. Sheathbills scavenge for all kinds of offal, mixing with nesting colonies of other antarctic birds, sucking eggs and killing small chicks. White looks belie dirty habits.

SHEATHBILLS   Chionididae

Sheathbills are something of a paradox being a connecting link between waders and gulls for they have only rudimentary webs between the three front toes and a well developed hind toe. When seen pecking about the shore line on the sub-antarctic and S. Indian Ocean islands scavenging amongst the most unpleasant offal, they look more like pigeons. Sheathbills are however able to swim in the sea, and may be seen occasionally out to sea on ice floes. They are not active birds, flying laboriously with a flapping flight on somewhat rounded wings.

The two separate species are very similar, those breeding in the sub-antarctic being distinguished by yellow bills, those breeding on islands in the southern area of the Indian Ocean by black bills.

Nesting and young

These nest in scattered pairs near an assured source of food such as a penguin colony. The nest is in a well-concealed site in a cavity or crevice among boulders. It consists of a collection of pebbles, bones, plant fragments and similar debris. The clutch of 2–4 eggs are creamy-yellowish, heavily spotted and blotched in purplish-brown. Incubation, shared by both birds, takes *c.* 4 weeks. The chicks have dull brownish down, becoming grey. Often only one of the brood is successfully reared. The young have no special juvenile plumage, moulting from down into the white adult plumage in *c.* 7–8 weeks.

YELLOW-BILLED SHEATHBILL *Chionis alba*   **Pl. 25**
Medium, 16 ins, 41 cm. Plumage white overall. The distinctive features are the bill and wattles. Bill short, stout and conical, black at tip shading to pinkish-yellow at base. The basal half of the upper mandible is covered by a horny sheath from which the bird derives its name. Beneath the eye is a bare pinkish crinkly wattle, and a second wattle on top of the base of the bill, giving the bird a 'scabby' appearance. Legs black; rudimentary webs between the three front toes; hind toe well developed.
RANGE: Confined to the Antarctic Peninsula and sub-antarctic islands. Breeds on Falkland Is. S. Georgia, S. Sandwich, S. Orkney and S. Shetland Is., and islands adjacent to Graham Land.   Map 173.

BLACK-BILLED SHEATHBILL *Chionis minor*   **Pl. 25**
Medium, 16 ins, 41 cm. General plumage white, similar to the Yellow-billed Sheathbill. Its bill however is black and legs vary in colour, usually black in those breeding in its northerly islands, and varying from brown to flesh-colour in those breeding further south.
RANGE: Breeds in Marion and Prince Edward Is., Kerguelen and Heard Is.   Map 174.

Long-tailed Skua chasing a tern.

Great Skua

SKUAS   Stercorariidae

Skuas are seen frequently by ships on the ocean routes for they remain largely at sea outside the breeding season when they undertake long oceanic migrations.

Three of the smaller skuas or 'jaegers' as they are often named, the Arctic Skua, the Pomarine Skua and the Long-tailed Skua breed in the arctic belt of the northern hemisphere and migrate southwards to winter in the far southern hemisphere.

The larger Great Skua of the northern hemisphere which breeds slightly south of the Arctic Circle and its counterpart of the southern hemisphere, the southern Great Skua, of which there are several races, resort to more temperate climates outside their breeding seasons and rarely cross the Equator. The southern Great Skua is almost identical with the Great Skua and the separate races in the southern hemisphere are closely similar, with the exception of McCormick's Skua, that their differences cannot normally be observed under sighting conditions at sea.

All four species are bold rapacious seabirds, betraying their profession as predators by the sharply hooked tip of the upper mandible, and their inveterate habit of harrying other seabirds to force them to jettison their food.

The Great Skua is a much larger and more heavily built brown bird with broad wings with pale wing patches, somewhat like a large brown gull. The smaller skuas are almost falcon-like in appearance with narrow sharply pointed wings and a strong rapid direct flight. The Long-tailed Skua very rarely occurs in a dark phase, but both the Arctic and Pomarine Skuas occur in both a light and a dark phase.

The Great Skua is quite a regular 'ship follower', often picking up a ship and remaining astern for several hours, waiting to harry other seabirds or land in the sea to gobble up refuse from the galley. The Pomarine Skua is also attracted to ships for short periods, but the Arctic and Long-tailed Skuas appear to pay little attention.

At sea the Arctic and Pomarine Skuas may easily be confused except in full adult plumage and then only if a clear sight of their protruding 'pin' tail feathers is possible.

Nesting and young

Nesting occurs on sea-coasts, offshore islands, tundra or moorland and mountain slopes. Although the Great Skua is a coastal nester and feeder, the smaller species often nest further inland and depend extensively on lemmings and small rodents for food while nesting. Nesting is often sociable, but the nests are well-spaced. The nest is a shallow hollow, usually in an exposed site on the ground commanding a good view around, and is unlined or sparsely lined with fragments of nearby vegetation. The clutch is usually of 2 eggs, which are dull olive, greenish or buff, with dark markings. Incubation is undertaken by both birds and lasts *c*. 4 weeks. The young are covered in dark brown down. They are fed by both parents and take 6–8 weeks to become independent.

GREAT SKUA *Catharacta skua*   **Pl. 26**
Medium–large, 21–24 ins, 53–61 cm. Wing-span 59 ins, 150 cm. The Great Skua of the northern hemisphere can be distinguished from somewhat similar northern gulls in brown immature plumage by its heavier build and, in particular, by the large white patches which show at the base of the primaries. Its wings are broad and rounded. It has a stout blackish bill, hooked at the tip, black legs and a short

wedge-shaped tail. At leisure its flight appears ponderous and heavy, but when harrying seabirds it shows great agility and speed. Young birds are similar

It obtains much of its food by pursuing other seabirds, causing them to disgorge their food, or by scavenging for offal, and frequently follows ships.

RANGE: Breeds in Iceland, the Faroes, Shetland and Orkney Is., and ranges widely across the N. Atlantic as far as Newfoundland and Nova Scotia. Outside the breeding season it disperses southwards, and has been observed as far south as the Equator. Map 175.

GREAT SKUA ('Southern Skua', southern form of Great Skua)　　　Pl. 26
　Catharacta skua

Medium–large, 21–24 ins, 53–61 cm. In the southern hemisphere, the Great Skua is represented by the Southern Skua showing similar plumage and characteristics. The southern Great Skua, of which a number of sub-species have been named but cannot be distinguished at sea, breeds on the Antarctic Peninsula, adjacent subantarctic islands, S. Shetlands, S. Orkneys, S. Sandwich Is., Marion I., Crozet, Kerguelen and Heard Is., S. Georgia, Falkland Is., Bouvet I. Tristan da Cunha, Gough, eastwards to the islands south and east of New Zealand. Map 175.

McCORMICK'S SKUA　*Catharacta maccormicki*　　　　　　　**Pl. 26**

Medium–large, 21 ins, 53 cm. This antarctic skua is similar but much lighter in colour than the Great Skua. The crown and upperparts are brown, the neck feathers partly straw-coloured, the forehead, sides of head and underparts pale brown, almost whitish, but normally browner on the abdomen. Bill stout and black, hooked at tip; legs black; tail short and round.

RANGE: Occurs on the antarctic continent and S. Shetlands. Unlikely to be seen on the sea routes. Map 177.

POMARINE SKUA　*Stercorarius pomarinus*　　　　　　　　　**Pl. 26**

Medium–large, 21–22 ins, 53–56 cm. Wing-span 48 ins, 122 cm. Noticeably smaller than the Great Skua, yet more stoutly built than the Arctic and Long-tailed Skuas, it occurs in both light and dark phases. *Light phase*: The top of the head is sooty-black contrasting with the straw-coloured sides of the head and collar. The neck and breast are white the remainder of the underbody whitish, flanks and under tail-coverts dusky or barred. Underwing and remainder of upperparts and upperwings dusky-brown. A rather faint white band appears at the base of the primaries and a dusky band usually shows across the breast. Bill brown with black hooked tip; legs black. The most distinctive feature is its long dark wedge-shaped tail which in full adult plumage, carries projecting central tail feathers extending to 2 ins with broad rounded and vertically twisted tips. *Dark phase*: In the dark phase the entire underparts are dark of the same tone as the upperparts.

Occasionally follows ships.

RANGE: Breeds in high arctic latitudes. Migrates to wintering areas through all oceans as far as 50°S. Map 178.

ARCTIC SKUA　*Stercorarius parasiticus*　　　　　　　　　**Pl. 26**

Medium size, 17–20 ins, 43–51 cm. Wing-span 40 ins, 102 cm. Smaller and more falcon-like than the Pomarine Skua but very similar in plumage pattern to the Pomarine both in its light and dark phases. *Light phase*: top of head, back, wings and tail ashy-brown, sides of head and neck yellowish, breast white, remainder of underbody whitish, under tail-coverts and underwing ashy-brown. A faint white band appears at the base of the primaries. Bill brown, hooked at tip; legs black. The tail is long and wedge-shaped and, in full adult plumage, carries two sharply pointed

Arctic Skua

Pomarine Skua

Long-tailed Skua

narrow tail feathers about 3 ins long. *Dark phase*: neck and underparts sooty-brown, slightly paler than upperparts. *Intermediate phase*: whitish-buff sides of head. Pale brown below.

RANGE: Breeds in high northern latitudes. Migrates to wintering areas as far as 60°S.   Map 179.

POMARINE and ARCTIC SKUAS – IMMATURE PLUMAGE – MOULT IN ADULTS

Immatures of both species are indistinguishable at sea, having brown heads, necks and wings and buffish-brown underparts, the underparts showing varying degrees of barring. In immatures the elongated central tail feathers have not developed.

Adults in moult lose their distinguishing elongated tail feathers, and at other times they may become broken. At such times differentiation between species at sea is almost impossible.

LONG-TAILED SKUA *Stercorarius longicaudus*   Pl. 26

Medium–large, 21–23 ins, including 6–8 ins tail and streamers, 53–58 cm. Wing-span 30 ins, 76 cm. The smallest and slenderest of the smaller skuas or jaegers and does not appear to occur in a dark phase. The top of the head is brownish-black, remainder of the upperparts greyish-brown with black primaries. The sides of the head and entire neck are yellowish, breast and underbody white, duskier on the flanks, underwings greyish-brown. No white band is noticeable on the upperwings, and no dark breast band is ever present. Bill brown with black hooked tip; legs bluish-grey. In adult plumage the very distinctive feature is the presence of two greatly elongated narrow pointed central tail streamers.

Young birds have greyer ashy-brown upperparts, and paler greyish-white under-parts, slightly barred, in comparison with young Pomarine and Arctic Skuas.

Tail streamers are not present in immatures.

RANGE: Breeds in arctic latitudes. Migrates to wintering areas south of the Equator.   Map 180.

GULLS Laridae

Gulls are primarily coastal seabirds, obtaining their food from the coastlines and inshore. They swim buoyantly however, and in certain areas they will follow fishing fleets far from land living off the refuse thrown overboard. They rarely dive below the surface. Many gulls disperse from their breeding areas to winter in warmer climates, some from the northern hemisphere undertaking long migrations and crossing the Equator. In general however, with the notable exception of the kittiwake they are not oceanic as a family and are seen rarely at sea far from land.

In adult plumage, with few exceptions, gulls have white wings, bodies and square tails, their upperwings varying from pearl grey to sooty-black. Males and females appear alike. Some however acquire dark hoods in the breeding season, and bills and legs vary in colour. In the majority of species the immature plumage is entirely different, being of a dark streaked and mottled brown, with dark bills and frequently dark bands on tails. The gradual change to adult plumage may take two to four years, and during this period specific identification often presents considerable difficulty.

Their flight is buoyant and elegant, sometimes circling and planing in updraughts of air currents, hovering over food or turning and twisting sharply. At eventide they are often seen winging their way gracefully to their night roosts.

Nesting and young

These nest colonially, or more rarely in single pairs, on a variety of sites – cliff ledges, or small projections built up with nest material, rock stacks, islands, cliff-tops, sandbanks and shingle banks on coasts and lakes, inland marshes and moors, and in some instances in trees. Nest material is carried to the site and the nest may be a substantial structure of plant material, sticks or seaweed. The clutch is usually 2–3 eggs, variable in colour but usually ranging from creamy to olive or buff, with dark markings. Both birds incubate for c. 3–4 weeks. The chicks are downy, grey or buffish with dark spots or mottling. They remain at or near the nest site. They are fed by both parents on regurgitated food, and become independent in c. 4–6 weeks. The cycle is usually annual, but may vary since the Silver Gull has six-month cycles in W. Australia and S. Africa.

PACIFIC GULL *Larus pacificus*   **Pls. 27, 34, 40**
Large, 25 ins, 64 cm. Wing-span 54 ins, 137 cm. This is a noticeably large black-backed gull with white head, neck and underparts. Mantle and upperwing-coverts black. The primaries and secondaries are also black, broadly tipped white. The large sturdy bill is deep-yellow with a red spot at the angle; legs yellow. Tail white, a distinctive feature being the presence of a sub-terminal black band.

Young birds are brown, the feathers with paler edges, primaries and tail brownish-black. Bill flesh-coloured with a black sub-terminal band; legs brown.

Distinguished from the Dominican Gull by its large bill and black band on tail.
RANGE: S. Australian and Tasmanian coasts.   Map 181.

Gulls are seldom found far from land. They like to look out over the sea for food from cliffs or any high vantage point.

MAGELLAN GULL *Gabianus scoresbyi*   **Pls. 30, 38**
Medium, 18 ins, 46 cm. Wing-span 40 ins, 102 cm. In adult southern summer plumage the head, neck and underparts pale grey. Upperparts and upperwings slaty-black; under-surface of wings dark grey. Primaries and secondaries show white tips. Tail white; bill stout, red; legs red. Young birds have head, neck and upper breast palish-brown; upperwings brown; upper tail-coverts, lower breast and abdomen white; tail white with broad black sub-terminal band. Bill brown with black tip; legs brown.
     Mainly confined inshore and on the shore line.
RANGE: Breeds in the Falkland Is., Tierra del Fuego, and on east coast of S. America northwards to Point Tombo, 44°S., 65°20′W.   Map 182.

IVORY GULL *Pagophila eburnea*   **Pls. 33, 39**
Medium, 16–18 ins, 41–46 cm. The adult plumage is entirely white. Eye large and black showing a distinct red eye-ring. Bill rather short, dark at base shading to yellow with a reddish tip. Legs short and black.
     Its short legs and habit of standing with tail depressed and head raised gives it an awkward appearance. On the wing however its flight is buoyant and graceful. Young birds show grey smudges on face and chin, the upperparts finely spotted with black, wing quills tipped black and tail showing a narrow sub-terminal black band.
RANGE: A species of the high arctic frequenting open leads in the pack ice outside the breeding season. Wanders southwards in small numbers in autumn and winter to Iceland, rarely further south, Alaska, Hudson Bay, Labrador and Bering Sea. Breeds on islands across the high arctic oceans.   Map 183.

DUSKY GULL *Larus fuliginosus*   **Pls. 30, 33, 38**
Small–medium, 15–17 ins, 39–43 cm. Adults have black heads with white eyelids, dark grey upperparts with grey rump and tail. Underparts grey, paler on abdomen. Bill dark, tip red. Legs black. Young birds are dark sooty-brown above, head, wing quills and tail blackish, and underparts grey. Bill and legs black.
RANGE: Local to Galapagos Is.   Not mapped.

GREY GULL *Larus modestus*   **Pls. 30, 38**
Medium, 18 ins, 46 cm. The gull in adult plumage is easily identified for with the exception of its head which is white in summer and palish-brown in winter, the whole plumage is leaden-grey, darker on the wing quills. The dark secondaries however have broad white tips which show a white band along the trailing edge of the wings in flight. The grey tail carries a broad black band. Bill and legs reddish-black.
     Young birds are generally brown with pale edges to feathers, the wings and tail darker. Bill and legs black.
     The contrast between the white head in summer, grey body and white band on the trailing edge of wings in flight is very noticeable.
RANGE: West coast of S. America. Breeds inland in the deserts of Peru and Chile.   Map 184.

HEERMANN'S GULL *Larus heermanni*   **Pls. 30, 38**
Medium size, 17 ins, 43 cm. Adults in summer plumage have head and upper neck white; in winter greyish-brown. Upperparts and upperwings slate-grey, wing quills tipped white. Lower neck, underparts and upper tail-coverts pale grey. Underwing brownish-grey. Bill red; legs black; tail dark, almost black with white tip. Young

birds are dark brown overall with some buff flecking; bill and legs black.
Easily distinguished by its grey colouring and white or greyish head.
RANGE: Pacific coast of N. America from Vancouver to southern Mexico. Breeds
on Mexican coast.   Map 185.

RED SEA BLACK-HEADED GULL or WHITE-EYED GULL
Larus leucophthalmus   **Pls. 32, 37, 40**

Small–medium size, 15.5 ins, 39 cm. In breeding plumage, head, nape, throat and
neck deep black. Eyelids white. No white ring around neck. Mantle and
upperwing-coverts slate-grey, in winter brownish-black. Primaries and secondaries
black, secondaries tipped white. Underparts of sides of breast slate-grey, remainder of underparts white. Underwings greyish. In winter head and throat pale
mottled-white and neck grizzled. Bill dusky-red, tip black. Legs yellowish. Immatures are brown above, underparts whitish, rump white, black band on tail, bills
greenish.
See Aden Gull (p. 95) for comparison.
RANGE: From Gulf of Suez south through Red Sea, Gulf of Aden and Somaliland
coast. Breeds in southern Red Sea.   Map 186.

ADEN GULL *Larus hemprichi*   **Pls. 32, 37, 40**

Medium, 17.5–18.5 ins, 44–47 cm. In breeding plumage head, nape and throat
coffee-brown. Eyelids white. A white ring shows around neck. Mantle and
upperwing-coverts greyish-brown. Primaries and secondaries brownish-black,
secondaries tipped white. Breast pale brown, abdomen and tail white. Underwings
greyish. In winter, head and throat mottled-brown and indistinct collar brownish-
grey. Bill greenish with sub-terminal black band and red tip. Legs yellowish.
Immatures are brown above, underparts whitish, tail black and bill greenish.
Aden Gulls and Red Sea Black-headed Gulls are very similar. When seen
together the Aden Gull looks decidedly larger.
A detailed comparison should be made.
RANGE: Southern Red Sea, coasts of S. Yemen, Oman and Persian Gulf, southwards from Somaliland to Zanzibar. Breeds throughout range.   Map 187.

SIMEON GULL *Larus belcheri*   **Pls. 30, 34, 38**

Medium, 20 ins, 51 cm. In adult summer plumage the head, neck, underparts and
rump are white; in winter the head becomes brownish-black showing white eyelids.
Mantle and upperwing-coverts sooty-black; primaries black, secondaries grey with
broad white tips. Bill yellow with a black band and red tip; legs yellow. Tail white
with a broad central black band.
Young birds have pale mottled-brown upperparts, black primaries, whitish
underparts, yellow bills with a black tip and greyish legs. The tail is black showing a
white tip.
Somewhat similar to the Dominican Gull but smaller and distinguished in adult
plumage by the black bar on the tail and black band on bill.
RANGE: West coast of S. America from Peru south to Coquimbo in Chile, breed-
ingly chiefly on rocky islands along coast of Peru. On east coast, the lesser
well-known Atlantic form ranges further south from Buenos Aires possibly to
Patagonia; breeding in 1963 established only on small low-lying island of San Blas,
south of Bahia Blanca.   Map 188.

JAPANESE GULL   *Larus crassirostris*   **Pls. 27, 34**
Medium, 19 ins, 48 cm. In adult summer plumage the head and underparts are
white, the upperparts slate-grey. The first two primaries are grey, remaining
primaries and secondaries black, all showing white tips. The tail is white with a
distinctive black sub-terminal central band. Bill yellow with a black cross-band and
red tip; legs yellow. In winter the head becomes greyish-brown.
   Young birds have dark brown upperparts with pale edges to feathers, darker
brown wings and tail, paler upperparts. Bills flesh-coloured with black tip; legs
flesh-coloured.   .
   The black band on the white tail is distinctive.
RANGE: Coasts of eastern Asia. Breeds on coasts of Japan and China.   Map 189.

AUDOUIN'S GULL   *Larus audouinii*   **Pls. 29, 35**
Medium–large, 20 ins, 51 cm. In adult summer plumage head, neck, underparts and
tail white; in winter head shows greyish streaks. Upperparts and upperwings very
pale grey; outer primaries black with white spot; inner primaries and secondaries
grey with white tips. Eye-ring red. Bill coral red with sub-terminal black band and
yellow tip; legs dark olive-green. Young birds have streaked whitish-grey heads
with dark spot behind eye, greyish-brown upperparts and upperwings, whitish
underparts, and are very similar but smaller than immature Lesser Black-backed
Gulls.
   In size it is midway between the Common Gull *Larus canus* and the Herring Gull
Larus argentatus. The colour of its stout red bill and eye-rim helps to distinguish
the adult.
RANGE: Mediterranean Sea. It appears to cling to rocky coastlines mainly along
the northern shore. A relatively rare species not yet reported on the main sea route
from Gibraltar to Port Said.   Map 190.

RING-BILLED GULL   *Larus delawarensis*   **Pls. 28, 35, 40**
Medium, 18.5 ins, 47 cm. Wing-span 48 ins, 122 cm. In adult plumage the Ring-
billed Gull closely resembles a Herring Gull but is distinctly smaller in size. It is
distinguished by the colour of the bill which is greenish-yellow and crossed by a
black band towards the tip. Its legs also are yellow or greenish in colour.
   Young birds have head and neck whitish-grey with some brown mottling, mantle
and upperwing-coverts brownish-grey with paler edging to feathers; underparts and
tail mottled whitish-brown; tail with narrow dark sub-terminal band; bill brown
with dark sub-terminal band; legs pinkish or flesh-grey.
   In flight the Ring-billed Gull is more buoyant than the Herring Gull, and shows
more black on the underside of the primaries. Young birds look much whiter than
young Herring Gulls.
RANGE: Breeds in central U.S.A. Occurs on both coasts of U.S.A. south to Texas
and Gulf of Mexico.   Map 191.

COMMON or MEW GULL   *Larus canus*   **Pls. 28, 35, 40**
Medium, 18 ins, 46 cm. Wing-span 48 ins, 122 cm. Head, neck, underparts and tail
white; in winter the head shows grey streaking. Upperparts pale grey; outer
primaries black with broad white tips, remainder of primaries and secondaries grey
with white tips. Bill and legs greenish-yellow.
   Young birds have greyish-white heads, remainder of upperparts mottled
greyish-brown, underparts whitish-brown mottling; bill brown with a black sub-
terminal bar; legs flesh-coloured. Tail whitish, mottled brown with dusky sub-
terminal band.

Adults differ from Ring-billed Gulls by greater amount of white on wing tips and lack of black band on bill.

RANGE: Widespread throughout global temperate N. latitude belts.   Map 192.

HERRING GULL *Larus argentatus*   **Pls. 28, 35, 40**
Medium–large, 22–24 ins, 56–61 cm. Wing-span 52 ins, 132 cm. In adult breeding plumage head and neck white, in winter showing pale grey streakings. Underparts and tail white. Mantle and upperwing-coverts grey. Primaries and secondaries black, tips white. Outermost primaries have white sub-terminal spots. Bill yellow with red spot at angle. Legs pinkish flesh-coloured. Immatures in first year are coarsely mottled-brown overall with brownish-black wing quills and tail, the latter barred. Bill black. As they grow older head, underparts and rump become progressively paler. Second year birds show tail with broad dark terminal band, the bill has semblance of a dark tip (compare second year Ring-billed Gull, p. 96).

First year immatures are virtually indistinguishable from similar immature Lesser Black-backed Gulls, which however grow darker as they grow older during transition to adult plumage. Through geographical distribution certain adult Herring Gulls show a somewhat darker mantle and yellow legs, and are best referred to as yellow-legged Herring Gulls.

RANGE: Widespread across the whole northern hemisphere, breeding throughout range.   Map 193.

THAYER'S GULL *Larus thayeri*   **Pls. 28, 35**
Medium–large, 22–24 ins, 56–61 cm. Very similar to Herring Gull, and Kumlien's Gull. Chief differences lie in the primaries usually grey compared to the black primaries of Herring Gull, but the white mirrors in wing tips show. The primaries are always darker than those of Kumlien's Gull.

RANGE: Arctic coasts of Canada and arctic islands to Baffin I.   Map 194.

LESSER BLACK-BACKED GULL *Larus fuscus*
(A) Medium–large, 20–24 ins, 51–61 cm. Wing-span 50 ins, 127 cm; (B) Adult breeding, head, neck, underparts and tail white; (C) Mantle and upperwing-coverts slate-grey, primaries black, first primary with a sub-terminal white spot, remainder white, secondaries and tertials grey, broad white tips; (D) Bill yellowish, red spot at angle; (E) legs yellowish; (F) Immatures in first winter have coarsely brown upperparts, mottled underparts, dark bills, tails blackish-brown. In second winter, head freckled, underparts white, tail white with black terminal band.

RANGE: N. Russia, Norway, Baltic, Germany, Holland, France, British Isles, Shetlands, Faroes, extending range to Iceland. A number disperse southwards in winter to Mediterranean, Atlantic coasts of Europe, N. Africa and E. Atlantic Is.

RACES:

   LESSER BLACK-BACKED GULL *Larus f. fuscus*   **Pls. 27, 34, 40**
   Scandinavia and Baltic. (C) Mantle and upperwing-coverts slaty-black, often look black at sea; (E) Bright yellow.   Map 195.

   LESSER BLACK-BACKED GULL *Larus f. graellsii*   **Pls. 27, 35, 40**
   British Isles, Germany, Holland, France, Shetlands, Faroes. (C) Mantle and upperwing-coverts dark slaty-grey; (E) Yellow.   Map 196.
   Note: First winter immatures are virtually indistinguishable from similar immature Herring Gulls *Larus argentatus*; second year immatures appear darker than second year Herring Gulls.

CALIFORNIA GULL *Larus californicus*   **Pls. 28, 35**
Medium, 20 ins, 51 cm. Wing-span 49 ins, 125 cm. For adult plumage see similar Herring Gull (p. 97). The California Gull is slightly smaller and differs only in showing a partially dusky sub-terminal band on its yellow bill and in its greenish, as opposed to flesh-coloured, legs.

Young birds cannot normally be distinguished from young Herring Gulls.

RANGE: Winters on Pacific coast of N. America from British Columbia to California. Breeds on inland lakes in western N. America.   Map 197.

WESTERN GULL *Larus occidentalis*   **Pls. 27, 34**
Medium–large, 21–22 ins, 53–56 cm. Wing-span 54 ins, 137 cm. In adult plumage the head, neck, underparts and tail are white. In winter the head and neck may carry grey streaks. Mantle and upperwing-coverts leaden-grey. The wing quite grey with white tips, the first four primaries however having black outer webs, and the leading primary a white sub-terminal spot. Bill yellow with a red spot at angle; legs flesh-coloured.

Young birds have brownish-grey plumage, the upperparts with white mottling; wing quills and tail black; legs brown.

Distinguished from the California Gull by its darker mantle and flesh-coloured as opposed to greenish-yellow legs.

RANGE: West coast of N. America, from British Columbia to California. Breeds on coasts and islands.   Map 198.

SOUTHERN BLACK-BACKED GULL *Larus dominicanus* **Pls. 27, 34, 40**
Medium–large, 23 ins, 58 cm. Wing-span 50 ins, 127 cm. A large gull. In adult plumage the head, neck, underparts and tail are white; mantle and upperwings sooty-black. The primaries and secondaries are black, the four outer primaries tipped white, secondaries broadly tipped white. The leading primary has an additional white sub-terminal patch. The tertials are also tipped white so that two white bands are seen on the upperparts when the wings are closed. Bill yellow with a red spot at angle; legs yellow or olive-green.

Young birds do not attain adult plumage until their third winter. Early plumage is brown all over the buff-edged feathers on upperparts, mottled brown on underparts, barred brown and white on rump and tail coverts. Tail is brown; bill blackish; legs greenish-yellow.

Known locally as the 'kelp gull'. The only large black-backed gull in the southern hemisphere with an entirely white tail.

RANGE: Both coasts of S. America, S. Africa, in New Zealand and many islands in the southern ocean belt. Recently extended northwards to New South Wales. Map 199.

SLATY-BACKED GULL *Larus schistisagus*   **Pls. 27, 34**
Medium–large, 24 ins, 61 cm. Wing-span 53 ins, 135 cm. See Herring Gull (p. 97). This gull can be distinguished from the otherwise similar Herring Gull by its much darker slate-coloured mantle and upperwing-coverts and larger size.

Young birds have noticeably paler light-brown upperparts than the Herring Gull, a conspicuous dark bar on the wing, underparts greyish, dark brown tail; bill black; legs brown.

RANGE: Coasts of N.E. Asia dispersing south to China and Japan. Breeds on coasts of Sea of Okhotsk, Kamchatka, Kuril Is. and northern Japan.   Map 200.

GREAT BLACK-BACKED GULL   *Larus marinus*   **Pls. 27, 34, 40**
Very large, 27–30 ins, 69–76 cm. Wing-span 65 ins, 165 cm. The largest black-backed gull.

In adult plumage the head, neck, underparts and tail are pure white; mantle and upperwings sooty-black, the primaries and secondaries tipped white. In winter some dusky streaks appear on the head and neck. The powerful massive bill is yellow with a red spot at angle; legs flesh-coloured.

Young birds are paler than the mottled brown young of Herring and Lesser Black-backed Gulls, and have whitish underparts. Their upperparts are brownish, primaries brownish-black; tail white with black mottling; bill brownish-black; legs pale flesh-coloured.

Its much greater size, almost black upperparts and slow deliberate flight distinguish it from smaller black-backed gulls.

RANGE: East and west coasts of N. Atlantic, some dispersing southwards in winter to Mediterranean and N. Atlantic Is. and on the east coast of N. America to Virginia.   Map 201.

GLAUCOUS-WINGED GULL   *Larus glaucescens*   **Pls. 29, 35**
Large, 25 ins, 64 cm. Wing-span 53 ins, 135 cm. Similar to the Herring Gull but with a paler grey mantle and upperwings, and dark grey (as opposed to black), primaries with white sub-terminal spots; secondaries grey with white tips. Bill yellow with red spots at angle; legs flesh-coloured.

Young birds in second winter are unusual in being grey overall with a darker grey tail, the throat and vent alone white. Bill dark; legs brown.

RANGE: Breeds on the N.E. coasts of Siberia and the N.W. coasts of Alaska and Aleutian Is., ranging southwards in winter to northern Japan and California.   Map 202.

GLAUCOUS GULL   *Larus hyperboreus*   **Pls. 29, 35, 40**
Very large, 28 ins, 71 cm. Wing-span 53 ins, 135 cm. An outstandingly large, stoutly built, pale winged gull with a stouter and longer bill than the similar and smaller Iceland Gull. Head and neck white in summer, in winter showing grey streaking. Remainder of body and tail white. Upperwings pale grey, wing quills white, wings broader than in Iceland Gull. Bill stout, yellow with red spot at angle. In breeding plumage eye ring is lemon yellow. Legs pink.

Immatures in first year are creamy-brown with some barring with flesh-coloured bills and dark tips. Tail shows no dark band. Second year birds are white overall, the upperparts gradually becoming pale grey.

See also Iceland Gull for comparison (p. 99).

RANGE: Arctic seas dispersing southwards in winter into the N. Atlantic and N. Pacific Oceans.   Map 203.

ICELAND GULL   *Larus leucopterus*
(A) Medium–large, 22 ins, 56 cm. Adult. (B) Summer head, neck white, in winter streaked, upper tail-coverts and tail white; (C) mantle, upperwing; coverts and wing quills pale grey with white tips; (D) in summer eye-ring red; (E) bill yellow, red spot at angle, legs pinkish-flesh colour; (F) Immatures first winter finely mottled overall pale brown, bill dusky with dark band towards tip. Second winter birds are almost pure white, bill yellowish, tip dark; (G) Flight: more buoyant and with faster wing-beats than Glaucous Gull *Larus hyperboreus*.

Smaller and slimmer, with relatively longer wings and a more slender bill than the larger Glaucous Gull which has a yellow eye-ring in the breeding season. Observed on the water its wing tips will be seen to project well beyond its tail.

RANGE: Breeds in Greenland, arctic Siberia and arctic Canada dispersing southwards in autumn and winter, occasionally as far south as Latitude of New York, rarely to the British Isles.

RACES:

ICELAND GULL *Larus l. leucopterus* Pls. 29, 33, 35, 40
Map 204.

KUMLIEN'S GULL *Larus l. kumlieni*
Breeds in Baffin I. and vicinity. Probably ranges eastwards and has been observed in the Belle I. Strait. (C) Wing quills slightly darker grey than Iceland Gull and shows grey spots towards white wingtips, but difficult to identify between the two, Kumlien's Gull being rarely seen. Map 205.

Iceland Gull (p.99)   Kumlien's Gull.

These two species are very similar. Iceland Gull shows red eye-ring in summer. Kumlien's Gull shows slightly darker wing quills with grey spots towards white tips.

GREAT BLACK-HEADED GULL *Larus ichthyaetus* Page 104; Pls. 32, 37

Large, 27 ins, 69 cm. Readily noticeable by its exceptionally large size in comparison with any other dark-hooded gull.

In adult summer plumage the head is deep black, and white crescentic patches show above and below the eye. The mantle and upperwings are grey; primaries white, outer primaries with sub-terminal black bars; inner primaries and secondaries grey, tipped white. Underparts and tail white. In winter the black head becomes white with some streaking. The bill is distinctive, yellow with a subterminal black band and broad red tip; legs greenish-yellow.

Young birds have mottled white heads, dark brown mantle and upperparts with buff streaking and paler wing feathers. Underparts and tail are white, the tail showing a broad sub-terminal black band; bill and legs greyish.

RANGE: Breeds in inland seas and lakes in southeastern Russia and central Asia. Winters on coasts in southern Red Sea, Persian Gulf, India, Sri Lanka, Bangladesh and Burma. Map 206.

LAUGHING GULL *Larus atricilla*   **Pls. 31, 36**
Medium, 16.5 ins, 42 cm. Wing-span 41 ins, 104 cm. In adult summer plumage the whole head and upper neck is greyish-black, showing white eyelids above the eye; the upperparts bluish-grey, the first five outer primaries black, inner primaries and secondaries grey, all with white tips. Lower neck and remainder of underparts and tail white. Bill in summer red, in winter blackish; legs reddish-brown. In winter the crown and sides of head and neck become white with some mottling.

Young birds have pale greyish-brown upperparts, with much darker primaries and secondaries, the latter tipped white. Tail grey with broad black sub-terminal band; breast brown, rump and remainder of underparts and under tail-coverts white. Bill black; legs brown.

In flight the white border on the trailing edge of the wings is conspicuous. In immatures the brown breast and white at base of tail is noticeable.
RANGE: Breeds on Atlantic coast of N. America from Nova Scotia to Texas and Caribbean, dispersing southwards in winter to Brazil, to Gulf of Panama and coast of Ecuador.   Map 207.

INDIAN BLACK-HEADED GULL *Larus brunnicephalus*
                                     Page 104 and Pls. 32, 37
Medium, 16–17 ins, 41–43 cm. In adult plumage the hood is brown, paler on forehead and blacker at neck. Mantle and upperwing-coverts blue-grey, wing-coverts at edge and bend of wing white. Outer primaries black, leading two with white patches near tips, inner primaries and secondaries grey. Underbody and tail white, underwing-coverts blue-grey. Bill and legs deep-red. In winter the hood disappears and head becomes white; dark patch behind eye.

Immature birds have head greyish-brown, mantle brownish, outer primaries brown; bill yellowish; legs orange.

Very similar to Northern Black-headed Gull but paler hood and can be distinguished by the large white patches near the tips of its black outer primaries.
RANGE: Coastal from Aden eastwards through India to Burma. Breeds in central Asia from Turkestan to Tibet.   Map 208.

GREY-HEADED GULL *Larus cirrocephalus*   **Pls. 30, 36, 38**
Small-medium, 16 ins, 41 cm. Wing-span, 40 ins, 102 cm. In adult summer plumage the head and throat to the middle of the nape is lavender-grey showing a clear cut white neck; in winter only a pale-grey half hood remains. The mantle and upperwing-coverts are grey; primaries black with a white sub-terminal patch on the outer two, the inner primaries and secondaries grey. Neck, underbody and tail white; underwing-coverts grey; bill and legs deep crimson-red. At rest the folded wings are seen to extend beyond the tail.

Young birds have mottled white heads, mottled grey-brown upperparts, outer primaries black, inner primaries and secondaries brown. Tail white with a dark terminal band. Bill yellow with dark tip; legs brown or yellowish.

In flight it is distinguished by its grey head and back, large white mirror on black outer primaries and distinct white fore edge to wing.
RANGE: Coasts of Peru, Southern Brazil, Argentine, W. and S.E. coasts of Africa. Breeds inland in tropical Africa and eastern S. America.   Map 209.

ANDEAN GULL *Larus serranus*   **Pls. 30, 36**
Medium, 19 ins, 48 cm. In adult plumage the head in summer is black, a white semi-circle behind the eye; in winter streaked white with a greyish smudge behind

the eye, and a square headed appearance due to a rather flat crown. The mantle and upperwing-coverts are pale pearl-grey, primaries black, leading primaries with large white sub-terminal patches, posterior ones with white tips, secondaries grey. The underwing-coverts are grey, pale at the axillaries, and the large white patch shows clearly on the underwing in flight. The neck, underbody and tail are white, the breast showing a rosy tint. Bill and legs dark red.

Young birds have the crown, neck and mantle mottled-brown, secondaries brown, underparts white, tail with a sub-terminal black band. Bill and legs brown.

In flight the gull appears to have a large wing spread. At a distance it looks rather like a large pale Northern Black-headed Gull, or Laughing Gull, the wings showing a distinct white leading edge. The broad white wing patches are distinctive.

RANGE: In winter to coasts of Peru and Chile south to Valparaiso. Breeds on lakes in the Andes. Map 210.

FRANKLIN'S GULL *Larus pipixcan* Pls. 30, 31, 36

Small–medium, 13.5–14 ins, 34–36 cm. Wing-span 35 ins, 89 cm. A small lightly built gull. In adult summer plumage the hood is deep black with white rim above and below the eye; in winter the hood recedes leaving only a dull black crown and forehead. Underparts and tail white. The upperparts are bluish-grey. First five primaries black with white tips, remaining primaries and secondaries grey tipped white. A white window separates the black primaries from the grey upper-wing-coverts on each wing. Bill dark red; legs reddish-brown.

Young birds have white foreheads, crowns and sides of head dusky, upperparts greyish-brown, wing-tips white, underparts white; tail grey with a broad sub-terminal black band; bill and legs brown.

Smaller but rather similar to Laughing Gull but with paler upperparts and distinguished in flight by the sharply divided black and white wing-tips. Immatures are very similar to immature Laughing Gulls, but young Laughing Gulls normally have all-brown heads and brown breasts as opposed to the pale foreheads and white underparts of young Franklin's Gulls.

RANGE: Breeds in interior of N. America and Canada and migrates southwards to Gulf coasts of Louisiana and Texas, wintering largely along the west coast of S. America. Map 211.

SILVER GULL *Larus novaehollandiae* Pls. 29, 38, 40

Small–medium, 14–15 ins, 36–38 cm. Wing-span 36 ins, 92 cm. In adult plumage the head, neck, underparts and tail are white; mantle, upperwing-coverts and underwing-coverts pearl-grey. The primaries are mainly black, white tipped, having basal areas white, the two outer black primaries having broad sub-terminal white bands. Bill, eyelids and legs scarlet.

Young birds have pale buff tips on the mantle and brown patches on the secondaries forming a dark band on the wing; tail white with narrow sub-terminal brown band; bill and legs brownish-black.

There are several forms, the Australian gull known as the Silver Gull; the New Zealand form, the Red-billed Gull; the S. African form, the Hartlaub's Gull. In Australia it is the only small gull. The outer and inner white flashes on the black primaries are noticeable in flight.

RANGE: Western, southern and all round coasts of Australia, coasts of New Zealand, western and southern coasts of southern Africa; also in New Caledonia. Map 212.

BLACK-BILLED or BULLER'S GULL *Larus bulleri* Pls. 29, 38

Small–medium, 14.5 ins, 37 cm. A delicately built gull. Head, neck, underparts and tail white, eyelid dark red; mantle and upperwing-coverts very pale pearly-grey. The first four outer primaries are white with black points and white tips, the remaining primaries and secondaries grey, thus a very broad white triangle, tipped black, appears on the forewing in flight. Bill black; legs dark reddish-black.

Young birds show buff mottling on upperparts, primaries with small white tips, bill reddish, tip black and legs pinkish-brown. In 2nd year bill becomes red causing confusion with Red-billed Gull (see Silver Gull).

Largely an inland gull of lakes and rivers, but occurs in small numbers occasionally in harbours and coasts in winter. Adults distinguished from Silver Gulls by black bills; immatures difficult to distinguish from immature Silver Gulls.

RANGE: New Zealand. Map 213.

MEDITERRANEAN BLACK-HEADED GULL Pls. 32, 37
Larus melanocephalus

Medium, 15.5–17 ins, 39–43 cm. Wing-span 36 ins, 92 cm. A medium sized black-headed gull resembling the Northern Black-headed Gull but distinguished from it in adult summer plumage by its black as opposed to coffee-brown head, in winter white streaked blackish. Small white crescentric patches show above and below the eye. Upperparts pale pearl-grey as opposed to blue-grey. Entirely pale wing quills with white tips, as opposed to the black tips in the Northern Black-headed Gull. Its bill is very stout, coral red with a black sub-terminal band; legs dark red.

Young birds are similar to young Northern Black-headed Gulls but show a brown band along the leading edge of the wing and dark band on tail.

In adult plumage a white band is noticeable along the leading edge of the pearl-grey wings.

RANGE: Mediterranean. Map 214.

PATAGONIAN BLACK-HEADED GULL Pls. 31, 36
Larus maculipennis

Small–medium, 14–15 ins, 36–38 cm. See Northern Black-headed Gull (below).

Somewhat smaller and more slightly built but in other respects both adult and immature plumage are very similar to the Northern Black-headed Gull. Outer primaries white at ends. The white underbody in adults sometimes show a rosy tint.

In view of its limited range on the coasts of S. America it cannot be confused with the northern species.

RANGE: Both coasts of S. America southward from southern Brazil, and from about 30°S. on the west coast. Breeds in Falkland Is., Patagonia, southern Chile, Argentine and Uruguay. Map 215.

NORTHERN BLACK-HEADED GULL Pls. 28, 31, 32, 37, 40
Larus ridibundus

Medium, 15–17 ins, 38–43 cm. Wing-span 36 ins, 92 cm. In adult summer plumage the head is coffee-brown with a narrow white eye-ring, white neck, underbody and tail. Mantle and upperwing-coverts blue-grey, the wing-coverts at the edge and bend of wing white. The outer primaries are mainly white with black tips, inner primaries and secondaries grey; underwing-coverts dark grey. Bill and legs deep-red. In winter the head becomes white with a dusky mark behind the eye.

Young birds have head greyish-brown, mottled brownish-grey upperparts, outer primaries black with white centres; tail white with sub-terminal blackish band; bill yellowish with dark tip; legs dull red.

The broad white leading edge of the leading black primaries and the slender red bill and red legs are noticeable in adults.

RANGE: Breeds inland from British Isles eastward through Europe to eastern Asia. Disperses southwards to winter to the Mediterranean, Red Sea, Persian Gulf, coasts of India, China and Japan.   Map 216.

Indian Black-headed Gull (p.101)

Mongolian Gull (below)   Great Black-headed Gull (p.100).

MONGOLIAN GULL   *Larus relictus*   **Drawing above**

Small numbers of this hitherto lost species of black-headed gull have been discovered recently breeding on Lake Alakul on the eastern border of Kazakstan (U.S.S.R.).

RANGE: Its range and distribution are as yet uncertain.   Not mapped.

BONAPARTE'S GULL   *Larus philadelphia*   **Pls. 31, 36**

Small–medium, 14 ins, 36 cm. Wing-span 32 ins, 82 cm. A small tern-like gull. In adult summer plumage the head is black, mantle and upperwing-coverts pearl-grey. Outer primaries black at tip with large white areas on inner webs, which show as a long white triangle at the front edge of the wing. Underparts, underwing-coverts and tail white; bill black; legs red. In winter plumage the head becomes white with a conspicuous black spot behind the eye, and the bill appears black.

Young birds have greyish-brown upperparts; forehead, neck and underparts white, dusky patch on side of head, and a dark sub-terminal band on the white tail; bill and legs dusky.

Distinguished by its black bill and reddish feet, pale upperparts, and in flight by the long triangle of white at the front edge of the wing.

RANGE: From breeding area migrates southwards along east and west coasts of N. America to Caribbean area and Gulf of Panama. Breeds in N.W. Canada. Map 217.

SLENDER-BILLED GULL *Larus genei* **Pls. 29, 37**
Medium, 15.5–18.5 ins, 39–47 cm. Wing-span 37 ins, 94 cm. In adult plumage the whole head, neck, underbody and tail are white, showing rosy tint except on head. The mantle and upperwing-coverts are pearl-grey. First four primaries white, tipped black, the leading primary with a black outer web; inner primaries and secondaries grey. Axillaries and underwing-coverts grey. The bill is noticeably slender and red; legs red.

Young birds are rather similar to adults but with grey markings on crown and nape; ashy-brown upperparts and white underbody; bill orange-yellow; legs yellow; lacks rosy tint. The white tail carries a black terminal band.

Always has a white head, is larger but somewhat similar to a Northern Black-headed Gull in winter plumage.

RANGE: Coasts of N.W. Africa, Mediterranean, Black Sea, Red Sea, Persian Gulf and Mekran coast. Breeds in Spain, Asia Minor, on coasts of Black, Azov and Caspian Seas, and in Persia and Baluchistan. Map 218.

LITTLE GULL *Larus minutus* **Pls. 31, 32, 37**
Small, 10–12 ins, 25–31 cm. Wing-span 25 ins, 64 cm. Much smaller than any other gull.

In adult summer plumage the head and upper neck are black, the lower neck, underbody and tail white. The mantle and upperwing-coverts are pale grey, wing quills grey, with no trace of black, and with broad white tips. The underbody sometimes shows a rosy tinge. The underwings are dark smoky-grey. Bill and legs deep red in summer. In winter plumage the head becomes white, the crown and nape shows a greyish-black patch; bill black.

Immatures in first plumage have a basically white head with dark brown markings on the crown, also through or near the eye and down the back of the neck. The mantle is dark brown, the central upperwing-coverts dark brown with pale edging, the forward triangle of the inner wing darker forming a dark zig-zag pattern across the wing resembling young kittiwakes. The underbody and underwing are white; tail white with a broad sub-terminal dark band; bill brownish; legs dull flesh-coloured.

Little Gulls appear very neat and compact. The head and tail appear to project less beyond the wings than other gulls; this is accentuated by the head being rounded rather than tapering into the short fine bill. In flight the wings appear broader and shorter from the carpal joint to the tip than in most gulls. On the ground the Little Gull's very short legs distinguish it, closely resembling the posture of a tern. The untidy dark markings about the head are a useful recognition feature in all plumages except full breeding plumage, and the dark slate-grey underwings in adults.

RANGE: Breeds in northern Europe from Holland and Denmark eastwards, and in Siberia to the Sea of Okhotsk. Disperses southwards in winter passing through British Isles to winter in the Mediterranean, Black Sea and Japan Sea. Map 219.

CHINESE BLACK-HEADED GULL *Larus saundersi* **Pls. 31, 37**
Small–medium, 12.5 ins, 32 cm. In adult summer plumage the head is bluish-black and a narrow white ring surrounds the eye, interrupted at the back. In winter the head is white with dusky patches. Neck, underparts and tail white. Upperparts dark pearl-grey; flight feathers mainly white, the first primary with a narrow black edge on outer web, other primaries with black inner webs and black sub-terminal bars.

Underwing-coverts grey. Bill black; legs red. Young birds have upperparts mottled brownish-grey, the first two primaries with black outer webs, remainder with black tips. Tail white with sub-terminal black band. Bill black; legs brownish.

Distinguished from Northern Black-headed Gull by its black as opposed to brown head in summer, darker mantle, black bill and large amount of white on primaries. Very similar to Bonaparte's Gull.

RANGE: Breeds inland in N. China and Mongolia and occurs on coasts of eastern Siberia, Korea and China, Japan and Taiwan.   Map 220.

SABINE'S GULL   *Xema sabini*   Pls. 33, 39

Small–medium, 13–14 ins, 33–36 cm. Wing-span 34 ins, 86 cm. In adult summer plumage the head and throat are slate-grey, the neck, underparts and forked tail pure white. In winter the head and throat become white leaving some dusky marking. The appearance of the upperparts in flight ismost striking. The grey mantle and wing-coverts form one triangle with its apex at the bend of the wing; the first four black primaries form a second triangle with its apex at the bend of the wing; the remaining very pale inner primaries and secondaries form a third white triangle between the grey mantle and black outer primaries, which show white tips. The tail is forked; bill black with yellow tip; legs dark.

Young birds have the whole upperparts ashy-brown, with a white forehead; underparts and tail white, a broad black terminal band across the forked tail; bill and legs brown.

The only gull with a forked tail except the Swallow-tailed Gull which is much larger and has a deeply forked tail. Both gulls occur off Ecuador and might be confused.

RANGE: Breeds in the high arctic and migrates south to winter off W. African coast and the west coast of S. America.   Map 221.

ROSS'S GULL   *Rhodostethia rosea*   Pls. 33, 39

Small–medium, 13–14 ins, 33–36 cm. Adults in summer plumage have head and neck whitish with a narrow black collar round the neck; in winter head and neck pale bluish grey. Eyelids red. Upperparts and upperwings pearl-grey, outer web of first primary black, secondaries with rosy-white tips. Underbody, rump and wedge-shaped tail rosy-white; underwing-coverts grey. Bill black; legs red

Young birds have crown, neck and mantle brownish-grey; forehead and sides of head dull white; outer primaries black, inner primaries and secondaries white. A dark band shows on upperwing-coverts. Underparts white; bill black; legs dark flesh-coloured; tail with broad black terminal band on central feathers. Immatures recall immature Sabine's Gull.

A rare small gull distinguished by its black collar, red eyelids, grey underwing and red legs.

RANGE: High arctic regions rarely wandering south of Arctic Circle.   Map 222.

COMMON KITTIWAKE   *Rissa tridactyla*   Pls. 33, 39

Medium, 15.5–16 ins, 39–41 cm. Wing-span 36 ins, 92 cm. This lightly built, largely oceanic gull can be distinguished in adult summer plumage by its white head and neck, white underparts, under surface of wings and white tail, and its pearl-grey upperparts. The tips of the outer four primaries are black, remaining primaries and secondaries grey. At close range its dark eye, slender greenish-yellow bill and dark legs are noticeable. In winter plumage the crown and sides of the head have dark grey streaking.

Young birds, known as 'tarrocks', are distinctive, having a dark band at the back of the neck, a conspicuous dark diagonal band across each upperwing, forming a '**W**' pattern, and a black band across the tail. Bill black.

The flight is light and buoyant, more often than not low over the sea. Outside the breeding season kittiwakes keep to the open ocean, and frequently pick up and follow ships in small flocks.

The solid black wing tips form a point in identification in flight.

RANGE: Arctic seas, N. Atlantic and N. Pacific Oceans.   Map 223.

RED-LEGGED KITTIWAKE *Rissa brevirostris*   Pls. 33, 39

Small–medium, 15 ins, 38 cm. Wing-span 36 ins, 92 cm. Adults are similar to the Common Kittiwake but differ in having a darker mantle and upperwing coverts, and red legs.

Young birds are similar to adults but upperparts are browner and a broad dark band shows across the nape; lack black diagonal band on upperwings and have plain white tails. Bills dark; legs brown.

RANGE: Ranges in high latitudes of N. Pacific Ocean and southern Bering Sea and only likely to be seen by ships undertaking extremely northerly passages. Breeds in Aleutian Is. and islands in the Bering Sea.   Map 224.

SWALLOW-TAILED GULL *Creagrus furcatus*   Pls. 33, 39

Medium–large, 20 ins, 51 cm. This rather large gull is unusual in that it looks more like a tern in flight on account of its long wings, long white forked tail and distinctive upper surface plumage.

In adult summer plumage the head and neck are dark grey with a white stripe on each side of the forehead. In winter the head becomes white with a dark ring round the eye and greyish collar. The eyelids are crimson. The mantle is grey; outer webs of outer primaries black, inner primaries and first few secondaries grey, remaining secondaries white, the wing-coverts also white. The effect in flight from above is to show a wide triangular white patch on the upperwings, against the outer black primaries.

The white throat and breast show a rosy tinge, the remainder of the underparts, tail and upper tail-coverts white. Bill dark greenish with a pale tip; legs pinkish-red. The tail is deeply forked.

Young birds have white mottled head, neck and upperparts mottled and barred brown and white; bill dark; legs greyish-white; tail white with black terminal band.

Much larger than Sabine's Gull, which occurs in the same area, but can be distinguished by the large white triangular patch on the upperwings and more deeply forked tail.

RANGE: Breeds only on the Galapagos Is. and ranges southwards along coasts of Ecuador and northern Peru.   Not mapped.

Like many seabirds, terns and noddies breed in large colonies – terns on the ground, noddies often in trees or shrubs.

TERNS and NODDIES Sternidae

TERNS

Terns with their graceful bodies, long pointed wings, finely tapering bills, deeply forked tails and buoyant flight have acquired the name of sea swallows. With the exception of one or two species such as the Sooty Tern and to a lesser extent the Brown-winged and Crested Terns which range often well out into the ocean, terns are seen by ships close to the coastlines and harbours, frequently hovering over shoals of small fish with bills pointing downwards, and plunging one after the other with a splash as they capture their sand eels or fry. Some species resort almost entirely to inland swamps, lagoons and rivers remote from the coasts.

The majority favour the warm water belts of the globe where great numbers colonise tropical islands. Certain species however that breed in the north temperate latitude belt are migratory, forsaking their breeding areas and migrating to warmer climates north and south of the Equator to winter. At such times, notably off the bulge of N. Africa, large numbers of different species may be seen. The Arctic Tern undertakes an enormous annual migration, leaving its breeding areas north of the Arctic Circle in late summer or early autumn and wintering as far south as sub-antarctic latitudes.

Nesting and young

Most species nest in colonies, often large, on open sites such as stretches of sand or shingle, or small islets, by the coast or on large lakes or marshes. The nests are often very close together and may be simply bare hollows, or may be lined with varying amounts of plant material if this is available close at hand. Marsh terns build shallow nests on floating marsh vegetation. Inca Terns nest in crevices or holes in rocks. Noddy Terns nest on trees, shrubs, rock ledges or rocky islets, carrying material to the site and building quite substantial nests. White Terns lay single eggs on tiny ledges or small level surfaces of rocks or trees where they seem precariously balanced. The clutch may be of 1–3 eggs, varying with different species, and the eggs are usually pale, creamy, yellowish or buffish, or sometimes olive or deep buff, and variably and cryptically patterned with dark markings. Both adults incubate for *c.* 3 weeks in most species and up to 5 weeks in Noddy and White Terns

The young are downy, usually pale in colour with dark spotting and mottling, the down sometimes in spiky tufts; but young noddies have dark brown down with whitish crowns. They may remain and hide near the nest site, but larger young of some species flock by the water's edge. Young White Terns have well-developed claws for clinging to their circumscribed sites. Young terns are fed by both parents and may fly at 4–5 weeks, but take much longer to become fully independent. There is evidence in some places of breeding of Sooty Terns occurring at nine-month and possibly six-month intervals. Six-month intervals in nest site occupation are known for some other species but it is not certain that the same individuals are involved each time.

WHISKERED TERN *Chlidonias hybrida* **Pl. 44**
Small–medium, 13 ins, 33 cm. Wing-span 27 ins, 69 cm. In adult summer plumage the top of the head is deep black level with the top of the eye. A conspicuous white streak extends from the base of the bill backwards below the black cap on each side. Upperparts slate-grey, primaries darker grey, inner webs of outermost primaries pale. Throat white, darkening to slate-grey on breast to deep blue-grey on flanks and abdomen. In winter the forehead and whole underbody become white, the crown streaked with black, darkest on nape. Upper tail-coverts and tail grey, outer feathers with white outer webs. Tail short, slightly forked, outer feathers rounded. Underwing-coverts and under tail-coverts white. Bill deep red, legs vermilion. Young birds similar to adults in winter, but upperparts and tail mottled-brown.

The winter plumage is hard to distinguish from the White-winged Black Tern in winter plumage.
RANGE: Widely spread throughout the warmer parts of eastern Europe and Asia, E. Indies, Australia and S. Africa. Frequents swamps and lagoons and rarely visits coasts. Map 225.

WHITE-WINGED BLACK TERN *Chlidonias leucoptera* **Pl. 44**
Small, 8.5–9.5 ins, 216–242 mm. Wing-span 26 ins, 66 cm. In adult summer plumage the head, neck, upper back and underparts black. Underwing linings also black (white in Black Tern *Chlidonias nigra*). Tail white (grey in Black Tern). The outstanding feature in flight is the broad white 'shoulder' or lesser upperwing-coverts, forming a distinctive pattern against the greyish-black primaries and secondaries.

In winter plumage the head is white, mottled black on crown. The upperparts including upperwings and tail slate-grey, the underparts and underwing linings white (similar to Black Tern). Bill red in summer, black in winter; legs orange. Young birds similar to adults in winter but upperparts have brown mottling. Tail grey, upper tail-coverts white.

Largely an inshore tern but sometimes seen in harbours.
RANGE: Ranges and breeds widely across central and southern Europe, extending to eastern Asia. Migrates southwards in winter and has been seen by ships at Aden, Persian Gulf, Malaysia and Borneo. Reaches S. Africa and Australia and occasionally to New Zealand. Map 226.

BLACK TERN *Chlidonias nigra*   Pl. 44
Small, 9.5–10 ins, 242–254 mm. Wing-span 26 ins, 66 cm. In adult summer plumage
head and neck are black; mantle, upperwings, and tail slate grey; the breast and
underbody black; under tail-coverts white. The underwings are light grey. In winter
plumage head and neck become mottled-white, the crown and nape appearing grey;
the chin, throat and underbody become white. A noticeable feature is the thin white
margin at the bend of the wing. Bill black; legs purplish-brown. The tail is only
slightly forked.
     Young birds are similar to adults in winter but head and mantle mottled-brown
and flanks greyer.
RANGE: Breeds mainly in inland swamps in Europe and N. America migrating
southwards to winter where it is seen frequently off the coasts in certain favoured
areas.   Map 227.

LARGE-BILLED TERN *Phaetusa simplex*   Pl. 45
Small–medium, 14.5 ins, 37 cm. Wing-span 36 ins, 92 cm. Top of head glossy-black.
A narrow white line shows above the bill. Mantle and tail slate-grey. Upperwing-
coverts white. Primaries dark brown, secondaries white. Underparts white. Bill
very stout, chrome-yellow. Legs olive, webs yellow. Tail short, nearly square.
Young birds have greyish upperparts mottled with brown, and white underparts.
     Distinguished by its stout yellow bill and square tail.
RANGE: Tropical S. America, breeding on rivers and estuaries in northern and
north-east S. America from Bolivia to southern Brazil and Argentine. Unlikely to
be seen at sea.   Map 228.

GULL-BILLED TERN *Gelochelidon nilotica*   Pl. 43
Medium, 15–16 ins, 38–41 cm. Wing-span 34 ins, 86 cm. In adult summer plumage
crown and sides of head deep glossy black; in winter forehead and crown white with
dark streaks, a black ear patch showing behind the eye. Upperparts and tail pale
grey. The tail is only partially forked. Underparts including under surface of wings
white. The stout bill is gull-like and black; legs blackish.
     Young birds are similar to adults in winter but head duller white with dusky
streaks, back and scapulars spotted-brown, stout bill and legs reddish-brown.
     Chiefly noticeable for its gull-like appearance, stout black bill and lightly forked
grey tail.
RANGE: South-east coast of N. America, California, Gulf of Mexico, W. Indies
and S. America, western and southern coasts of Europe, N. Africa. E. to Indo
China, Australia. Chiefly inland on lakes, marshes and estuaries. Breeds throughout range.   Map 229.

CASPIAN TERN *Hydroprogne caspia*   Pl. 41
Medium–large, 19–22 ins, 48–56 cm. Wing-span 53 ins, 135 cm. The largest of the
terns, almost the size of a Herring Gull.
     In adult summer plumage forehead, sides of head to below eye, crown and nape
black, the feathers at the nape elongated. In winter the forehead is streaked and
crown greyish. Upperparts ash-grey, upper tail-coverts white, tail grey and only
slightly forked. The inner webs of primaries slate-grey. Underparts white. Bill very
stout, heavy and coral-red; legs black.
     Young birds are similar to adults in winter but with upperparts lightly mottled
brownish; bill dull orange; legs blackish-brown. The flight is powerful, somewhat

gull-like and frequently at a considerable height.

The large size and very large red bill distinguish it. In flight when viewed from below the ends of the primaries look conspicuously dark.

RANGE: N. America, Europe, Africa, Asia, Australia and New Zealand.   Map 230.

INDIAN RIVER TERN   *Sterna aurantia*   Pl. 45

Medium, 15–17 ins, 38–43 cm. In adult breeding plumage top of head and circle around eye greenish-black; in winter crown grey and forehead white. Upperparts and tail dark pearl-grey. Outer primaries pale brown. Throat, underwing-coverts and under tail-coverts white, breast and abdomen pale pearl-grey. Bill stout, orange-yellow with a dusky tip in winter. Legs orange-red. Tail very long and deeply forked. Immatures have forehead, crown and head buffish with brown flecking, and dull yellow bills.

Its deeply forked tail and stout orange-yellow bill assists identification. Resorts chiefly to rivers and estuaries, sometimes seen off coasts.

RANGE: Tropical Asia from Persia through India, Sri Lanka, and Burma to Singapore. Breeds on islands on lakes and rivers.   Map 231.

SOUTH AMERICAN TERN   *Sterna hirundinacea*   Pl. 42

Medium, 16 ins, 41 cm. Wing-span 33 ins, 84 cm. See Arctic Tern (below). Except for its larger size and very slightly curved bill the plumage and characteristics of the South American Tern are entirely similar to the Arctic Tern. Its upperwings are distinctly paler.

RANGE: East and west coast of S. America.   Map 232.

COMMON TERN   *Sterna hirundo*   Pls. 42, 43

Small–medium, 12.5–15 ins, 32–38 cm. Wing-span 31 ins, 79 cm. In adult summer plumage the top of the head is black, in winter brown and forehead streaked with white. Mantle and upperwings French-grey, outer primaries with black outer web. Forked tail grey. Throat, rump, under tail-coverts and underwings white; breast and abdomen pale grey, white in winter. Bill scarlet with black tip; legs coral-red. In winter the bill becomes mainly black but always retains some red, legs duller red.

Young birds have forehead and front of crown white, remainder of crown streaked, the mantle mottled ashy-brown showing a dark band in the region of the shoulder. Underparts white; bill brownish; legs flesh-coloured.

Very similar to Arctic Tern and almost impossible to distinguish at sea, doubtful sightings usually quoted as 'comic' tern. Eastern races of Common Tern are darker with a dark bill.

RANGE: Eastern N. America, temperate Europe and Asia. Breeds widely throughout range, and extends southwards from many breeding areas as far as southern Africa and Australia.   Map 233.

ARCTIC TERN   *Sterna paradisea*   Pls. 41, 42

Small–medium, 13–15 ins, 33–38 cm. Wing-span 31 ins, 79 cm. Top of head black showing a narrow white streak running from the base of the bill to the nape below the black cap. In winter plumage the crown and forehead are mottled white. Upperparts pearl-grey, secondaries with white margins. Throat, breast and underbody French-grey. Tail deeply forked, outermost tail feathers very long with dark grey outer webs. Bill blood-red; legs very short and coral-red. In winter bill and legs change by stages to black.

Young birds similar to adults in winter plumage but with ashy-brown mantle, and black bill and legs.

Distinguished from Common Tern by red bill without black tip, longer outer tail feathers and darker grey underparts. It is however extremely difficult to distinguish between Common and Arctic Terns at sea and in their winter or juvenile plumage.

Whether Arctic Terns during their great trans-global migrations pass along the east coast of S. America may not yet be established owing to confusion between the extremely similar South American Tern.

RANGE: Breeds from arctic coasts of Alaska, Canada, Greenland, Europe, Siberia, including British Isles. Migrates to winter in extreme southern continental latitudes, reaching the antarctic ice edge.   Map 234.

1 Common Tern (p.111). Tail not extending beyond wing-tips.
2 Arctic Tern (p.111). Tail slightly larger than Common Tern's.
3 Roseate Tern (p.113). Tail streamers extending well beyond wing-tips.

ANTARCTIC or WREATHED TERN *Sterna vittata*   Pl. 42
Small—medium, 16 ins, 41 cm. Wing-span 31 ins, 79 cm. In adult southern summer plumage forehead, crown and nape black; a broad white stripe extends from the gape below the eye to the nape. In winter plumage forehead and crown white. Upperparts and upperwings pale bluish-grey, outer webs of outermost primaries black. Rump and tail white, outer webs of tail feathers pale grey; tail deeply forked. Throat and underparts pearl-grey; under tail-coverts white. Bill coral red; legs orange-red. Young birds similar to adults in winter but have pure white underparts. Flight undulating.
RANGE: Southern oceans and antarctic seas. Breeds at Tristan da Cunha, Gough, Kerguelen, St. Paul and Amsterdam Is., S. Georgia, S. Sandwich Is., S. Orkneys, S. Shetlands, the antarctic continent and the sub-antarctic islands of New Zealand.   Map 235.

KERGUELEN TERN *Sterna virgata*   Pl. 42
Small—medium, 13 ins, 33 cm. Wing-span 31 ins, 79 cm. In adult plumage the top of head black with a broad white moustachial streak between the black crown and grey throat on each side. Upperparts, underparts and tail pearl-grey. Bill red; legs orange. Young birds are similar but forehead brownish, crown, nape and upperparts mottled brownish.
RANGE: Breeds at Marion, Crozet Is., Kerguelen and Heard Is. in S. Indian Ocean.   Map 236.

FORSTER'S TERN *Sterna forsteri*   Pl. 42
Small, 10–11 ins, 25–28 cm. Wing-span 30 ins, 76 cm. Top of head black in summer, whitish in winter with large black patch on each side of face. Upperparts and upperwings pearl-grey; primaries silvery-grey, inner border of inner web of outer

primary white. Rump and underparts white; tail pale grey. Bill orange with black
tip; legs orange; tail deeply forked. In winter the bill becomes black. Young birds
have browner upperparts, shorter tails and a dark patch through eye and ear.

Very similar to Common Tern. From above however the primaries of Forster's
Tern are lighter than rest of wing in contrast to Common Tern, and the tail of the
Common Tern is whiter contrasting with the grey of its back.

RANGE: Breeds in marshes along east coast of U.S.A. from Maryland to Texas
migrating southwards in winter when it may be seen in Panama zone and western
California.   Map 237.

TRUDEAU'S TERN *Sterna trudeaui*   Pl. 43
Small, 10–11 ins, 25–28 cm. Wing-span 30 ins, 76 cm. Top of the head, sides and
chin white. A noticeable black streak runs through the eye. Upperparts and
upperwings pale pearl-grey, shading into white above rump. Primaries and secondaries grey, secondaries showing broad white edges. Breast and underbody grey.
Under-surface of wings white. Bill yellow with broad sub-terminal black band; legs
orange; forked tail grey; outer tail feathers white. Young birds are similar but crown
greyish; upperparts with some brown mottling; tail dark grey with white outer
edges; bill dusky; legs yellowish.

RANGE: S. American coasts from Rio de Janeiro to northern Patagonia on the east;
coast of Chile on the west. Breeds inland in Argentina. Occasionally resorts to
coasts and harbours.   Map 238.

ROSEATE TERN *Sterna dougalli*   Pl. 42
Small–medium, 15 ins, 38 cm. Wing-span 30 ins, 76 cm. In adult summer plumage
forehead, crown and nape black; in winter forehead and crown speckled white. The
mantle and upperparts are very pale pearl-grey, primaries slightly darker, the outer
web of the outer primary noticeably darker. Underparts, rump and long deeply
forked tail white. In summer the underparts show a distinct rosy tint. Bill varies
from dark red to red at base with dark tip, and is often black in winter; legs dark red.

Young birds similar to adults in winter but upperparts mottled ashy-brown
showing a dark band on the upperwing coverts. Bill and legs dark.

In appearance it looks much whiter than the Common and Arctic Terns and its
very long forked tail is conspicuous. At rest the tail extends well beyond the wing
tips.

RANGE: Breeds on east coast of U.S.A. southwards through W. Indies to Venezuela, Azores, Madeira, British Isles, southern Europe, northern Africa, islands
in Indian Ocean eastwards, western and northern Australia, and New
Caledonia.   Map 239.

WHITE-FRONTED TERN *Sterna striata*   Pl. 43
Medium, 16–17 ins, 41–43 cm. In adult plumage the forehead is white, the crown
and nape black. In winter the white on the forehead is extended and the crown
mottled. Upperparts pearl-grey, outer web of outer primary brownish-black, inner
webs of primaries with white edges to the tips. Underparts, including under-surface
of wings white, the breast sometimes showing a pink tint. Bill black; legs reddish-
brown. Tail white, deeply forked.

Young birds have crown and nape streaked and spotted with white, black and
buff, upperparts barred and mottled, a broad band of dark brown on the shoulders
of the wings and a dusky edging to the fork of the tail.

Distinguished in adult plumage from the Black-fronted Tern by its white forehead. The commonest tern around the New Zealand coast, many dispersing during the southern autumn (see below). Marine in habits.

RANGE: Breeds in New Zealand, Chatham and Auckland Is. In the autumn large numbers migrate to coasts of Tasmania, Victoria and New South Wales, being plentiful between May and November.   Map 240.

WHITE-CHEEKED TERN   *Sterna repressa*   Pl. 42

Small–medium, 12.5–14.5 ins, 32–37 cm. In adult summer plumage forehead, crown and nape black. Upperparts and tail darkish-grey, secondaries smoky-grey. Underparts grey, much darker than in Common Tern. Underwing-coverts and under tail-coverts pale grey. A white area shows between the dark cap and the grey underparts. Tail forked, bill slender, coral-red with dark tip, legs red. In winter forehead and crown become mottled and streaked white. Young birds similar but forehead and crown grey and a dark band on upperwing-coverts. Underparts white. Bill blackish, legs dusky-yellow.

Similar but darker than Common Tern.

RANGE: Red Sea, Persian Gulf to west coast of India. Breeds on coast of N.E. Africa, southern Arabia, Persian Gulf and Laccadive Is.   Map 241.

BLACK-NAPED TERN   *Sterna sumatrana*   Pl. 43

Small–medium, 13.5–14.5 ins, 34–37 cm. Wing-span 24 ins, 61 cm. Head and neck white with a triangular black spot in front of the eye and a black band round the nape. Mantle, upperwings and rump pale pearl-grey. Underparts white, sometimes showing a rosy flush. The white tail is long and deeply forked, the central tail feathers grey. Bill black with yellow tip; legs black.

Young birds have the top of the head grey-brown mottling, with a black patch on the nape. Upperparts barred greyish-brown; primaries grey with inner margins white. Bill yellow; legs yellowish-brown.

Favours lagoons and usually keeps close inshore. The black band round the nape is distinctive.

RANGE: Tropical islands in Indian and Pacific Oceans and off northern Australia and the Great Barrier Reef. Breeds throughout range.   Map 242.

BLACK-BELLIED TERN   *Sterna melanogastra*   Pl. 45

Small–medium, 12–13 ins, 31–33 cm. In adult breeding plumage top of head black; in winter crown and forehead greyish with dark streaking, showing a dark patch round eye. Upperparts and tail pearl-grey. Throat and underwings white. Foreneck and breast pearl-grey. Abdomen and under tail-coverts brownish-black, in winter greyish. Bill orange-yellow. Legs red. Tail deeply forked, outer tail feathers white.

Smaller than Indian River Tern with more slender bill, and can be confused when in winter plumage. An inland species resorting to rivers and marshes, and unlikely to be seen on coasts.

RANGE: Similar to Indian River Tern (p. 111).   Map 231.

ALEUTIAN TERN   *Sterna aleutica*   Pl. 44

Small–medium, 13.5 ins, 34 cm. Forehead white. Crown and nape black, a line from bill to eye black. Upperparts and upperwings medium grey, primaries dark grey, outer primary black, remainder of wing quills grey with white inner webs. Tail white. Foreneck, breast and abdomen pale grey; underwing and under tail-coverts white. Bill and legs black. Young birds have greyish-brown head and upperparts, dark grey wing quills and grey rump and tail; underparts white. Bill dusky; legs reddish-yellow.

Distinguished from Common and Arctic Terns by its white forehead and darker overall colour contrasting with white underwings and black bill and legs.

RANGE: Breeds on coasts of Alaska and eastern Siberia. A rare straggler to Japan.   Map 243.

SPECTACLED TERN *Sterna lunata*   Pl. 44

Small—medium, 14–15 ins, 36–38 cm. Wing-span 29 ins, 74 cm. See Brown-winged or Bridled Tern (below). The characteristic plumage of the Brown-winged Tern is repeated in the Spectacled Tern which can be distinguished however apart from its black crown, nape and stripe from bill to eye, by its grey upperparts and tail as opposed to the dark brownish-grey upperparts and tail of the Brown-winged Tern. Its outer tail feathers are white.

Young birds have mottled grey-brown crowns and upperparts; underparts white.

RANGE: Tropical Pacific Ocean, more abundant in the central Pacific and relatively rare in the western Pacific where the Brown-winged Tern is the common species.   Map 244.

BROWN-WINGED or BRIDLED TERN *Sterna anaethetus*   Pl. 44

Small—medium, 14–15 ins, 36–38 cm. Wing-span 30 ins, 76 cm. Liable to be confused with the Sooty Tern.

Crown and nape black and a black band extends on each side from bill to eye. Between the bands a narrow white patch on the forehead (narrower than in Sooty Tern) extends beyond the level of the eyes, giving it a 'bridled' appearance. Upperparts brownish-grey, a whitish band showing around the nape. White piping on leading margin of wing. Underparts and under tail-coverts white. Tail deeply forked, greyish-brown. Bill and legs black. Flight similar but more graceful than Sooty Tern with a quicker wing-beat. Immatures have mottled-brown heads and mantles and greyish underparts.

See Sooty Tern for comparison (below).

RANGE: Widespread throughout the tropical and sub-tropical zones of the Atlantic, Indian and Pacific Oceans, west and north coasts of Australia. Breeds throughout range.   Map 245.

SOOTY TERN *Sterna fuscata*   Pl. 44

Medium, 17 ins, 43 cm. Wing-span 34 ins, 86 cm. The first impression is of a tern with black upperparts and white underparts. Crown and nape black and a black band extends on each side from bill to eye. Between the bands the forehead is white, terminating at the eye. Upperparts dark brownish-black, a white piping showing clearly in flight at close range along the leading margin of the wing. Underparts and under tail-coverts greyish-white. Tail dark, deeply forked, outer webs of outer tail feathers white, showing as a white piping. Bill and legs black. Flight buoyant and undulating, steady wing-beats appearing to pause on completion of down stroke. Capable of soaring in updraughts on motionless wings. Immatures are sooty-brown overall with white tips to feathers on mantle.

See Brown-winged or Bridled Tern for comparison (above). The Sooty Tern is the most truly oceanic of all terns, and frequently follows ships at night.

RANGE: Widespread throughout the tropical zones of the Atlantic, Indian and Pacific Oceans. Breeds throughout range.   Map 246.

Sooty Terns fishing. This species is one of the few terns to be found at sea far from land.

FAIRY TERN *Sterna nereis*   **Pl. 43**
Small, 10 ins, 25 cm. Wing-span 21 ins, 53 cm. Crown and nape black; forehead white with a black band extending forward from the eye and just short of the bill. Upperparts very pale pearl-grey; underparts and tail white, outer tail feathers not markedly elongated. Bill wholly yellow; legs orange. In winter bill tip black.
   Young birds very similar with dusky bills and legs.
   Differs from Little Tern in larger size, much paler upperparts and in adults totally bright yellow bill. Young birds are virtually impossible to distinguish from young Little Terns.
RANGE: Breeds on southern and western coasts of Australia and New Caledonia, and a few pairs in North Island, New Zealand.   Map 247.

BLACK-FRONTED TERN *Chlidonias albostriata*   **Pl. 43**
Small–medium, 12 ins, 31 cm. In adult summer plumage forehead, top of head and nape deep velvety-black, a broad white stripe showing beneath the black head and nape. Mantle, upperwings and tail blue-grey. The rump and under tail-coverts are white, the breast and abdomen blue-grey. The white rump is noticeable in flight. Bill and legs bright orange-red. In winter the top of the head and nape become pale grey.
   Young birds are similar to adults in winter plumage but show some brown mottling on upperwings and tail. Bill yellowish with dark tip; legs bright orange-red.
RANGE: Largely an inland tern breeding in the South Island of New Zealand but moves north during the southern autumn and occurs off the west coast of North Island at this period. Confined to New Zealand.   Map 248.

AMAZON TERN *Sterna superciliaris*   **Pl. 45**
Small, 9 ins, 23 cm. In breeding plumage, crown, nape and a band from bill to eye black. Forehead white. In winter, crown and nape become white with dark speck-

ling. Mantle and upperparts grey; four outer primaries greyish-black. Underparts white. Bill wholly greenish-yellow. Legs dull yellow. Tail white, forked. Young birds have dusky crowns, darker around back of head, upperparts mottled greyish-brown. Bills and legs dull yellow.

A fresh water tern extending far inland up S. American rivers.

RANGE: Breeds on sandbanks of rivers of eastern S. America from the Orinoco to the La Plata rivers.   Map 249.

DAMARA TERN *Sterna balaenarum*   **Pl. 43**
Small, 8.5–9 ins, 216–229 mm. Wing-span 20 ins, 51 cm. In adult summer plumage the top of the head is black, in winter the forehead and crown mottled-white. Mantle and upperparts pale-grey; underparts white, slightly grey on breast. Tail grey; bill black with yellow base; legs yellow.

Young birds are similar to adults in winter but upperwings darker grey.

Very similar to the Little Tern but distinguished by its black forehead and black bill. Its range does not overlap with that of the Little Tern.

RANGE: Confined to the western coast of southern Africa.   Map 250.

CHILEAN TERN *Sterna lorata*   **Pl. 43**
Small, 9.5 ins, 24 cm. In adult plumage this little tern has the crown and nape black, a white forehead and a black band from the eye to the bill narrowing towards the bill. Mantle, upperwings, rump and forked tail slate-grey, the outer web of the leading primary black. Throat and underwing-coverts white; breast and abdomen pale grey. Bill greenish-yellow with black tip; legs brown.

This is a small very grey looking tern, darker and slightly larger but which might be confused with the Little Tern which occasionally overlaps its northern range in winter months.

RANGE: Breeds on the coasts of Peru, ranging southward to northern Chile.   Map 251.

LITTLE TERN *Sterna albifrons*   **Pl. 43**
Small, 8–11 ins, 205–280 mm. Wing-span 20 ins, 51 cm. In adult summer plumage crown, nape and a band from the bill to the eye black; forehead white. In winter the crown and nape become white with dark speckling. Mantle and upperparts pale pearl-grey; underparts and forked tail white. Bill yellow with black tip; legs yellow. In winter the bill tends to become black.

Young birds have whitish-buff crowns with a darker patch from the eye around the back of the head, upperparts greyish, mottled with buff and dark areas on the fore edge of the wings; bills black; legs dull yellow.

Distinguished by its small size, narrow wings, yellow bill with black tip, yellow legs and white forehead. Its light buoyant flight with quicker wingbeats than other terns is noticeable at a distance.

RANGE: Widespread throughout temperate and tropical parts of the world.   Map 252.

CRESTED TERN *Thalasseus bergii*   **Pl. 41**
Medium, 18–19 ins, 46–48 cm. Wing-span 43 ins, 109 cm. In adult summer plumage the forehead is white, crown and nape black with elongated feathers which can be raised to form a crest. In winter the crown is mainly white. Upperparts and tail pearl-grey, secondaries with white tips; sides of head, neck and underparts white.

Bill powerful, greenish-yellow; legs brownish-black; tail deeply forked.

Young birds are similar but forehead and crown white with brownish-black mottling; mantle and upperparts with buffish-white mottling; bill greenish-yellow; tail darker grey than in adults.

One of the largest terns, distinguished from the Lesser-crested Tern by its larger size, darker grey colour, white forehead (the Lesser-crested Tern's forehead is black), and greenish-yellow bill (the Lesser-crested Tern's bill is bright orange).
RANGE: Ranges throughout islands and coasts of the Indian Ocean, Persian Gulf, tropical Pacific, coasts of Australia, Tasmania and S. Africa.   Map 253.

ROYAL TERN *Thalasseus maximus*   Pl. 41
Medium, 19 ins, 48 cm. Wing-span 43 ins, 109 cm. In adult summer plumage, crown and nape are black, feathers on the nape noticeably elongated forming a partial crest. The forehead may be black but frequently white. In winter the forehead is white, crown streaked. Upperparts pale grey, outer primary darker grey. Underparts, rump, edge of wing and deeply forked tail white. Bill large, red; legs black.

Young birds are similar to adults in winter but upperparts show dusky spotting, tail feathers dusky-white, bill and legs yellow.

The more heavily built Caspian Tern is similar but has an even stouter bright red bill, and a much less deeply forked tail. The Royal Tern is the commonest tern in the W. Indies.
RANGE: Coasts of N. and S. America from Virginia to Peru, from West Indies southwards on east coast of S. America to Point Tombo, Argentine, 44°S., 65°20′W. Also on N.W. coast of Africa. Breeds from Virginia to Mexico, West Indies, and in N.W. Africa.   Map 254.

LESSER-CRESTED TERN *Thalasseus bengalensis*   Pl. 41
Small–medium, 15–16 ins, 39–41 cm. Wing-span 35 ins, 89 cm. See Crested Tern, p. 117 – very similar but smaller than Crested Tern. In adult summer plumage the Lesser-crested Tern's forehead is black (white in Crested Tern), and the upperparts are a paler grey. The colour of their bills is different, the Lesser-crested Tern's being orange (greenish-yellow in Crested Tern). In both cases the legs are black.

In flight both species have a steady measured wing-action, slightly hesitant on completion of the down stroke, giving the appearance of a powerful and yet graceful flight.
RANGE: Red Sea, east coast of Africa, Arabian Sea, Persian Gulf, islands in Indian Ocean, coasts of India, islands in E. Indies and northern Australia.   Map 255.

CHINESE CRESTED TERN *Thalasseus zimmermanni*   Pl. 41
Small–medium, 15 ins, 38 cm. Forehead, crown and nape black, feathers on nape elongated; hindneck white. Upperpart and upperwings very pale grey; first five primaries very dark grey with white wedges on inner webs. Underparts and tail white. Bill yellow with broad black tip; legs black.

Distinguished from Lesser-crested Tern by its heavier yellow bill with broad black tip. A little known species.
RANGE: Coasts of China.   Map 256.

CAYENNE TERN *Thalasseus eurygnatha*   Pl. 41
Medium, 17 ins, 43 cm. Wing-span 37 ins, 94 cm. Similar to Royal Tern but

distinguished from it by its long pale yellow bill and black legs. Tail deeply forked. Young birds similar to young Royal Terns but bill black.

The only tern in S. America with a pale yellow bill.

RANGE: From Colombia eastwards, Lesser Antilles, and east coast of S. America. Breeds throughout range as far south as Santa Cruz, Argentine, 44°S., 65°20'W. Map 257.

ELEGANT TERN *Thalasseus elegans* Pl. 41

Medium size, 16.5 ins, 42 cm. Similar to Royal Tern but distinctly smaller. Bill longer and more slender. Upperparts and upperwings pale grey (darker than Royal Tern); tail deeply forked (whiter than Royal Tern); bill orange-red; legs black. Young birds similar to young Royal Terns but bills blackish and shorter than in adults.

RANGE: West coast of Americas from Lower California to Chile. Breeds on coasts of lower California. Map 258.

SANDWICH TERN *Thalasseus sandvicensis* Pls. 41, 43

Medium, 16–18 ins, 41–46 cm. Wing-span 37 ins, 94 cm. In adult summer plumage forehead, crown and nape black, the feathers on the back of the crown elongated and erected as a crest at times. In winter the forehead and crown become streaked white. The upperparts are pale pearl-grey, primaries with white margins on inner webs, the outer primary dark slate-grey on the outer web. Underparts and tail white. The bill is long, slender, black with a yellow tip; legs comparatively long and black; tail less deeply forked than normal in terns. The flight is more gull-like than in other common terns.

Young birds have brownish foreheads, crown white, heavily streaked, upperparts with black and white mottling and slate-grey tails. Underparts white; bill and legs dark.

The crested effect of the elongated feathers on the crown and the long black bill with its yellow tip help to identify it.

RANGE: Coasts of N. and S. America from Carolina to Peru and Argentina. Coasts of S. Africa, Persian Gulf. British Isles, west and southern Europe to Black Sea. Map 259.

INCA TERN *Larosterna inca* Pl. 44

Medium, 16 ins, 41 cm. A most distinctive species with an overall dark slate-blue plumage, darker on crown and nape and paler and bluer on the throat, breast and underwing-coverts. The four outer primaries and the secondaries are broadly tipped white. The stout bill which curves slightly downwards is scarlet, and fleshy yellow wattles occur on each side at the base of the gape. A striking narrow white feathered 'handlebar' moustache leads back and down from the wattles, curving upwards like a ram's horn at the bend of the wing. Legs bright red; tail medium-forked.

Young birds are similar, but somewhat browner with duller coloured bills and legs.

RANGE: West coast of S. America. Map 260.

WHITE TERN *Gygis alba* Pl. 43

Small, 10.5–13 ins, 27–33 cm. Wing-span 28 ins, 71 cm. Adult snow white overall with a black ring round the eye. Bill black, blue at base, legs vary between black and pale blue, webs whitish-yellow. Tail slightly forked. Young birds similar but show a black spot behind the eye and black shafts to wing quills and tail feathers. Its flight is light, often rising and sinking, and erratic, diving to surface to catch fish but never submerging.

Quite closely related to the noddies (see below), this beautiful tern is often called the White Noddy. It lays a single egg either on a bare branch or ridge of rock and appears exceptionally tame and confiding at its breeding quarters.

RANGE: Distributed throughout tropical islands in the Atlantic, Indian and Pacific Oceans. Breeds throughout range. Map 261.

NODDIES

The brown plumaged noddies, one species of which is however blue-grey, are distributed throughout islands in the tropical and sub-tropical belts of the oceans but behave somewhat differently from most other terns. They nest amongst the branches of trees and bushes making crude nests of sticks and seaweed. They rarely dive below the surface but feed largely on small fry skipping above the water, and may often be observed in large flocks where fish are jumping under attack from tuna, bonito and other large game fish. In courtship the noddy displays by nodding the head vigorously towards the female from which its name has doubtless been derived. Unlike other terns noddies have wedge-shaped tails, the outer tail feathers becoming progressively shorter, with only a shallow 'V' shaped cut in the centre. Flight is swift, erratic and normally low over the sea. Noddies do not range far from the coast.

BLUE-GREY NODDY *Procelsterna cerulea*   **Pl. 44**
Small, 10–11 ins, 25–28 cm. Wing-span 24 ins, 61 cm. Forehead and throat pale grey; crown and nape grey; a narrow black ring around eye. Upperparts smoky-grey, secondaries with white tips. Underparts and tail grey, tail slightly forked. Some paler birds have paler underparts and underwings. Bill black; legs black with yellow webs to feet.

Young birds are darker grey with dark primaries.

Easily recognised by its grey appearance.

RANGE: Confined to central and southern Pacific Ocean. Breeds throughout range. Map 262.

COMMON or BROWN NODDY *Anous stolidus*   **Pl. 44**
Small–medium, 14.5–16 ins, 37–41 cm. Wing-span 33 ins, 84 cm. Top of head lavender-grey, paler on forehead. White arc above and below eyes. Upperparts dark brown, primaries and tail almost black. Underparts dark brown, underwings paler. Bill black; legs brownish-black; tail rather long, wedge-shaped with shallow 'V' cut in centre. Young birds lighter brown with greyish cap.

Larger and not so dark as White-capped Noddy which also has a white cap. Bill stouter than other noddies. Ranges up to 50 miles from land.

RANGE: Widely distributed in tropical and sub-tropical Atlantic, Indian and Pacific Oceans, west and north coasts of Australia. Breeds throughout range. Map 263.

WHITE-CAPPED NODDY *Anous minutus*   **Pl. 44**
Small–medium, 13–14 ins, 33–36 cm. Wing-span 28 ins, 71 cm. Smaller than Common Noddy with top of head white and overall plumage almost black. White

arc above and below eyes. Bill black, legs brown. Tail wedge-shaped, slightly forked. Top of head is whiter than either Lesser or Common Noddy.

RANGE: Distributed widely through Caribbean, tropical Atlantic and tropical Pacific Oceans. Less numerous than Common Noddy throughout its range. Map 264.

LESSER NODDY *Anous tenuirostris*   **Pl. 44**

Small–medium, 12–13 ins, 31–33 cm. Wing-span 28 ins, 71 cm. Top of head greyish-white. White arc below eyes. Overall plumage sooty-brown, primaries darker. Bill black, legs blackish-brown. Tail wedge-shaped slightly forked. Top of head is paler than that of Common Noddy. White-capped Noddy has almost pure white at top of head.

RANGE: Indian Ocean. Breeds on Maldives, Chagos, Cargados Carajos, Mauritius, Seychelles, Abrolhos (W. Australia) and possibly other islands. Map 265.

Black Skimmers. Adults in breeding plumage. These birds collect food by skimming the water with their lower mandibles while on the wing.

SKIMMERS Rynchopidae

Skimmers, with their long narrow wings, black or dark brown upperparts, white foreheads and underparts, short legs and short forked tails, superficially resemble dark terns. Their structural peculiarities however, adapted to their remarkable method of fishing, places them in a family of their own.

When feeding they fly with steady wing-beats very close to the surface, their longer lower mandible cutting the water. To achieve this their wing strokes terminate above the horizontal. When the lower mandible strikes a fish the upper mandible snaps shut like a trap door. Their bills are so constructed that the outer edges of both mandibles are compressed to knife-like edges, broader towards the mouth, the edges of the lower mandible closing into grooves within the upper mandible. When a fish is caught it is usually tossed in the air and swallowed on the wing, the lower bill returning immediately to scoop through the water.

Skimmers usually feed in the evenings or by moonlight, when shrimps and fish rise to the surface, and rest in flocks on sandbanks by day. Their usual habitats are lakes and rivers, but they also resort to the coast and are occasionally seen at sea.

Nesting and young

These nest sociably on coastal and river sandbanks, but although large numbers may be present the nests are well-spaced. The nest is a bare, shallow hollow with 2–4 eggs, cryptically coloured and similar to those of terns. The young are downy, with a finely mottled pattern for concealment on a sandy background. They are precocial, leaving the nest soon after hatching and can swim well at an early age. They are fed at first on regurgitated, and later on whole fish, brought by the parents. The bill is unspecialised at first and the elongated lower mandible does not develop until the chick is well-grown.

BLACK SKIMMER *Rynchops nigra*   Pl. 45
Medium, 19 ins, 48 cm. Wing-span 45 ins, 114 cm. Crown, nape, upperparts and upperwings black; in winter a whitish collar around the neck. Secondaries have broad white tips. Forehead and underbody white. Underwings and under tail-coverts whitish-grey. Bill long, lower mandible extending beyond upper mandible, bright red at base, merging into black at forward end. Legs short, red. Tail slightly forked, brown with white edges, outer tail feathers white. Young birds mottled brown above, underparts mottled-grey. Bills shorter, brown. Legs dusky red.
RANGE: Rivers, lakes and coasts of the Americas from Massachusetts to Buenos Aires and from Ecuador to Chile. Breeds from Massachusetts to Texas, in winter from S. Carolina to the Gulf of Mexico. From Columbia southwards to the Argentine.   Map 266.

AFRICAN SKIMMER *Rynchops flavirostris*   Pl. 45
Small–medium, 14 ins, 36 cm. Wing-span 42 ins, 107 cm. Crown, nape and upper-wings brown, feathers with buff edges; in winter a whitish collar around the neck. Secondaries have broad white tips. Forehead and underbody white. Underwings dusky-brown. Bill long, upper mandible orange-red, lower mandible orange at base merging into yellow at forward end. Legs short, red. Tail slightly forked, greyish. Young birds similar but forehead streaked grey. Bill yellowish, with dark tip.
RANGE: Rivers, lakes and coasts throughout tropical Africa, from Senegal to the Orange River across Africa, and from the Nile to the Zambesi.   Map 267.

INDIAN SKIMMER *Rynchops albicollis*   Pl. 45
Small–medium, 16 ins, 41 cm. Wing-span 43 ins, 109 cm. Crown and nape dark brown. Hindneck, rump and tail white. Remainder of upperparts dark brown, primaries blackish. Secondaries have broad white edges. Forehead and underparts white, underwings grey. Bill orange, tip yellow. Legs red. Young birds have streaked foreheads, paler brown upperparts with paler mottled feathering and a brown tip to tail feathers.
RANGE: Rivers and lakes in India and Burma. Breeds on sandbanks.   Map 268.

A breeding colony of Auks and Guillemot. Killiwakes.

ALCIDS Alcidae

The family *Alcidae*, auks, guillemots, razorbills, auklets, puffins and murrelets, are all seabirds of the high latitudes in the colder water of the northern hemisphere where they replace the penguins and diving-petrels of the southern hemisphere.

They are rather stoutish-bodied, medium to small sized birds; in colouring mostly black above and white below, some dark with white wing patches and with varying shaped and coloured bills and legs. Outside the breeding season they spend much of their time in flocks at sea at no great distance from the land, diving below water using their wings to propel them in search of fish. They swim high in the water and when taking wing fly with rapid 'whirring' wingbeats for short distances low over the sea. When disturbed they will often splash along the surface before diving.

Most species breed in colonies on ledges or clefts in cliffs, making no nest and laying their eggs on the bare rock. Puffins however nest in burrows scraped out of springy turf along cliffs making a sparse nest of grasses and feathers.

It is by no means easy to identify individual species at sea.

Nesting and young

The nesting habits vary, but most species are sociable in their nesting. Nest material may be accumulated if it is available close to the nest site. Only one or two eggs are laid, large for the size of the birds, and both parents take a share in incubating eggs and caring for the young. The young usually have thick, soft and dark coloured down. Guillemots and razorbills tend to crowd on open rock ledges and niches of cliffs, and on flat-topped stacks. The large single pear-shaped egg is very varied in colour and pattern. It is laid on a bare ledge often crowded with birds and the considerable variation may enable birds to recognise their own eggs. The young leave for sea at 2–3 weeks, only partly grown, and accompanied by the parents. The other species nest in rock crevices, cavities or burrows dug by the birds. These are usually on islands, or boulder-beaches, cliff-tops and screes on the coast, exceptionally on higher ground further inland. Black Guillemots have two heavily spotted eggs in a rock crevice, puffins and auklets have a single faintly marked or unmarked egg, and the Little Auk has an unmarked blue egg. The young of these remain in the nest until fledged, at about 3–4 weeks for the Little Auk, 5–6 for the Black Guillemot, and *c.* 7 for the Atlantic Puffin.

Most murrelets and auklets nest in burrows, the former having speckled eggs and those of the latter being plain and whitish. The young of Ancient and Crested Murrelets are exceptionally precocious, leaving the burrow for the sea within two days of hatching. Kittlitz's Murrelet nests on bare rocky slopes high on mountains near the sea, while the Marbled Murrelet nests on platforms of twigs, moss or old nests in coastal forests.

LITTLE AUK or DOVEKIE *Plautus alle*   **Pl. 46**
Very small, 8 ins, 203 mm. Wing-span 12 ins, 31 cm. Head, neck, upper breast and upperparts black; in winter the throat and ear-coverts become white. Secondaries and scapulars show white streaks visible at short range. Lower breast and underparts white. Bill very short, thick, black, yellow inside mouth; legs flesh-coloured.

Young birds similar to adults in winter but have browner upperparts.

Distinguished by its very small stubby appearance and short stout bill. Swims very low in the water and dives when alarmed. Frequently seen in the N. Atlantic on the routes from the British Isles to the Gulf of St. Lawrence, and has been seen off New York in winter.

RANGE: N. Atlantic and adjacent arctic seas. Disperses southwards in winter to the latitude of the British Isles and New York. Occasionally driven ashore or further south during gales.   Map 269.

RAZORBILL   *Alca torda*   **Pl. 46**

Medium, 16.5 ins, 42 cm. Wing-span 26 ins, 66 cm. Head, neck and upperparts black with a somewhat 'bull-necked' appearance. A narrow white line extends from bill to eye. In winter the cheeks and foreneck become white; underparts and underwing-coverts white. Secondaries tipped white, showing a white line when the bird is on the water. Bill stout, compressed, black and crossed by a conspicuous white band; legs black.

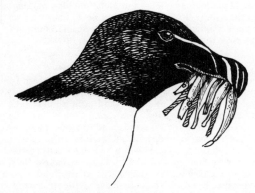

Razor-billed Auk with bill full of food for young.

Young birds similar to adults in winter but with a smaller black bill lacking the white line.

When on the water it carries its tail cocked in the air.

RANGE: N. Atlantic and adjacent arctic seas. Some disperse southwards in winter to latitude of New York and Straits of Gibraltar.   Map 270.

BRUNNICH'S GUILLEMOT or THICK-BILLED MURRE   **Pl. 46**
   Uria lomvia

Medium, 18 ins, 46 cm. In breeding plumage head, neck and upperparts black, the whole head dark. Breast and underbody white. In winter it retains the sides of the face below the ear-coverts black, the throat and neck white like the rest of the underbody. The tips of the secondaries are white forming a thin white line. Bill noticeably stouter than Common Guillemot, pointed, a pale streak running back along the base of the upper mandible. Legs yellow in front, black behind. Tail short and round.

Young birds similar to adults but browner and bills shorter.
See also Common Guillemot or Murre (below) for comparison.
RANGE: Similar to Common Guillemot or Murre but confined to higher arctic latitudes.   Map 271.

COMMON GUILLEMOT or MURRE *Uria aalge*   Pls. 46, 48
Medium, 17 ins, 43 cm. Wing-span 42 ins, 107 cm. In breeding plumage head, neck and upperparts dark chocolate-brown. Some birds known as 'Bridled Guillemots' have a white ring round the eye and a white stripe running back from the eye. Breast and underbody white. In winter the ear-coverts, throat and front of neck are white like the rest of the underbody, and a black streak runs backwards from the eye over the ear-coverts. The tips of the secondaries are white forming a thin white line. Bill black, long, fine and pointed. Legs brownish to yellowish. Tail short and round.
Birds in the higher northern latitudes have black as opposed to the browner plumage of birds further south. Young birds similar to adults but underparts dusky-white, bills shorter and legs paler.
The neck is rather long and slender in comparison with other auks. See also Brunnich's Guillemot for comparison (above).
RANGE: N. Atlantic and N. Pacific Oceans and adjacent arctic seas, dispersing southwards in winter to the Straits of Gibraltar, Maine, California, northern Japan.   Map 272.

BLACK GUILLEMOT *Cepphus grylle*   Pl. 46
Small–medium, 12–14 ins, 30–36 cm. Adults in summer are uniformly black except for a conspicuous broad white patch on the wing. Axillaries and underwing-coverts white. In winter the crown, hindneck, back and upperparts are white with dark speckling; primaries and secondaries black; wing patch and underparts white. Bill pointed, black outside, inside vermilion; legs red.
Young birds similar to adults in winter but with black mottling on wing patch and underparts.
RANGE: N. Atlantic and adjacent arctic seas. Southwards to Massachusetts, and the latitude of the British Isles. Breeds in Greenland, arctic coasts of Canada, Gulf of St. Lawrence south to Maine, arctic coasts of Europe, Siberia, Norway, Baltic, Iceland and British Isles.   Map 273.

PIGEON GUILLEMOT *Cepphus columba*   Pl. 46
Small–medium, 14.5 ins, 37 cm. The Pacific representative of the Black Guillemot with a very similar summer and winter plumage. The white wing patch is divided into two or three black transverse patches. In winter the wings are sometimes entirely black. Underwing-coverts and axillaries brownish-grey (white in Black Guillemot). Bill black, legs bright red. Young birds similar to young Black Guillemots in winter plumage, but the white feathers are tipped black, sometimes making young birds look almost black.
RANGE: N. Pacific and Bering Sea extending from Wrangel I. southward to the Kuril Is., eastwards to the Aleutian Is. and southwards to Sta. Barbara Is., California. In winter to Japan and Lower California.   Map 274.

SPECTACLED GUILLEMOT *Cepphus carbo*   Pl. 46
Small–medium, 14.5 ins, 37 cm. In summer the overall plumage is slaty-black, the shoulders and underwing-coverts brownish. A conspicuous white ring surrounds

the eyes. In winter the chin, throat and underbody white; underwing-coverts brownish. Bill black; legs red.

Young birds similar to adults in winter plumage but with grey forenecks.

Resident in Japan.

RANGE: Western N. Pacific. Okhotsk Sea and Sea of Japan to Bering Sea. Map 275.

MARBLED MURRELET *Brachyramphus marmoratus* **Pl. 48**

Small, 9.5–10 ins, 24–25 cm. Head, neck and upperparts dark brown, the back, rump and upper tail-coverts with buff barring in summer plumage. Scapulars white. Underparts white with greyish-black patches and barring in summer; underwing-coverts greyish-black. In winter a white ring shows around the eye and a white band across the nape. Bill slender, black; legs flesh-coloured.

Young birds have dusky upperparts; white on nape and scapulars, and dusky-white underparts.

When on the water the white band on each side above the wings is noticeable and it carries its bill and tail cocked up. Has been observed off Vancouver I. and north Japan.

RANGE: N. Pacific. Breeds in Kamchatka and the Kuril Is. in the western Pacific and on the west coast of N. America from Unalaska to Vancouver I. Map 276.

KITTLITZ'S MURRELET *Brachyramphus brevirostris* **Pl. 48**

Small, 9.5 ins, 24 cm. In summer plumage cheeks, chin and neck pale buff. Upperparts dusky with buff streaking. Underparts whitish with black bars on chest and sides. Axillaries and underwing-coverts dark brownish-grey. In winter upperparts slate-grey spotted white, a white collar on nape, sides of head and underparts white. A grey crescent in front of eye and grey bars on sides of breast. Bill black; legs pale brown. Tail edged and tipped white.

RANGE: N. Pacific and Bering Sea extending from arctic coasts of Siberia and the Kuril Is., eastwards to the Aleutian Is. and Alaska. In winter to Japan. Map 277.

XANTUS'S MURRELET *Brachyramphus hypoleucus* **Pl. 48**

Small, 8.5 ins, 216 mm. Upperparts and flanks slate-grey, darker on wings. Underparts and underwings white. Bill small, slender, black, bluish at base. Legs pale blue. Tail short, round. Young birds similar.

Distinguished from Craveri's Murrelet by white underwings.

RANGE: West coast of U.S.A. from San Francisco to southern lower California. Breeds on Sta. Barbara and Los Coronados Is. Map 278.

CRAVERI'S MURRELET *Brachyramphus craveri* **Pl. 48**

Small, 8.5 ins, 216 mm. Upperparts slaty-black. Underparts white with brownish-grey flanks. Underwings brownish-grey. Bill small, slender, black. Tail short and round. Young birds similar but sides and breasts with blackish spots.

Distinguished from Xantus' Murrelet by darker upperparts and underwings.

RANGE: Both coasts of Lower California. Breeds on islands in the Gulf of California. Map 278.

ANCIENT MURRELET *Synthliboramphus antiquus* **Pl. 48**

Small, 10.5 ins, 27 cm. Wing-span 17 ins, 43 cm. In breeding plumage throat, face, head and hindneck black. A white stripe shows on each side of the crown. Sides of neck white. Upperparts slaty-blue, tail and wings black. Underparts and underwing-coverts white, sides and flanks black. Bill short, stout, whitish; feet grey. In winter the throat becomes white and chin greyish.

Young birds similar to adults in winter plumage.

Distinguished by the blue appearance of upperparts and sharply defined white sides to neck and stripe on crown.

RANGE: N. Pacific and Bering Sea. A common winter visitor to north Japan and reaches the coast of California in winter.   Map 279.

CRESTED MURRELET *Synthliboramphus wumizusume*   **Pl. 48**
Small, 10.5 ins, 27 cm. Forehead, crown and nape slaty-black, cheeks and throat slate-grey. In summer a crest of loose black feathers curving back from crown; a broad white stripe of feathers running back from eye and meeting at back of head. Upperparts blue-grey; underparts white. Bill very short, stout, yellow; legs yellow. Young birds are similar to adults in winter but head and upperparts brownish-grey.

Distinguished by its grey upperparts and, in summer plumage, by its black crest and white stripe along the side of head.

RANGE: Breeds only in Japan.   Map 280.

CASSIN'S AUKLET *Ptychoramphus aleuticus*   **Pl. 48**
Small, 9 ins, 230 mm. This very small Pacific Ocean auklet has dusky-grey upperparts; chin, throat and foreneck brownish; sides and flanks grey, remainder of underbody white. Underwing-coverts greyish-brown. It shows white spots above and below the eye. Bill pointed, black; legs bluish. Young birds similar.

RANGE: West coast of U.S.A. from Aleutian Is. to Lower California.   Map 281.

PARAKEET AUKLET *Cyclorrhynchus psittacula*   **Pl. 48**
Small, 10.5 ins, 27 cm. Wing-span 18 ins, 46 cm. Upperparts slaty-black. Chin, throat, foreneck, sides and flanks greyish-brown in summer, in winter all white. In breeding plumage only elongated white plumes extend from behind the eye downwards across the black cheeks. Bill very stubby, small and deep, orange-red, the lower mandible curving upwards. Legs pale bluish. Young birds similar to adults in winter without plumes, and with a smaller brownish bill.

Its flight is reported as stronger and usually higher above the sea than other species.

RANGE: N. Pacific and Bering Sea from N.E. Siberia, Kuril Is. eastwards to Aleutian Is. In winter to northern Japan and California.   Map 282.

CRESTED AUKLET *Aethia cristatella*   **Pl. 47**
Small, 10.5 ins, 27 cm. Upperparts slaty-black. A distinctive forward curving brown crest of plumes projects from forehead, and elongated white plumes extend backwards and downwards from behind the eye. Underparts, forehead and underwings brownish-grey. Bill short, deep, compressed, orange-red with pale tip. Legs bluish-grey. Young birds similar but without crest or plumes, and with smaller dull brown bills.

RANGE: N. Pacific, Bering Sea and adjacent arctic sea. In winter to Japan and Kodiak I.   Map 283.

LEAST AUKLET *Aethia pusilla*   **Pl. 47**
Very small, 6.5 ins, 165 mm. Smaller than any other auk. In summer, upperparts slaty-black, scapulars partly white, secondaries tipped white. Throat white, underparts white with dark blotches which sometimes appear as a dusky band around the foreneck. Underwing-coverts white. A row of elongated white plumes stretches

from behind the eye extending downwards across the dark cheeks, and another row from the corner of the gape. In summer also some white pointed feathers occur on the forehead. Bill small, stubby, red; legs brown. Winter, lacks white plumes; bill black.

Young birds similar to adults in winters.

RANGE: Bering Sea and adjacent parts of N. Pacific. Reported to occur in flocks in the northern quarter of the N. Pacific in winter, and a regular winter visitor to north Japan.   Map 282.

WHISKERED AUKLET *Aethia pygmaea*   Pl. 47

Very small, 7.5 ins, 191 mm. Upperparts dusky-grey. A blackish forward curving crest projects from forehead. Two elongated white plumes on each side in front of eye, one extending upwards and curving forwards, another extending backwards and downwards. Chest grey, lower underbody and under tail-coverts white. Underwing-coverts brown. Bill short, bright red with a pale tip and blunt horny knob at base. Legs bluish. Young birds similar but without crest, plumes, or knob on smaller dusky bill.

Differs from Crested Auklet by smaller size, differing white plumes, by knob on bill in summer and white under tail-coverts.

RANGE: N. Pacific and southern Bering Sea from Kamchatka and Kuril Is. eastward to Aleutian Is. and coast of Alaska.   Map 283.

RHINOCEROS AUKLET *Cerorhinca monocerata*   Pl. 47

Small–medium, 14 ins, 36 cm. Upperparts sooty-black. Underparts white with brownish-grey chin, throat, chest, sides and flanks. Underwings brownish-grey. A line of white elongated straight plumes extends from the eye across the cheeks, and another from the bill below the eye. Bill rather long, orange-yellow with a horny projection on the top of the base of the upper mandible in the breeding season. Legs yellow. Young birds similar to adults in winter without the white plumes, and with a smaller duller bill.

RANGE: N. Pacific Ocean from the coast of Kamchatka and the Kuril Is. Also from the west coast of Alaska south to Washington. In winter to Japan and Lower California.   Map 284.

ATLANTIC PUFFIN *Fratercula arctica*   Pl. 47

Small–medium, 11.5–14 ins, 29–36 cm. Wing-span 18 ins, 46 cm. In adult summer plumage the crown, nape and upperparts black, cheeks and throat white with a darker streak behind the eye, a blue horny triangle above eye, and narrow rectangle below eye, eye-ring red. Underparts white. The remarkable laterally-compressed parrot-like triangular bill is pale blue at base, bright red at tip and crossed by yellow bands. Legs bright red. In summer a yellow wattle patch occurs at base of gape. After the breeding season the face becomes grey, basal part of the bill sheath is shed and the bill becomes smaller and yellower, and the wattle shrivels.

Young birds are similar to adults in winter plumage, with browner upperparts and more 'normal' slender bills.

In the N. Atlantic, while the guillemot and razorbill have been observed well out at sea, the Puffin appears usually to remain closer to the coast.

RANGE: Both sides of the N. Atlantic and adjacent arctic seas. Some disperse southwards in winter to the Straits of Gibraltar and Massachusetts.   Map 285.

HORNED PUFFIN *Fratercula corniculata*   Pl. 47

Small–medium, 14–16 ins, 36–41 cm. Wing-span 22 ins, 56 cm. Chin and crown greyish-brown, neck and upperparts black. Cheeks and underbody white; a fleshy excrescence occurs over the eye. Underwing-coverts greyish-brown. The very large triangular bill is red at tip, yellow at base; legs red. In winter cheeks grey; bill reduced, red at tip, dusky at base.

Young birds are similar to adults with grey cheeks and much reduced brownish bills.

A common winter visitor to north Japan.

RANGE: N. Pacific and Bering Sea from arctic coasts of Siberia eastwards to Aleutian Is. and S.E. Alaska. Disperses southwards to Kuril Is. and British Columbia.   Map 286.

Atlantic Puffins inspecting nesting burrows.

TUFTED PUFFIN   *Lunda cirrhata*   Pl. 47

Medium, 16 ins, 41 cm. In adult summer plumage the forehead and cheeks are white and long yellow drooping tufts extend behind the eye down the sides of the head. Eye-ring red. Upperparts black; underparts greyish brown. In winter chin, throat and foreneck sooty-brown. The very large laterally compressed triangular bill is greenish-yellow at the base and bright red at the forward end; a red wattle patch occurs at the base of the gape. Legs bright red. In winter the overall plumage is duller, the bill reduced, bluish at base and red at tip, the plumes are not present and the whole head and face dark. Young birds have yellowish bills.

RANGE: N. Pacific and Bering Sea from north coasts of Siberia and Kuril Is., eastwards to Aleutian Is., Alaska and west coast of America to Sta. Barbara Is., California.   Map 287.

Plate 1   **PENGUINS**

Flightless birds, confined to the southern oceans except for the Galapagos Penguin.
May be seen swimming far from land.

1 EMPEROR PENGUIN *Aptenodytes forsteri*   page 7
Very large; orange-yellow neck band; red slash lower mandible; long
bill.   Map 2.

2 KING PENGUIN *Aptenodytes patagonica*   7
Large; orange neck band extends to foreneck; orange-reddish slash
lower mandible; long bill.   Map 1.

3 GENTOO PENGUIN *Pygoscelis papua*   7
White band over back of head; bill red, tip black; legs orange.
Map 3.

4 ADELIE PENGUIN *Pygoscelis adeliae*   7
White eyelids; bill stubby, brick-red, tip dark; legs pinkish-
white.   Map 4.

5 CHIN-STRAP or BEARDED PENGUIN   8
Pygoscelis antarctica
Black line surrounds white throat; bill black; legs pinkish-
white.   Map 5.

6 JACKASS PENGUIN *Spheniscus demersus*   11
Single black horseshoe band; bill black, grey band; legs black.   Map
14.

7 HUMBOLDT PENGUIN *Spheniscus humboldti*   11
Single black horseshoe band; bill stout, blackish, base flesh-colour;
legs blackish.   Map 15.

8 MAGELLAN PENGUIN *Spheniscus magellanicus*   11
Black band around foreneck; black horseshoe band below; bill blackish; legs mottled blackish.   Map 16.

9 GALAPAGOS PENGUIN *Spheniscus mendiculus*   11
Small; black band around foreneck; black horseshoe band below; bill
black above, yellow below; legs black, mottled white. Confined to
Galapagos Is.

Plate 2   **PENGUINS**

1 **ROCK-HOPPER PENGUIN** *Eudyptes crestatus*
Yellow plumes from each side behind nostrils; iris red; bill orange
red; legs flesh-colour. In the background, a Rock-hopper group with
one young.   Map 9.

2 **MACARONI PENGUIN** *Eudyptes chrysolophus*
Golden plumes from centre of forehead; bill black, tip red; legs
pinkish.   Map 10.

3 **SNARES CRESTED PENGUIN** *Eudyptes robustus*
Narrow yellow crest, end bushy; bill reddish-brown; legs flesh-
colour.   Map 7.

4 **FIORDLAND CRESTED PENGUIN**
Eudyptes pachyrhynchus
Similar to Snares Crested Penguin; yellow plumes straight, shorter;
bill reddish-brown; legs pale flesh-colour.   Map 6.

5 **ERECT-CRESTED or BIG-CRESTED PENGUIN**
Eudyptes sclateri
Bright yellow crest curves upwards; iris red; bill reddish-brown; legs
pale-flesh colour.   Map 8.

6 **ROYAL PENGUIN** *Eudyptes schlegeli*
Side of face white; long orange plumes curve downwards; iris red; bill
pale reddish-brown; legs flesh-colour. Breeds only on Macquarie I.

7 **YELLOW-EYED PENGUIN** *Megadyptes antipodes*
Crown and face pale golden; pale yellow band circles crown; bill
flesh-colour, dull brown on culmen and tips of lower mandible; legs
flesh-colour.   Map 11.

8 **LITTLE or BLUE PENGUIN** *Eudyptula minor*
Upperparts slate-blue; iris silver-grey; bill black; legs pale flesh-
colour.   Map 12.

9 **WHITE-FLIPPERED PENGUIN** *Eudyptula albosignata*
Upperparts pale slate-grey; iris silver-grey; bill black; legs pale flesh
colour.   Map 13.

Plate 3   **ALBATROSSES**

Oceanic birds of great size and wing-span. Often follow ships, alighting briefly astern to feed on garbage.

1   SHORT-TAILED ALBATROSS *Diomedea albatrus*   page 17

  a Adult above. Mainly white above and below; wing quills, leading wing-coverts and tail band dark; bill and legs flesh-colour; under-wings white.   Map 20.

  b Immature below. Sooty-brown overall; bill and legs flesh-colour.

2   ROYAL ALBATROSS *Diomedea epomophora epomophora*   17

  a Adult above. Always mostly white; primaries black; thin dark margin to trailing edge of underwing; black cutting edge to both mandibles; bill faintly pink; legs bluish-white.   Map 18.

  b Northern race *Diomedea e. sandfordi*   17
    Adult above. Slightly smaller than 2a. Upperwings show less white, sometimes entirely dark.   Map 18.

3   WANDERING ALBATROSS *Diomedea exulans*   16

  a Adult above. Slight speckling on back and shoulders; bill and legs pale flesh-colour.   Map 17.

  b Adult below. Thin dark margin to trailing edge of underwing often shows.

  c Immature above. Bill whitish; tail brown.

  d Immature below. Face and throat white; central linings of underwings white; underbody and tail brown.

Plate 4   **ALBATROSSES**

1 BULLER'S ALBATROSS *Diomedea bulleri*   page 19
 a Adult above. Forehead white; head and neck blue-grey; dark patch at
   eye; yellow band along upper and lower mandibles; tail sooty-
   brown.   Map 24.

 b Adult below. Dark margin to leading edge of underwing; fine margin
   on trailing edge; legs bluish-white.

2 LAYSAN ALBATROSS *Diomedea immutabilis*   18
 a Adult above. Back and upperwings dark sooty-brown; bill greyish;
   base of bill yellow; dark band on tail.   Map 22.

 b Adult below. Broad dark underwing margins; legs flesh-colour.

3 SHY or WHITE-CAPPED ALBATROSS *Diomedea cauta*   19
 a Adult above. Large, forehead white; in New Zealand area crown and
   neck also white; back and upperwings greyish-brown; bill greenish-
   grey, tip orange; orange stripe behind base of lower mandible.   Map
   25.

 b Adult below. Very narrow dark margins to underwings.

 c Adult. Form with grey cap and yellow bill.

4 WAVED ALBATROSS *Diomedea irrorata*   17
   Adult above. Map 19.

Plate 5   **ALBATROSSES**

1 BLACK-BROWED ALBATROSS *Diomedea melanophris*   page 18

  a Adult above. Dark streak around eye; bill stout, yellow, pink tip; legs bluish-white; tail slaty-black. Map 23.

  b Adult below. Broad dark margins to leading and trailing edges of underwing.

  c Immature below. Crown and hindneck greyish, merging into white; broad smudgy margins to underwing; bill greyish-black.

2 GREY-HEADED ALBATROSS *Diomedea chrysostoma*   20

  a Adult above. Whole head and neck dusky-grey; white around back of eye; yellow bands above and below bill, tip bright pink. Map 27.

  b Adult below. Dark margins to underwing, wider from bend of wing on leading edge.

3 YELLOW-NOSED ALBATROSS *Diomedea chlororhynchos*   19

  a Adult above. Dark patch at eye; bill slender, black, yellow band on ridge of upper mandible, tip bright orange; legs flesh-colour. Map 26.

  b Adult below. Clearly defined thin dark margins to underwing, leading margin broader.

Plate 6   **ALBATROSSES**

1 SOOTY ALBATROSS *Phoebetria fusca*   page 20
Adult above. White ring around eye; yellow groove along side of
lower mandible; tail long, wedge-shaped. Map 28.

2 LIGHT-MANTLED SOOTY ALBATROSS   21
Phoebetria palpebrata
Adult above. Paler, greyer than Sooty Albatross; white ring around
eye; pale blue groove along side of lower mandible; tail long,
wedgeshaped. Map 29.

3 BLACK-FOOTED ALBATROSS *Diomedea nigripes*   17
 a Adult above. White area around bill; bill dark brown; legs black.
Map 21.

 b Immature above. Broad whitish area around and above bill; upper
tail-coverts whitish.

4 NORTHERN GIANT PETREL *Macronectes halli*   24
Above for size comparison. See also Pl. 7. Map 31.

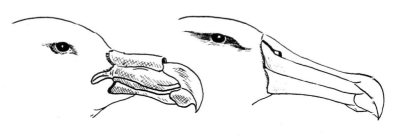

GIANT PETRELS   SHY ALBATROSS

The large, squat, plated bill of the Giant Petrels immediately distinguishes them from any Albatross. In flight the Giant Petrels appear
ungainly, with awkward flapping or rather stiff-winged gliding.

Plate 7   **PETRELS and SHEARWATERS**

Oceanic birds, smaller than albatrosses with which they share a tube-nose (see p. 13). Generally seen flying close over the sea surface.

1 WHITE-CHINNED PETREL *Procellaria aequinoctialis*   page 29
  a Above. Heavy build; white on chin noticeable; long massive yellowish bill.   Map 45.

  b White on chin frequently much reduced in birds breeding on New Zealand islands.

  c, d Variable heads. Peculiar to birds breeding on Tristan da Cunha; sometimes seen in South Atlantic.

2 PARKINSON'S PETREL *Procellaria parkinsoni*   29
Dark blackish-brown overall; bill bluish-horn, tip black; legs black. Map 46.

3 WESTLAND PETREL *Procellaria westlandica*   29
See Parkinson's Petrel. Bill yellowish.   Map 47.

4 WEDGE-TAILED SHEARWATER *Puffinus pacificus*   31
  a Above, dark phase. Dark chocolate-brown overall; bill long, slender, grey; tail long, wedge-shaped; legs flesh colour.   Map 53.

  b Below, pale phase. Slightly paler above than 4a; dark margins to underwings; bill and legs flesh-colour.

5 CHRISTMAS SHEARWATER *Puffinus nativitatis*   32
Above. Smaller, paler chocolate-brown than 4a; bill long, slender, dark; legs brown; tail rounded.   Map 57.

6 NORTHERN GIANT PETREL *Macronectes halli*   24
Below. Outsize; darker body and head than 7a, darker yellowish-brown bill. See also Pl. 6.   Map 31.

7 SOUTHERN GIANT PETREL *Macronectes giganteus*   24
  a Below. Outsize; very large plated bill; dark feathers around pale eye; legs sooty-black.   Map 30.

  b Immature above. Rich dark chocolate-brown; eye dark.

  c White phase with chick. Occasional in southerly breeding colonies.

Plate 8   SHEARWATERS

1 SHORT-TAILED SHEARWATER *Puffinus tenuirostris*   page 32
  a Below. Greyish lining to underwing; bill slender, dark; legs bluish-grey; tail short, round.   Map 56.

  b Above.

2 SOOTY SHEARWATER *Puffinus griseus*   32
  a Below. Larger than 1. Silvery lining to underwing; pale under chin. Map 55.

  b Above.

3 PALE-FOOTED SHEARWATER *Puffinus carneipes*   30
  a Below. Underbody and wings chocolate-brown; bill straw-colour, tip brown; legs yellowish-flesh-colour; tail short, round.   Map 51.

  b Above.

4 PINK-FOOTED SHEARWATER *Puffinus creatopus*   30
  a Below. Underbody whitish, underwing mottled-white; bill pink, tip black; legs pink.   Map 50.

  b Above.

5 GREY-BACKED SHEARWATER *Puffinus bulleri*   31
  a Below. All white underparts; bill long, bluish; legs flesh-colour. Map 54.

  b Above. Dark '**W**' pattern; dark wedge-shaped tail.

6 WHITE-FACED or STREAKED SHEARWATER   29
  Calonectris leucomelas
  a Below. Underwing linings white, darker streaked margins; legs flesh-colour; tail brown.   Map 48.

  b Above.

Plate 9   **PETRELS and SHEARWATERS**

1 **BULWER'S PETREL** *Bulweria bulwerii*   page 44
Above. Paler band on upperwing.   Map 94.

2 **JOUANIN'S PETREL** *Bulweria fallax*   43
Above. Larger than 1. Short thick black bill.   Map 93.

3 **GREAT SHEARWATER** *Puffinus gravis*   31
a Below. White neck under dark cap.   Map 52.

b Above. Dark cap; white band across rump.

4 **CORY'S SHEARWATER** *Calonectris diomedea*   30
a Below. Bill stout, yellow; legs pinkish.   Map 49.

b Above.

5 **LITTLE SHEARWATER** *Puffinus assimilis assimilis*   33
a Below. Small; white extends into head; legs bluish. Map 66.

b Madeiran race.   *Puffinus a. baroli*   34
Below. More white in front of eye.   Map 66.

c Cape Verde Is. race.   *Puffinus a. boydi*   34
Below. Darker under tail.   Map 66.

d Little Shearwaters are sharply black and white. They often fly with dropping legs like storm-petrels.

6 **MANX SHEARWATER** *Puffinus puffinus puffinus*   32
a Below. Dark of head extends below eye; legs pinkish.   Map 58.

b **Levantine Shearwater** *Puffinus p. yelkouan*   33
Below. Dark area further below eye.   Map 59.

c **Balearic Shearwater** *Puffinus p. mauretanicus*   33
Below. Underparts mottled brown.   Map 60.

d **Black-vented Shearwater** *Puffinus p. opisthomelas*   33
Below. Under tail-coverts and flanks dark.   Map 63.

e **Manx Shearwater** Above.

f **Manx Shearwater** Swimming.
Townsend's and Newell's Shearwaters (see p. 33) are similar.

7 **AUDUBON'S SHEARWATER** *Puffinus l'herminieri l'herminieri*   34
Below. Compare Pl. 10, No. 9.   Map 67.

8 **HEINROTH'S SHEARWATER** *Puffinus heinrothi*   34
Below. Known only from single specimen near New Britain.

Plate 10   PETRELS and SHEARWATERS

Plate 11   **PETRELS**

1 NORTHERN FULMAR *Fulmarus glacialis*   page 25
 a Pale phase.

 b Dark phase. There is also a rare all-white phase. Map 32.

2 SOUTHERN FULMAR or SILVER-GREY PETREL   25
Fulmarus glacialoides
Paler than 1a. No dark phase.   Map 33.

3 SNOW PETREL *Pagadroma nivea*   25
All white; black bill; dark grey legs.   Map 35.

4 WHITE-NECKED PETREL *Pterodroma externa*   38
 a Above. Upperparts medium-grey; dark '**W**' pattern across wings;
 white collar round neck.   Map 84.

 b Below. Dark margin between bend of wing and leading primary.

5 WHITE-HEADED PETREL *Pterodroma lessoni*   35
 a Above. Hindneck pale grey; dark patch at eye.   Map 70.

 b Below. Underwing grey; legs flesh-colour.

6 KERGUELEN PETREL *Pterodroma brevirostris*   36
Map 75.

7 BLUE PETREL *Halobaena caerulea*   26
Small; dark '**W**' pattern across wings; legs blue; tail square, white
tips.   Map 37.

8 DOVE PRION *Pachyptila desolata*   28
 a Above. Small; black patch at eye; black terminal band on tail; tail
 wedge-shaped.   Map 40.

 b Below. Underparts and underwings white.

 The following are not illustrated separately, as being indistinguish-
 able in the field from Dove Prion:
  Broad-billed Prion *Pachyptila vittata*   Page 28,   Map 38.
  Salvin's Prion *Pachyptila salvini*   Page 28,   Map 39.
  Thin-billed Prion *Pachyptila belcheri*   Page 28,   Map 41.
  Fairy Prion *Pachyptila turtur*   Page 28,   Map 42.
  Fulmar or **Thick-billed Prion** *Pachyptila crassirostris*   Page 28,
  Map 43.

9 CAPE PIGEON or PINTADO PETREL *Daption capensis*   25
 a Above. Typically piebald black and white.   Map 34.

 b Below.

 c Swimming.

10 ANTARCTIC PETREL *Talassoica antarctica*   26
Underwing-coverts white.   Map 36.

Plate 12   PETRELS

Plate 13   **STORM-PETRELS**

Small oceanic birds. Flight close to the sea and fluttering; they sometimes follow ships.

1 **WILSON'S STORM-PETREL** *Oceanites oceanicus*   page 46
Long legs, webs yellow, extend beyond tail in flight; tail square.
Map 95.

2 **ELLIOT'S STORM-PETREL** *Oceanites gracilis*   46
Very small; centre of underbody white; tail square, slightly indented; webs yellow.   Map 96.

3 **BRITISH STORM-PETREL** *Hydrobates pelagicus*   48
Very small; small patch of white feathers at base of underwing; legs
short; tail square.   Map 102.

4 **MADEIRAN STORM-PETREL** *Oceanodroma castro*   49
Larger than 3; sooty-brown; broad white rump band; slight cleft in
tail.   Map 105.

5 **LEACH'S STORM-PETREL** *Oceanodroma leucorhoa*   49
 a Blackish-brown; oval white rump patch with indistinct dark centre
line feathers; tail forked.   Map 106.

 b Dark form. Dark rump; Southern and western tropical Pacific.

6 **GALAPAGOS STORM-PETREL** *Oceanodroma tethys*   48
Very small; sooty-black; triangular white rump patch; legs very
short; slight cleft in tail.   Map 104.

7 **WHITE-BELLIED STORM-PETREL** *Fregetta grallaria*   47
Indistinct white rump patch; underbody, under tail-coverts and
inner underwing-coverts white; tail square. See drawing of bill,
p. 47.   Map 99.

8 **BLACK-BELLIED STORM-PETREL** *Fregetta tropica*   47
Similar to 7; centre of abdomen usually divided lengthwise by dark
feathers. See drawing of bill, p. 47.   Map 100.

9 **WHITE-FACED STORM-PETREL** *Pelagodroma marina*   47
Distinctive brown and grey pattern above; white face, dusky eye
patch; white underbody and underwing-coverts; legs long, webs
yellow.   Map 98.

10 **WHITE-THROATED STORM-PETREL**   48
Nesofregetta fulginosa
 a Sooty-black above; narrow white rump patch; tail deeply forked;
white underparts variable; broad sooty breast band or dark streaking
on throat; underwing greyish; legs long.   Map 101.

 b Swimming.

Plate 14   **STORM-PETRELS and DIVING-PETRELS**

Diving-petrels are small, stubby oceanic birds; flight is whirring and close above the sea, with frequent dives below the surface.

Plate 15   **TROPIC-BIRDS**

Unmistakable white-looking oceanic birds, with long streaming tail-feathers. Flight strong and steady at some height above the sea. All swim with their tails cocked.

1 RED-BILLED TROPIC-BIRD *Phaethon aethereus*   page 57
  a Adult above. Black band over and beyond eye; upperparts finely barred black; bill coral red.   Map 119.

  b Adult below. Legs dull yellow, feet black; webs black.

  c Immature above. Upperparts barred black; indistinct band through eye; bill yellow; tail streamers absent or short.

2 RED-TAILED TROPIC-BIRD *Phaethon rubricauda*   57
  a Adult. Black crescent before and over eye; totally white upperparts; bill usually orange-red; legs blue; tail streamers very long, deep red. Map 120.

  b Immature. Upperparts thickly barred; indistinct eye stripe; bill black; tail streamers absent or short.

  c Adult in rosy plumage.

  d Adult swimming.

3 WHITE-TAILED TROPIC-BIRD *Phaethon lepturus lepturus*   57
  a Adult. Black crescent over and beyond eye; upperparts white with black band across upperwings; bill yellow; tail streamers very long, white.   Map 121.

  b Immature. Upperparts more lightly barred; dark eye stripe; bill yellow; tail streamers absent or short.

  c **Christmas Tropic-bird** *Phaethon l. fulvus*   57
  Adult. Sub-species of 3a distinguished by golden tinted plumage. Breeds only on Christmas I., Indian Ocean; limited range.

Plate 16   **PELICANS**

Very large inshore birds of the tropics, with unmistakable pouched bill.

1 DALMATIAN PELICAN *Pelecanus crispus*   page 61
  a Adult breeding. Grey bill; pouch orange; legs lead-grey. Yellow on breast absent in winter.   Map 125.

  b Immature. Greyish-brown, wings paler; pouch yellowish.

  c In flight below. Black tips of primaries only visible; compare 2c.

2 WHITE PELICAN *Pelecanus onocrotalus*   59
  a Adult. Grey bill; pouch yellow; legs pink. Sometimes shows rosy tint on white feathers.   Map 122.

  b Immature. Upperparts, neck and wings brown; underparts whitish; bill dull greyish-blue.

  c In flight below. Black primaries and secondaries very evident; legs pink.

3 PINK-BACKED PELICAN *Pelecanus rufescens*   60
  Adult. Overall plumage similar but a little greyer than 2a, pink tints showing; bill pale yellow; pouch flesh-colour; legs pale flesh-colour.   Map 123.

4 GREY PELICAN *Pelecanus philippensis*   60
  Adult. Overall plumage grey, paler below; bill pink; pouch purple; legs dark brown.   Map 124.

Plate 17   **PELICANS**

1 **AUSTRALIAN PELICAN** *Pelecanus conspicillatus*   page 61
   Adult. Blue sides to bill; pouch flesh colour; legs slate-blue; feathering on face distinctive; black tail-band and rump patch.   Map 126.

2 **AMERICAN WHITE PELICAN** *Pelecanus erythrorhynchus*   61
 a Adult breeding. White with black wing quills; crest on back of head;
   yellow on breast and wing-coverts; bill and pouch orange; legs
   orange; horny knob on bill.   Map 127.

 b Immature. Similar to adults in winter plumage.

 c Adult winter in flight. Horn on bill absent.

3 **BROWN PELICAN** *Pelecanus occidentalis*   62
 a Adult breeding. Reddish-brown neck, white band down sides of neck.
   Map 128.

 b Adult winter. White head and neck.

 c Immature. Brown on back, underparts white.

 d Adult in flight. Legs slate-black.

 e Diving.

4 **CHILEAN PELICAN** *Pelecanus thagus*   63
   Adult breeding. Similar but much larger than 3a; underparts greyish-
   brown streaked white; yellow feather tuft on foreneck.   Map 129.

Plate 18   **GANNETS and BOOBIES**

Large offshore birds, cigar-shaped, with long narrow wings and long dagger-shaped bills.

1 NORTHERN GANNET *Sula bassana*   page 65
a Adult.   Map 130.

b Adult with gular stripe.

c Immature in flight. Upperparts greyish-brown, white speckling; underparts white, brown speckling.

d Sub-adult.

e Adult in flight. Primaries only blackish-brown; tail white.

f Juvenile in flight

2 CAPE GANNET *Sula capensis*   66
a Adult.   Map 131.

b Adult with gular stripe.

c In flight. Primaries, secondaries and all tail feathers brown.

3 AUSTRALIAN GANNET *Sula serrator*   66
a Adult.   Map 132.

b Adult in flight. Tail: central feathers blackish-brown, outer feathers white; primaries and secondaries blackish-brown.

c Immature diving.

4 BLUE-FACED or MASKED BOOBY *Sula dactylatra*   67
a Adult.   Form with legs blue, bill blue-grey.   Map 135.

b Adult. Form with legs orange; bill yellow.

c In flight. Primary, secondaries and tail chocolate-brown.

d Juvenile.

e Sub-adult.

Plate 19 **BOOBIES**

1 RED-FOOTED BOOBY *Sula sula* page 68

  a Adult, white phase. Mainly white, wing quills blackish-brown; tail white; legs coral red; bill blue, base pink, black stripe below lower mandible. Eye ring and skin around eye bright blue. Map 136.

  b Intermediate phase. Variable, but red legs are diagnostic.

  c Intermediate phase in flight.

  d Adult, white phase in flight.

  e Brown phase, diving.

  f Juvenile. Legs greenish-yellow; bill dark.

2 ABBOTT'S BOOBY *Sula abbotti* 67

  a Adult female. Black thigh patches on underbody; black skin around eye conspicuous; bill: male blue-grey, female rosy; broad black tips. Breeds only on Christmas I., Indian Ocean; limited range.

  b Adult above. Upperwing-coverts show white speckling.

  c Adult in flight below. Black thigh patch.

3 PERUVIAN BOOBY *Sula variegata* 67

  a Adult. Bill blue; legs bluish-black. Map 134.

  b Adult in flight.

4 BLUE-FOOTED BOOBY *Sula nebouxii* 66

  a Adult. Bright blue legs; blue bill; brown tail. Map 133.

  b Adult in flight.

5 BROWN BOOBY *Sula leucogaster* 68

  a Adult. Map 137.

  b Variable colours of bills and legs; chocolate-brown upperparts.

  c With grey on head.

  d Adult above, in flight.

  e Adult below, in flight. Clear cut line between brown breast and white underparts.

  f Immature below. Dark underneath.

Plate 20 CORMORANTS

Long-necked inshore birds often seen perched on buoys with wings extended to
dry, or swimming and diving from the surface.

1 COMMON CORMORANT *Phalacrocorax carbo carbo* page 72
  a Adult breeding. Chin, sides of face white; white patch on flanks. See
  also Pl.23. Map 141.

  b Immature in flight.

  c Adult winter in flight. White flank patch absent.

  d Breeding in trees, Far East.

  e Continental Race *Phalacrocorox c. sinensis* 72
  Head and neck whitish; dark band encircles throat patch. Map 142.

2 WHITE-NECKED CORMORANT *Phalacrocorax lucidus* 72
  a Adult. Top of head, back of neck and upperparts black, upperwings
  with bronze tint; face, front of neck and breast white; white patch on
  flanks evident in breeding plumage. Map 143.

  b In flight.

3 BANK CORMORANT *Phalacrocorax neglectus* 73
  a Adult. Map 147.

  b In flight. White patch above rump.

4 JAPANESE CORMORANT *Phalacrocorax capillatus* 73
  a Adult breeding. White filo plumes on head and neck; white feathers
  extend over lower mandible; compare 1a. Map 148.

  b Immature.

5 CAPE CORMORANT *Phalacrocorax capensis* 73
  a Adult. Skin on face and throat yellow. Smaller than 2a and 3a. Map
  145.

  b In flight.

6 SOCOTRA CORMORANT *Phalacrocorax nigrogularis* 73
  Very large; entirely dark; wing-coverts with bronze tint. Map 146.

7 FLIGHTLESS CORMORANT *Nannopterum harrisi* 79
  Outsize; wings greatly reduced. Confined to Galapagos Is.

Plate 21 CORMORANTS

1 DOUBLE-CRESTED CORMORANT page 71
Phalacrocorax auritus
a Adult breeding. Crest each side of head; naked skin on throat orange. Map 138.

b Immature.

c Submerged. Adult breeding with white on crest.

2 BIGUA CORMORANT *Phalacrocorax olivaceus* 72
a Adult breeding. White tuft of feathers each side of head; naked skin on face and throat yellow; tail noticeably long. Map 139.

b Immature.

3 RED-FACED CORMORANT *Phalacrocorax urile* 74
a Adult breeding. Tufts on crown and nape; forehead bare; skin forehead and face red; bill blue. Map 152.

b Immature.

c Adult. White patch on flank in breeding plumage.

4 PELAGIC CORMORANT *Phalacrocorax pelagicus* 74
a Adult breeding. Smaller but similar to 3a; large white patch on flank; bill very slender, blackish-brown. Map 151.

b Immature.

c Adult in flight.

5 SHAG or GREEN CORMORANT *Phalacrocorax aristotelis* 74
a Adult breeding. Crest on crown noticeable; naked skin around bill yellow. Map 150.

b Immature.

6 BRANDT'S CORMORANT *Phalacrocorax penicillatus* 74
a Very large; white hair-like plumes on sides of face and back; naked skin of face and throat blue. Throat fawn-coloured. Map 149.

b Immature.

7 RED-LEGGED CORMORANT *Phalacrocorax gaimardi* 76
a Adult. White patch on side of neck; bright red legs noticeable; bright yellow bill. Map 159.

b Immature. White patches on sides of neck.

Plate 22 CORMORANTS

Plate 23   **CORMORANTS**

1 JAVANESE CORMORANT *Halieter niger*   page 79
  a Adult breeding. Scapulars greyish; naked skin throat and face black;
    legs black.   Map 165.

  b Winter.

2 PIGMY CORMORANT *Halietor pygmaeus*   79
  a Adult breeding. Head and neck brown, scapulars and wing-coverts
    greyish.   Map 166.

  b Adult winter.

  c In flight.

  d Immature.

3 INDIAN CORMORANT *Phalacrocorax fuscicollis*   72
  a Adult breeding. Tuft of white feathers at side of head; naked skin of
    face green.   Map 144.

  b Immature.

4 COMMON CORMORANT *Phalacrocorax carbo carbo*   72
    Adult winter for size comparison. See also Pl.20.   Map 141.

5 LITTLE PIED CORMORANT *Phalacrocorax melanoleucus*   78
  a Adult. White throat. See also Pl.22.   Map 163.

  b Immature for size comparison.

6 REED CORMORANT *Halietor africanus*   Adult breeding   79
  a Tuft on forehead; long tail; back and wing often very pale; red skin on
    face and pouch.   Map 164.

  b Sub-adult.

  c Immature.

7 LITTLE BLACK CORMORANT *Phalacrocorax sulcirostris*   72
  a Adult breeding. Indistinct white plumes on side of head and
    eye.   Map 140.

  b Immature. Similar to 7a but duller brownish-black; plumes absent.

Plate 24   **FRIGATE-BIRDS**

Large black birds, with long forked tails, usually seen high overhead, in harbours and at sea.

1 CHRISTMAS FRIGATE-BIRD *Fregeta andrewsi*   page 81
  a Adult male. Foreneck and breast back; pouch bright red; bill black. Not mapped. Breeds only on Christmas I., Indian Ocean; limited range.

  b Adult female. Throat black; bill reddish; legs white.

2 LESSER FRIGATE-BIRD *Fregata ariel*   83
  a Adult male. White patches under wings; bill grey; pouch bright red. Map 169.

  b Adult female. Throat black; chestnut collar on hindneck; bill bluish; red under throat; legs red.

3 MAGNIFICENT FRIGATE-BIRD *Fregata magnificens*   83
  a Adult male in courtship display
    Similar to 5a, 5b, but lacks brown band across upperwing-coverts.   Map 167.

  b Adult female. White collar around neck; foreneck and throat dark; underparts white; abdomen and flanks black; bill horn-colour.

4 ASCENSION FRIGATE-BIRD *Fregata aquila*   81
  a Adult male. Black overall; red pouch; red legs. Breeds only on Ascension I.; limited range.

  b Adult female. Black; breast dark brown; legs red.

  c Male and female, very rare form with white breast and abdomen.

5 GREAT FRIGATE-BIRD *Fregata minor*   83
  a Adult male. Red pouch only seen on display.   Map 168.

  b In flight. Brown band across upperwings.

  c Adult female. Throat and foreneck greyish; lower neck, breast and sides white; legs reddish or bluish.

Plate 25   PHALAROPES and SHEATHBILLS

Phalaropes: Small delicate waders, breeding in the high tundra but wintering in flocks at sea.

Sheathbills: White, pigeon-like birds, confined to sub-antarctica; usually inshore but also on ice-floes.

1 WILSON'S PHALAROPE *Steganopus tricolor*   page 85
  a Adult winter. No white wing bar.   Map 171.

  b Adult winter. Long needle-like bill.

  c Adult male breeding.

  d Adult female breeding. Black stripe eye to side of neck; chestnut stripe on side of back.

2 GREY PHALAROPE *Phalaropus fulicarius*   85
  a Adult winter. White wing bar; bill much shorter than 1a.   Map 170.

  b Adult winter. Dark stripe through eye; patch on cheek; bill yellow, tip black.

  c Adult male breeding.

  d Adult female breeding. Richer colour than males; legs yellowish.

3 RED-NECKED PHALAROPE *Lobipes lobatus*   85
  a Adult winter. White wing bar conspicuous.   Map 172.

  b Adult winter. Dark stripe through eye; patch on cheek; upperparts darker than 2b, more streaked; bill finger than 2b, bluish-grey.

  c Adult male breeding.

  d Adult female breeding. Chin and throat white; rufous band down sides and front of neck.

4 YELLOW-BILLED SHEATHBILL *Chionis alba*   87
  Bill pinkish-yellow, tip black; legs black.   Map 173.

5 BLACK-BILLED SHEATHBILL *Chionis minor*   87
  Bill black; legs flesh-colour.   Map 174.

Plate 26   SKUAS

Migratory hawk-like birds; flight high and swift, harrying other sea-birds for food. White flash on wings.

1 ARCTIC SKUA *Stercorarius parasiticus*   page 90
 a Adult, dark phase. Sharply pointed protruding tail feathers; tail wedge-shaped. Map 179.

 b Adult, pale phase. Dark top of head, yellow sides and neck, white patch on primaries.

 c Adult, intermediate phase. Chasing an immature Ivory Gull.

2 POMARINE SKUA *Stercorarius pomarinus*   90
 a Adult, dark phase. Blunt-twisted protruding tail feathers; tail wedge-shaped. Map 178.

 b Adult, pale phase. Dark band on breast; flanks dusky.

3 LONG-TAILED SKUA *Stercorarius longicaudus*   91
 a Adult. Smaller, paler above than other skuas; very long pointed central tail feathers. Map 180.

4 Immature of Arctic, Pomarine and Long-tailed Skua; but Long-tailed Skua has paler upperparts and greyish-white slightly barred under-parts. Central tail feathers undeveloped.

5 GREAT SKUA (Southern Skua in Southern Hemisphere)   90
 Catharacta skua
 Adult below. Large, stoutly built; white patches on wings; bill stout. Maps 175 and 176.

6 McCORMICK'S SKUA *Catharacta maccormicki*   90
 Paler and smaller than 5. Forehead, sides of head and underparts pale brown. Map 177.

Plate 27   GULLS

Inshore birds with white underparts and grey or black upperwings and square tails; stance upright. Immatures speckled brown (see also Pl.40). For gulls in flight see Pls. 34–40.

1 PACIFIC GULL *Larus pacificus*   page 93
   Adult. Large bill; black tail band. See also Pls.34, 40.   Map 181.

2 GREAT BLACK-BACKED GULL *Larus marinus*   99
 a Adult. Large; pink legs. See also Pls.34, 40.   Map 201.

 b 2nd year.

3 LESSER BLACK-BACKED GULL *Larus fuscus fuscus*   97
 a Adult. Scandinavian race. Bright yellow legs. See also Pls.34,
    40.   Map 195.

 b *Larus fuscus graellsii*   97
    Adult. British race. Paler on back; yellow legs. See also Pls.35, 40.
    Map 196.

  c 2nd year, *Larus fuscus graellsii*

4 WESTERN GULL *Larus occidentalis*   98
   Adult. Slate-grey back; pinkish legs. See also Pl.34.   Map 198.

5 SLATY-BACKED GULL *Larus schistisagus*   98
   Adult. Dark-grey back; pink legs. See also Pl.34.   Map 200.

6 JAPANESE GULL *Larus crassirostris*   96
   Adult. Black band on yellow bill, tip red; pale yellow legs; black band
   on tail. See also Pl.34.   Map 189.

7 SOUTHERN BLACK-BACKED GULL *Larus dominicanus*   98
   Adult. Greenish-yellow legs; white tail. See also Pls.34, 40.   Map
   199.

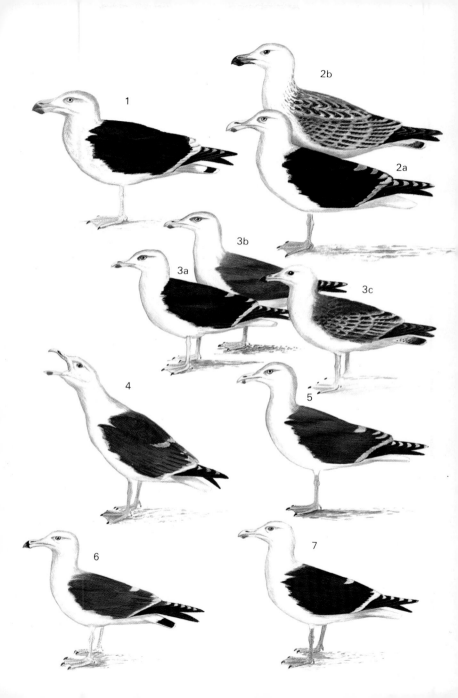

1 HERRING GULL *Larus argentatus*   page 97

a Adult. Legs pinkish flesh-colour. See also Pls. 35, 40.   Map 193.

b Adult. Upperparts slightly darker than 1a; legs yellow.

c Immature 1st winter. Bill black.

d Immature 2nd winter. Bill dull yellow, tip black; black tail band.

2 THAYER'S GULL *Larus thayeri*   97

Adult. Pinkish legs; paler wing-tips than 1a. See also Pl.35.   Map 194.

3 CALIFORNIA GULL *Larus californicus*   98

a Adult. Similar to 1a except legs greenish. See also Pl.35.   Map 197.

b Immature 1st winter. Coarsely mottled brown; bill dull yellow, tip black.

c Immature 2nd winter. Bill dull yellow, tip black; paler than 3b with broad dark tail band.

4 RING-BILLED GULL *Larus delawarensis*   96

Adult summer. Similar but smaller than 1a except bill greenish-yellow, black sub-terminal band; legs greenish-yellow. See also Pls.35, 40.   Map 191.

5 COMMON or MEW GULL *Larus canus*   96

a Adult breeding. Outer primaries black, broad white tips, remaining quills grey, tip white; bills and legs greenish-yellow. See also Pls. 35, 40.   Map 192.

b Adult winter. Grey streaking on head, face and nape.

6 NORTHERN BLACK-HEADED GULL *Larus ridibundus*   103

Adult winter for comparison
See also Pls.31, 32, 37, 40.   Map 216.

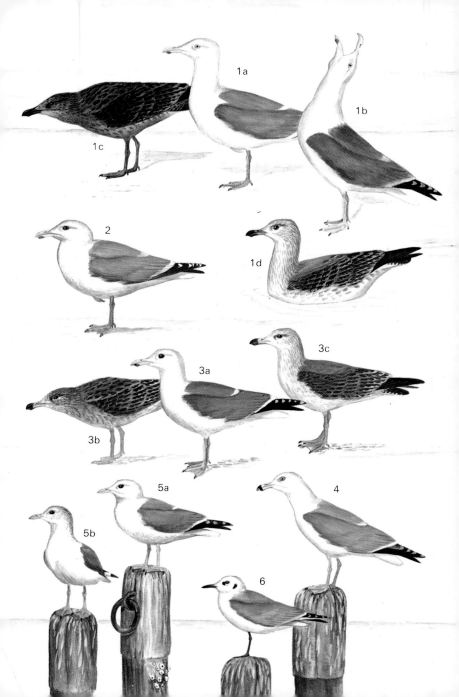

Plate 29 GULLS

1 GLAUCOUS-WINGED GULL *Larus glaucescens* page 99

a Adult breeding. Larger but similar to Herring Gull (Pl.28) except dark grey primaries, white spots, grey secondaries, white tips. See also Pl.35. Map 202.

b Immature 1st winter.

2 ICELAND GULL *Larus leucopterus leucopterus* 99

a Adult breeding. Smaller than 3a; white tips to wing quills; red eye ring; very pink legs. See also Pls.33, 35, 40. Map 204.

b Immature 2nd winter. Almost pure white; bill pale, tip dark; legs dusky pink; tail white.

3 GLAUCOUS GULL *Larus hyperboreus* 99

a Adult breeding. Very large, stoutly built; stout bill; wings broader than 2a; yellow eye-ring; compare 2a. See also Pls.35, 40. Map 203.

b Immature 2nd winter. White over all; bill yellow, tip black.

4 SLENDER-BILLED GULL *Larus genei* 105

a Adult breeding. Rosy tint on underbody; bill slender, red; legs red. See also Pl.37. Map 218.

b Immature. Crown and nape grey; upperparts ashy-brown; bill orange-yellow; legs yellow; lacks any rosy tint.

5 AUDOUIN'S GULL *Larus audouinii* 96

a Adult breeding. Eye-ring red; upperparts very pale grey; bill coral-red, black sub-terminal band; legs dark olive-green. See also Pl.35. Map 190.

b Immature. Greyish-brown upperparts; greyish-white underparts; bill dusky yellow; black sub-terminal band; black tail band.

6 SILVER GULL *Larus novaehollandiae* 102

a Adult breeding. Outer and inner white flashes on primaries in flight; bill, eyelids and legs scarlet. See also Pls.38, 40. Map 212.

b Immature. Buff markings on mantle; secondaries form dark band on wings; bill and legs brownish-black.

c South African form. Adult breeding.

7 BLACK-BILLED or BULLER'S Gull *Larus bulleri* 103

a Adult breeding. Broad white triangle tipped black on forewing shows in flight; bill and legs black. See also Pl.38. Map 213.

b Immature 2nd year. Bill reddish, tip black; legs pinkish.

Plate 30   GULLS

1 MAGELLAN GULL *Gabianus scoresbyi*   page 94
a Adult breeding. White tips to wings; head, neck and underbody pale grey; bill stout, red; legs red; tail white. See also Pl.38.   Map 182.

b Immature. Bill brown, tip black; lower breast, abdomen, upper tail-coverts and tail white, sub-terminal black band.

2 GREY GULL *Larus modestus*   94
a Adult breeding. Head white; white band on trailing edge of wings seen in flight; broad black band on tail. See also Pl.38.   Map 184.

b Adult winter. Head dark greyish-brown.

c Immature.

3 HEERMANN'S GULL *Larus heermanni*   94
a Adult breeding. Head and upper neck white; bill red; legs black; white tip to tail. See also Pl.38.   Map 185.

b Adult winter.

c Immature.

4 GREY-HEADED GULL *Larus cirrocephalus*   101
a Adult breeding. Grey head and throat; white neck; bill and legs crimson-red; in flight large white area on primaries, white fore edge to wing, white mirror on outer primaries. See also Pls.36, 38.   Map 209.

b Immature. Bill yellow, tip black; dark tail band.

5 DUSKY GULL *Larus fuliginosus*   94
Adult breeding. White eyelids; bill red; legs black. See also Pls.33, 38. Not mapped. Breeds only on Galapagos Is.

6 ANDEAN GULL *Larus serranus*   101
a Adult breeding. Rosy tint on breast; bill and legs dark red; broad white wing patches and white leading edge show in flight. See also Pl.36.   Map 210.

b Adult winter. Dusky smudge at eye; forehead and crown streaked white.

c Immature. Sub-terminal black band on tail; bill yellow.

7 SIMEON GULL *Larus belcheri*   95
a Adult breeding. Bill yellow; black band, tip red; tail black, tip white; legs yellow. See also Pls.34, 38.   Map 188.

b Adult winter. Brownish-black head; eyelids white.

c Immature 2nd year. Bill yellow, tip black; legs greyish.

8 FRANKLIN'S GULL *Larus pipixcan*   102
Adult winter. For comparison. See also Pls.31, 36.   Map 211.

Plate 31   **GULLS**

1 NORTHERN BLACK-HEADED GULL *Larus ridibundus*   page 103
a Adult breeding. Head coffee-brown; white eye-ring; bill and legs deep red. See also Pls.28, 32, 37, 40.   Map 216.

b Juvenile. Bill yellow, tip black.

c Immature 1st winter. Bill yellow, tip black; black band on tail.

d Sub-adult 1st summer. Bill dull reddish-black; black band on tail.

e Adult winter. Dusky patch behind eye.

2 PATAGONIAN BLACK-HEADED GULL   103
Larus maculipennis
a Adult breeding. Similar to 1a; sometimes shows rosy tint; outer primaries white at ends; bill dark red. See also Pl.36.   Map 215.

b Immature 1st winter.

3 BONAPARTE'S GULL *Larus philadelphia*   104
a Adult breeding. Head black; bill black; legs red. In flight long triangle of white at front edge of wing. See also Pl.36.   Map 217.

b Adult winter. Black patch behind eye.

c Immature. Bill and legs dusky; black sub-terminal band on tail.

4 CHINESE BLACK-HEADED GULL *Larus saundersi*   105
a Adult breeding. Similar to 3a; much white shows on primaries. See also Pl.37.   Map 220.

b Adult winter.

c Immature. Black sub-terminal band on tail.

5 FRANKLIN'S GULL *Larus pipixcan*   102
a Adult breeding. Small, light build; deep hood; white eye rims; in flight, white area between black wing-quills and grey coverts; bill and legs dark red. See also Pls.30, 36.   Map 211.

b Adult winter.

c Immature. Whitish forehead; dusky crown; broad black tail band.

6 LAUGHING GULL *Larus atricilla*   101
a Adult breeding. Head and neck dark greyish-black; in flight white border on trailing edge of wing conspicuous; bill red; legs reddish-brown. See also Pl.36.   Map 207.

b Adult winter. Crown and sides of head mottled; bill blackish.

c Immature. Black sub-terminal band.

d Immature 2nd winter.

7 LITTLE GULL *Larus minutus*   105
Immature. For comparison. See also Pls.32, 37.   Map 219.

Plate 32   GULLS

1 MEDITERRANEAN BLACK-HEADED GULL   page 103
Larus melanocephalus
  a Adult breeding. Entirely pale wing quills, tips white; bill coral red; black sub-terminal band; legs dark red. See also Pl.37.   Map 214.
  b Adult winter. Dark patch behind eye.
  c Immature. Bill and legs dusky; black sub-terminal band on tail.

2 NORTHERN BLACK-HEADED GULL *Larus ridibundus*   103
Adult breeding. Coffee-brown head; outer primaries white, tips black. See also Pls.28, 31, 37, 40.   Map 216.

3 INDIAN BLACK-HEADED GULL *Larus brunnicephalus*   101
  a Adult breeding. Brown hood, blacker at neck; large white patches near tips of black primaries. See also Pl.37.   Map 208.
  b Adult winter. White head, dark patch behind eye.
  c Immature.Bill yellowish; legs orange; black band on tail.

4 LITTLE GULL *Larus minutus*   105
  a Adult breeding. Very small; entirely pale wing quills, tips white; underwings dark grey; bill and legs deep red. See also Pls.31, 37.   Map 219.
  b Adult winter. Greyish-black patch on crown; bill black.
  c Juvenile. Dark zig-zag pattern across upperwing in flight; black band on tail.
  d 1st winter.

5 GREAT BLACK-HEADED GULL *Larus ichthyaetus*   100
  a Adult breeding. Very large size; primaries white, outer quills, black bars; bill yellow, black band, red tip; legs greenish. See also Pl.37.   Map 206.
  b Adult winter. Head white, streaked; bill yellow, black band.
  c Juvenile. Broad black band on tail; bills and legs greyish.

6 RED SEA BLACK-HEADED or WHITE-EYED GULL   95
Larus leucopthalmus
  a Adult breeding. Deep black hood; eyelids white; sides of breast slate-grey; bill red, tip black. See also Pls.37, 40.   Map 186.
  b Adult winter. Head and neck grizzled.
  c Immature. Rump white; tail black band.

7 ADEN GULL *Larus hemprichi*   95
  a Adult breeding. Coffee-brown hood; white ring around neck; bill greenish, sub-terminal black band, red tip; eyelids white. See also Pls.37, 40. Map 187.
  b Adult winter. Neck brownish-grey.
  c Immature. Brown above; underparts white; tail black.

Plate 33   **GULLS**

1   IVORY GULL   *Pagophila eburnea*   page 94

  a Adult breeding. Entirely white; red eye-ring; bill short, dark at base, shading yellow, reddish tip; legs short, black. See, Pl.39.   Map 183.

  b Immature. Upperparts finely speckled black; black band on tail.

2   ICELAND GULL   *Larus leucopterus leucopteras*   99

  Immature 2nd year. Compare 1a. See also Pls.29, 35, 40.   Map 204.

3   COMMON KITTIWAKE   *Rissa tridactyla*   106

  a Adult breeding. Lightly built, black wing tips; slender greenish-yellow bill; dark legs. See also Pl.39.   Map 223.

  b Immature. Dark band at back of neck; bill black; dark diagonal band across upperwings; black band on tail; bill black.

4   RED-LEGGED KITTIWAKE   *Rissa brevirostris*   107

  a Adult breeding. Similar to 3a; mantle darker; legs red. See also Pl.39.   Map 224.

  b Immature. Broad dark band across nape; upperwings show no diagonal bands; legs dark brown.

5   ROSS'S GULL   *Rhodostethia rosea*   106

  a Adult breeding. Black collar around neck; very short black bill; legs red; rosy tint often absent. See also Pl.39.   Map 222.

  b Adult winter. Black collar indistinct.

  c Immature. Dark band on upperwing-coverts shows in flight; bill black; black band on central tail feathers.

6   SABINE'S GULL   *Xena sabini*   106

  a Adult breeding. Head and throat slate-grey; bill black, tip yellow; tail white, forked. Three triangular patches, grey, black and white show on upperparts in flight. See also Pl.39.   Map 221.

  b Adult winter.

  c Immature. Upperparts ashy-brown; black band across forked tail.

7   SWALLOW-TAILED GULL   *Creagrus furcatus*   107

  a Adult breeding. White patch on forehead; bill dark greenish, tip pale; tail white, forked; legs pinkish-red; white triangular patch on upperwings in flight; very large eyes. See also Pl.39. Breeds only on Galapagos Is.

  b Immature. Mottled brown and white above; black band across tail.

8   DUSKY GULL   *Larus fuliginosus*   94

  Immature. All dark brown; compare 7b. See also Pls.30, 38. Breeds only on Galapagos Is.

Plate 35 ADULT GULLS IN FLIGHT – WINTER PLUMAGE

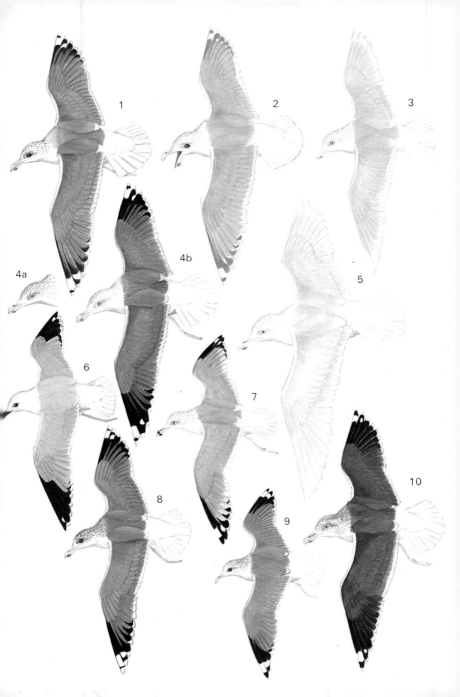

Plate 36   **GULLS IN FLIGHT**

Plate 37   **GULLS IN FLIGHT**

1   NORTHERN BLACK-HEADED GULL *Larus ridibundus*   page 103
   a Breeding head. See also Pls.28, 31, 32, 40.   Map 216.

   b Winter. Conspicuous white leading edge to wings.

2   INDIAN BLACK-HEADED GULL *Larus brunnicephalus*   101
   a Breeding head. See also Pl.32.   Map 208.

   b Winter. Large white patches show on forewing and wing tips.

3   MEDITERRANEAN BLACK-HEADED GULL   103
   Larus melanocephalus
   a Breeding head. See also Pl.32.   Map 214.

   b Winter. Entirely pale upper and underwings.

4   SLENDER-BILLED GULL *Larus genei*   105
   Winter. White leading edge to wings; legs yellow in summer. See
   Pl.29.   Map 218.

5   LITTLE GULL *Larnus minutus*   105
   a Breeding head. See also Pls.31, 32.   Map 219.

   b Winter below. Sooty-grey underwings.

   c Immature above. '**W**' pattern on upperparts; black band on tail.

6   GREAT BLACK-HEADED GULL *Larus ichthyaetus*   100
   a Breeding head. See also Pl.32.   Map 206.

   b Winter. Broad white area on forewing; black band on bill; bill and legs
   greenish-yellow.

7   CHINESE BLACK-HEADED GULL *Larus saundersi*   105
   a Breeding head. See also Pl.31.   Map 220.

   b Winter. White leading edge to wings.

8   RED SEA BLACK-HEADED or WHITE-EYED GULL   95
   Larus leucopthalmus
   a Breeding head. Deep black hood; bill red, tip black. See also Pls.32,
   40.   Map 186.

   b Winter. Sides of breast dusky.

9   ADEN GULL *Larus hemprichi*   95
   a Breeding head. Coffee-brown hood, white band around neck; bill
   greenish, with black band, red tip. See also Pls.32, 40.   Map 187.

   b Winter. Indistinct band around neck; breast brown.

Plate 38   GULLS IN FLIGHT

1 SILVER GULL *Larus novaehollandiae*   page 102
  a Breeding head, South African form. Lavender ring sometimes
     encircles neck. See also Pls.29, 40. Map 212.

  b Winter. Broad white area on forewing.

2 GREY-HEADED GULL *Larus cirrocephalus*   101
     Breeding head. For comparison. See also Pls.30, 36.   Map 209.

3 BLACK-BILLED or BULLER'S GULL *Larus bulleri*   103
     Winter. Bill black; outer primaries white, small black border. See also
     Pl.29.   Map 213.

4 DUSKY GULL *Larus fuliginosus*   94
     Winter. See also Pls.30, 33. Breeds only on Galapagos Is.

5 GREY GULL *Larus modestus*   94
  a Breeding head. See also Pl.30.   Map 184.

  b Winter.

6 MAGELLAN GULL *Gabianus scoresbyi*   94
  a Immature. Head, neck and upper breast brown; broad black sub-
     terminal band on tail; bill and legs dark. See also Pl.30.   Map 182.

  b Winter above. Head dusky; bill and legs red.

  c Summer below. Underwing coverts grey.

7 SIMEON GULL *Larus belcheri*   95
  a Immature head (Pacific). Yellow bill, dark tip. See also Pls.30, 34.
     Map 188.

  b Immature head (Atlantic).

  c Summer head. Yellow bill, black band, red tip.

8 HEERMANN'S GULL *Larus heermanni*   94
  a Breeding head. See also Pl.30.   Map 185.

  b Adult winter. Dark wings and tail.

  c Immature.

Plate 39   **GULLS IN FLIGHT**

1 SABINE'S GULL *Xema sabini*   page 106
  a Adult winter. See also Pl.33.   Map 221.

  b Breeding head.

  c Immature. Ashy-brown above; similar wing pattern to 1a; black band
     on forked tail.

2 ROSS'S GULL *Rhodostethia rosea*   106
  a Adult winter. Wedge tail. See also Pl.33.   Map 222.

  b Breeding head. Also occurs without rosy tint.

  c Immature.

  d Adult breeding.

3 SWALLOW-TAILED GULL *Creagrus furcatus*   107
  a Adult winter. Compare upperwing pattern with 1a; tail forked. See
     also Pl.33. Breeds only on Galapagos Is.

  b Breeding head.

4 RED-LEGGED KITTIWAKE *Rissa brevirostris*   107
  a Adult breeding. Red legs. See also Pl.33.   Map 224.

  b Immature. Black band on neck; no dark bands across wings; bill and
     legs dark.

5 COMMON KITTIWAKE *Rissa tridactyla*   106
  a Adult breeding. See also Pl.33.   Map 223.

  b Immature. Black band on neck; diagonal dark bands over wings; bill
     and legs dark; black band on tail.

  c Adult below. White underwing, black tips.

6 IVORY GULL *Pagophila eburnea*   94
  a Adult breeding. See also Pl.33.   Map 183.

  b Immature.

Plate 40   GULLS IN FLIGHT: 1ST YEAR WINTER

Plate 41   **TERNS**

Sometimes called "sea swallows" for their slender build, dipping flight and deeply forked tails. Mainly inshore birds when not migrating. They hover and dive steeply for food.

1 CASPIAN TERN *Hydroprogne caspia*   page 110
   a Adult breeding. Very large tern; bill very stout, coral red; legs black; tail only slightly forked.   Map 230.

   b Adult winter head.   **c** Immature.   **d** Adult breeding in flight.

2 ARCTIC TERN *Sterna paradisea*   111
   Size comparison. See also Pl.42.   Map 234.

3 ROYAL TERN *Thalasseus maximus*   118
   a Adult breeding. Crested head; white front to cap.   Map 254.

   b As 3a but white front to cap absent.   **c** Winter head.   **d** In flight. Pale underwing.

4 ELEGANT TERN *Thalasseus elegans*   119
   a Adult breeding. Smaller than 3a, upperparts darker; bill long, slender, orange-red.   Map 258.

   b Winter head.

5 CRESTED TERN *Thalasseus bergii*   117
   a Adult breeding. Large; forehead white; crested head; bill greenish-yellow; legs dark.   Map 253.

   b Autumn head.   **c** Winter head.

6 Immatures on *Thalasseus* terns. For varying bill colours, see the individual species.

7 LESSER-CRESTED TERN *Thalasseus bengalensis*   118
   a Adult breeding. Forehead black; bill orange. Compare 5a.   Map 255.

   b Winter head. Compare 5c.

8 CHINESE CRESTED TERN *Thalasseus zimmermanni*   118
   a Adult breeding. Upperparts very pale grey. Note bill.   Map 256.

   b Winter head.

9 CAYENNE TERN *Thalasseus eurygnatha*   118
   a Adult breeding. Similar to 3a except bill long, slender, pale yellow.   Map 257.

   b Winter head.

10 SANDWICH TERN *Thalasseus sandvicensis*   119
   Adult breeding summer head. See also Pl.43.   Map 259.

11 A *Thalasseus* tern with crown feathers erect in display.

Plate 42   **TERNS**

1 ROSEATE TERN *Sterna dougalli*   page 113
  a Adult breeding. Much whiter than 2a, 3a; rosy tint on underparts; long deeply forked tail.   Map 239.
  b Winter head.
  c At rest. Tail projects beyond wings; legs red.

2 COMMON TERN *Sterno hirundo*   111
  a Adult breeding. Bill scarlet, tip black; legs red. See also Pl.43.   Map 233.
  b Winter head, bill mainly black.
  c At rest. Wing tip and tail equal length.

3 ARCTIC TERN *Sterna paradisea*   111
  a Adult breeding. Bill and legs red; legs very short. See also Pl.41. Map 234.
  b Winter head. Bill blackish.
  c At rest. Short red legs; tail a little longer than wing tip.

4 ANTARCTIC or WREATHED TERN *Sterna vittata*   112
  a Adult breeding. White stripe from gape to nape; deeply forked tail; bill and legs red.   Map 235.
  b Winter head.
  c At rest.

5 FORSTER'S TERN *Sterna forsteri*   112
  a Adult breeding. Very pale; bill orange, black tip; deeply forked tail. Map 237.
  b Winter head.
  c At rest.

6 SOUTH AMERICAN TERN *Sterna hirundinacea*   111
  a Adult breeding. Pale upperwings.   Map 232.
  b Winter head.
  c At rest.

7 WHITE-CHEEKED TERN *Sterna repressa*   114
  a Adult breeding. Upperparts darkish-grey; underparts and tail grey; white area below cap.   Map 241.
  b Winter head.
  c At rest.

8 KERGUELEN TERN *Sterna virgata*   112
  Adult breeding. Map 236.
  b Winter head.
  c At rest.

Plate 43   **TERNS**

1 BLACK-FRONTED TERN *Chlidonias albostriata*   page 116
  a Adult breeding. Broad white stripe beneath cap; white rump seen in flight; bill and legs orange-red. **b** Winter head.   Map 248.

2 TRUDEAU'S TERN *Sterna trudeaui*   113
  a Adult breeding. Small, pale pearl-grey; black streak through eye; bill yellow, broad black central band; forked tail grey. **b** Winter head. Map 238.

3 WHITE-FRONTED TERN *Sterna striata*   113
  a Adult breeding. White forehead; black bill; legs reddish-brown. **b** Winter head.   Map 240.

4 BLACK-NAPED TERN *Sterna sumatrana*   114
  a Adult breeding. Very pale; black spot at eye; black band around nape; bill black, tip yellow; legs black. **b** Juvenile head.   Map 242.

5 FAIRY TERN *Sterna nereis*   116
  a Adult breeding. Small, pale; white forehead; bill yellow; tail lightly forked.   Map 247.

6 LITTLE TERN *Sterna albifrons*   117
  a Adult breeding. Smaller than 5; white forehead, black band bill to eye; bill yellow, tip black; legs yellow. Compare Pl.45, No.3. **b** Immature.   Map 252.

7 CHILEAN TERN *Sterna lorata*   117
  a Adult breeding. Very small; white forehead, black band bill to eye; appears slate-grey; white throat; legs brown. Compare 6a.   Map 251.

8   Winter plumage.

9 DAMARA TERN *Sterna balaenarum*   117
  a Adult breeding. Very small; black forehead; black bill. Compare 6a. **b** Winter head.   Map 250.

10 GULL-BILLED TERN *Gelochelidon nilotica*   110
  a Adult breeding. Bill stout, gull-like, black; legs blackish; tail lightly forked, pale grey.   Map 229.   **b** Winter head.   **c** Adult. Long legs; gull-like appearance.   **d** Immature.

11 SANDWICH TERN *Thalasseus sandvicensis*   119
  a Adult breeding. Crest on crown; bill long, slender, black, tip yellow; legs black. See also Pl.41. Map 259.   **b** Winter head.   **c** At rest.   **d** Immature.

12 COMMON TERN *Sterna hirundo*   111
  Immature for size comparison. See also Pl.42.   Map 233.

13 WHITE TERN *Gygis alba*   119
  a Adult breeding.   Map 261.   **b** Immature. Fawn speckled on head, back and wings.   **c** At nest on bare branch.

Plate 44   **TERNS and NODDIES**

Noddies are inshore tropical birds. Brown plumage with whitish caps and notched (not forked, except for Blue-grey Noddy) tails. Flight low over the water, dipping for food.

Plate 45   INLAND TERNS and SKIMMERS

Inland Terns overfly marshes, lagoons and rivers.
Skimmers have same habitat but distinctive feeding flight (usually at dark or on moonlit nights) with lower mandible skimming the surface.

1 INDIAN RIVER TERN *Sterna aurantia*   page 111
  a Adult breeding. Bill stout, yellow; tail very long, deeply forked.   Map 231.

  b Adult winter in flight. Crown grey, forehead white, winter, dusky tip on bill.

2 BLACK-BELLIED TERN *Sterna melanogastra*   114
  a Adult winter. Smaller than 1b; bill slender.   Map 231.

  b Adult breeding. Black abdomen.

3 AMAZON TERN *Sterna superciliaris*   116
  Adult breeding. Very small; white forehead; bill yellow, no black tip; almost identical with Little Tern (Pl.43).   Map 249.

4 LARGE-BILLED TERN *Phaetusa simplex*   110
  a Adult breeding. Bill very stout; tail short, nearly square.   Map 228.

  b Adult winter in flight.

  c Adult breeding in flight.

5 INDIAN SKIMMER *Rynchops albicollis*   123
  a Adult breeding. Back of neck white; upperparts dark brown.   Map 268.

6 Skimmers in flight

7 AFRICAN SKIMMER *Rynchops flavirostris*   123
  Adult breeding. Back of neck brown; upperparts brown.   Map 267.

8 BLACK SKIMMER *Rynchops nigra*   123
  a Immature.   Map 266.

  b Adult breeding. Back of neck black; upperparts black.

9 Skimmers
  Winter head, adults. All have whitish collars in winter.

Plate 46   **AUKS and GUILLEMOTS**

The Auk Family (Auks, Guillemots, Puffins, Auklets and Murrelets – Pls.45–48) are offshore and oceanic, black-and-white looking birds; confined to the northern hemisphere. Short stubby wings, fast whirring flight, diving from the surface to pursue their food under water.

1 COMMON GUILLEMOT or MURRE   *Uria aalge*   page 127
 a Adult breeding. Dark chocolate-brown above; neck long; bill long, pointed. See also Pl.48.   Map 272.

 b Bridled form. White ring at eye; white stripe from eye.

 c Adult winter. Throat and front of neck white.

 d Adult in flight.

2 BRUNNICH'S GUILLEMOT or THICK-BILLED MURRE   126
   Uria lomvia
 a Adult breeding. Black above; bill stouter than 1a, pale streak backwards from base of bill.   Map 271.

 b Adult winter. Black sides of face lower than 1c, otherwise similar.

3 RAZORBILL   *Alca torda*   126
 a Adult breeding. Thick neck; white line bill to eye; white band across stout flattened bill.   Map 270.

 b Adult winter. Cheeks and foreneck white; tail cocked, swimming.

 c Immature 1st winter. Bill smaller; white line and bill band absent.

4 LITTLE AUK or DOVEKIE   *Plautus alle*   125
 a Adult breeding. Very small, stubby; bill very short; dives freely; head, neck, upper breast black.   Map 269.

 b Adult winter. Throat and ear-coverts white; underparts white.

5 BLACK GUILLEMOT   *Cepphus grylle*   127
 a Adult breeding. Map 273.

 b Adult winter.

 c Adult in flight. White underwing-linings.

6 Black and **Pigeon Guillemots**
   Immature plumage. Both species similar.

7 PIGEON GUILLEMOT   *Cepphus columba*   127
 a Adult breeding. Similar to 5a, except black transverse bars on white area.   Map 274.

 b Adult winter.

8 SPECTACLED GUILLEMOT   *Cepphus carbo*   127
 a Adult breeding. Conspicuous white eye-ring.   Map 275.

 b Adult winter.

Plate 47 **PUFFINS and AUKLETS**
See notes on Plate 46

1 ATLANTIC PUFFIN *Fratercula arctica*   pag≥ 130
 a Adult breeding. Large parrot-like bill; face white.   Map 285.

 b Adult winter. Duller bill without sheath; face greyish.

 c Immature. Bill more slender, dark; face darker.

 d Adult in flight.

2 HORNED PUFFIN *Fratercula corniculata*   130
 a Adult breeding. Very triangular yellow-red bill; cheeks white.   Map 286.

 b Adult winter. Reduced bill, blue-red; head dark; indistinct eye patch.

 c Immature. Bill more slender, dark.

3 TUFTED PUFFIN *Lunda cirrhata*   131
 a Adult breeding. Huge bill, greenish-red; long yellow drooping plumes.   Map 287.

 b Adult winter. Bill reduced, greyish-red; head and face dark; plumes absent.

 c Immature. Bill yellowish.

 d Adult in flight.

4 RHINOCEROS AUKLET *Cerorhinca monocerata*   130
 a Adult breeding. White plumes across cheeks; yellow horn on orange bill.   Map 284.

 b Adult winter. Plumes absent; bill yellow.

5 WHISKERED AUKLET *Aethia pygmaea*   130
 a Adult breeding. Very small; groups of drooping white plumes adorn head; bill bright red.   Map 283.

 b Immature. Plumes absent; bill dusky-yellow.

6 CRESTED AUKLET *Aethia cristatella*   130
 a Adult breeding. Dark crest curves forward over red, deeply compressed bill; white plumes behind eye.   Map 283.

 b Adult winter. Crests much reduced; bill yellow.

 c Immature. Slaty-black; crest absent.

7 LEAST AUKLET *Aethia pusilla*   129
Adult breeding. Very small; black above; white throat; white plume behind eye; speckled underparts. See also Pl.48.   Map 282.

Plate 48   **AUKLETS and MURRELETS**
See notes on Plate 46

1 CASSIN'S AUKLET *Ptychoramphus aleuticus*   page 129
  a Adult breeding. Small; dusky; whitish central underparts.   Map
  281. **b** Winter in flight. Light throat.

2 LEAST AUKLET *Aethia pusilla*   129
  a Adult breeding. Very small; black above; white plume behind eye;
  white throat; speckled underparts; bill red. See also Pl.47.   Map
  282. **b** Adult winter. Black bill **c** Winter in flight. Scapulars
  white.

3 MARBLED MURRELET *Brachyramphus marmoratus*   128
  a Adult breeding. Dark brown above, speckled below; whitish
  scapulars.   Map 276. **b** Adult winter. White eye-ring; white side
  of neck; scapulars white; white underparts. **c** Adult in flight,
  winter.

4 KITTLITZ'S MURRELET *Brachyramphus brevirostris*   128
  a Adult breeding. Dusky above, barred brown below; bill stumpy,
  black.   Map 277. **b** Adult winter. Slate-grey above, spotted white;
  white face and collar; white underparts. **c** Winter in flight. Note
  white spots on upperparts.

5 XANTUS'S MURRELET *Brachyramphus hypoleucus*   128
  a Adult breeding. Underparts white. Map 278. **b** Adult in flight
  below. White underwing linings.

6 Xantus's and **Craveri's Murrelets**
  In flight above.

7 CRAVERI'S MURRELET *Brachyramphus craveri*   128
  a Adult breeding. Similar to 5a, 5b, except underwing linings dark.
  Map 278. **b** Adult in flight below. Underwing linings dark.

8 CRESTED MURRELET *Synthliboramphus wumizusume*   129
  Adult breeding. Black crest; white stripe on head below black
  crest.   Map 280.

9 ANCIENT MURRELET *Synthliboramphus antiquus*   128
  a Adult breeding. Upperparts slate-blue; white stripe across crown;
  white sides of neck; bill whitish.   Map 279. **b** Adult winter.
  Throat white; white stripe absent. **c** Adult winter in flight.

10 PARAKEET AUKLET *Cyclorrhynchus psittacula*   129
  a Adult breeding. Bill very stubby, compressed, bright red; white
  plumes across cheeks; chin, throat, foreneck brownish.   Map
  282. **b** Adult winter. White chin, throat. **c** Adult winter in flight
  above. White throat. **d** Adult summer in flight below. Dark throat

11 COMMON GUILLEMOT or MURRE *Uria aalge*   127
  For size comparison. See also Pl.46. Adult winter.   Map 272.

WORLD DISTRIBUTION MAPS

On the following two pages are mapped the 104 principal groups of islands on which seabirds breed. Then follow the distribution maps for individual species. Here **solid red** indicates principal breeding areas and the shaded areas of **light red** the oceanic (non-breeding) distribution. Red lines indicate migratory or dispersal routes. On certain maps figures indicate months of the year in areas where migratory species may be expected. E.g. 6–8=June–August inclusive.

The maps have all been drawn to show the mean distribution areas. They do not take account of occasional sightings of a bird far outside its normal range.

MAP CAPTIONS. The figures following each bird's map number and common name are references: in normal type to its text description, in **bold** type to its colour plate.

Under each map is given: the map number (referred to in the main text and in the index); the bird's common name; and references to its text description (in normal type) and its colour plate (in **bold** type).

BIRDS NOT MAPPED are listed below. These are either species whose status is uncertain or birds whose breeding is confined to a single island and whose oceanic range normally extends at no great distance to seaward.

ROYAL PENGUIN *Eudyptes schlegeli*, p.9 Macquarie I, New Zealand Seas
GALAPAGOS PENGUIN *Spheniscus mendiculus*, p.11 Galapagos Is, tropical East Pacific
HEINROTH'S SHEARWATER *Puffinus heinrothi*, p.34 One specimen only known from coast of New Britain, West S. Pacific
BECK'S PETREL *Pterodroma rostrata becki*, p.37 Two specimens only known off Solomon Is. West S. Pacific
REUNION PETREL *Pterodroma aterrima*, p.37 Reunion I, West Indian Ocean
JAMAICA PETREL *Pterodroma hasitata caribbaea*, p.39 Status in doubt, formerly bred on Jamaica
BERMUDA PETREL *Pterodroma cahow*, p.39 Bermuda Is, West N. Atlantic
CHATHAM ISLAND PETREL *Pterodroma axillaris*, p.40 Chatham I, New Zealand Seas
MACGILLIVRAY'S PETREL *Bulweria macgillivrayi*, p.44 One specimen only known from Fiji Is, S. Pacific
GUADALOUPE STORM-PETREL *Oceanodroma macrodactyla*, p.49 Possibly extinct. Bred on Guadaloupe I, East N. Pacific
CHRISTMAS TROPIC-BIRD *Phaethon lepturus fulvus*, p.57 Christmas I, East Indian Ocean
ABBOTT'S BOOBY *Sula abbotti*, p.67 Christmas I, East Indian Ocean
CAMPBELL ISLAND CORMORANT *Phalacrocorax carunculatus campbelli*, p.76 Campbell I, New Zealand Seas
PITT ISLAND CORMORANT *Phalacrocorax punctatus featherstoni*, p.77 Chatham I, New Zealand Seas
FLIGHTLESS CORMORANT *Nannopterum harrisi*, p.79 Galapagos Is, tropical East Pacific
ASCENSION FRIGATE-BIRD *Fregata aquila*, p.81 Ascension I, S. Atlantic
CHRISTMAS FRIGATE-BIRD *Fregata andrewsi*, p.81 Christmas I, East Indian Ocean
DUSKY GULL *Larus fuliginosus*, p.94 Galapagos Is, tropical East Pacific
MONGOLIAN GULL *Larus relictus*, p.104 Status in Mongolia uncertain
SWALLOW-TAILED GULL *Creagrus furcatus*, p.107 Galapagos Is, tropical East Pacific

Key to principal islands

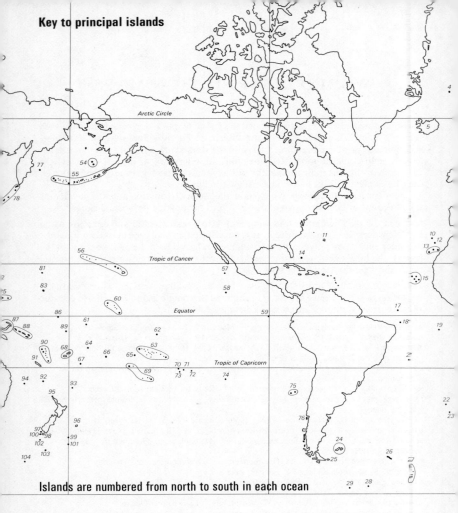

Islands are numbered from north to south in each ocean

Arctic and N. Atlantic
1 Franz Joseph Land
2 Spitzbergen
3 Bear I
4 Jan Mayen
5 Iceland
6 Faroes
7 Shetland Is
8 Balearic Is
9 Azores
10 Madeira
11 Bermuda
12 Salvage Is
13 Canary Is
14 Bahama Is
15 Cape Verde Is
16 Sao Tome I
17 St Paul Rocks

S. Atlantic
18 Fernando de Noronha
19 Ascension I
20 St Helena
21 Trinidad – Martin
   Vas
22 Tristan da Cunha
23 Gough I
24 Falkland Is
25 Staten I
26 South Georgia
27 South Sandwich Is

28 South Orkney Is
29 South Shetland Is
30 Bouvet I

N. Indian Ocean
31 Kuria Muria Is
32 Socotra I
33 Laccadive Is
34 Andaman Is
35 Maldive Is

S. Indian Ocean
36 Seychelles
37 Amirantes
38 Chagos Arch
39 Cocos Keeling Is
40 Christmas I

41 Alegela I
42 Providence I
43 Aldabra Is
44 Comoro Is
45 Cargados Carajos Is
46 Mauritius
47 Reunion I
48 Amsterdam
49 St Paul
50 Crozet Is
51 Marion Is
52 Kerguelen Is
53 Heard Is

N. Pacific east of 180°
54 Pribilof I

230

55	Aleutian Is	69	Austral Is	83	Marshall Is	**New Zealand Seas**
56	Hawaiian Is	70	Oeno I	84	Palau I	95	Three Kings Is
57	Revilla Gigedo I	71	Henderson I	85	Caroline Is	96	Chatham Is
58	Clipperton I	72	Ducie I	86	Gilbert Is	97	Solander I
59	Galapagos Is	73	Pitcairn I	**S. Pacific west of 180°**		98	Stewart I
60	Line Is – Christmas I	74	Easter I	87	New Britain	99	Bounty Is
S. Pacific east of 180°		75	Juan Fernandez Is	88	Solomon Is	100	Snares Is
61	Phoenix Is	76	Mocha I	89	Ellice Is	101	Antipodes Is
62	Marquesas Is	**N. Pacific west of 180°**		90	New Hebrides	102	Aukland Is
63	Tuamotu Arch	77	Kommandu I	91	New Caledonia Is	103	Campbell I
64	Samoan Is	78	Kuril Is	92	Norfolk I	104	Macquarie I
65	Society Is	79	Bonin Is	93	Kermadec Is		
66	Cook Is	80	Volcano I	94	Lord Howe I		
67	Tonga Is	81	Wake I				
68	Fiji Is	82	Mariana Is – Guam				

1. King Penguin, 7.1

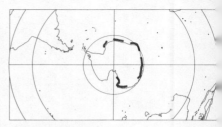

2. Emperor Penguin, 7.1

3. Gentoo Penguin, 7.1

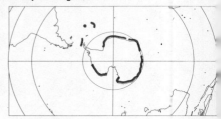

4. Adelie Penguin, 7.1

5. Chin-strap or **Bearded Penguin, 8.1**

6. Fiordland Crested Penguin, 8.2

7. Snares Crested Penguin, 8.2

8. Erect-crested or **Big-crested Penguin, 8.2**

9. Rock-hopper Penguin, 9.2

10. Macaroni Penguin, 9.2

11. Yellow-eyed Penguin, 10.2

12. Little or Blue Penguin, 10.2

13. White-flippered Penguin, 10.2

14. Jackass Penguin, 11.1

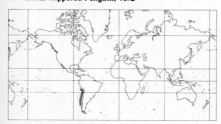

15. Humboldt Penguin, 11.1

16. Magellan Penguin, 11.1

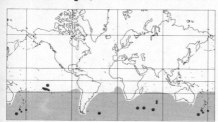

17. Wandering Albatross, 16.3

18. Royal Albatross, 17.3

19. Waved Albatross, 17.4

20. Short-tailed Albatross, 17.3

234

21. Black-footed Albatross, 17.6

22. Laysan Albatross, 18.4

23. Black-browed Albatross, 18.5

24. Buller's Albatross, 19.4

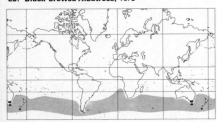

25. Shy or White-capped Albatross, 19.4

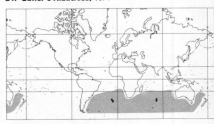

26. Yellow-nosed Albatross, 19.5

27. Grey-headed Albatross, 20.5

28. Sooty Albatross, 20.6

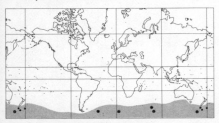

29. Light-mantled Sooty Albatross, 21.6

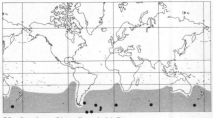

30. Southern Giant Petrel, 24.7

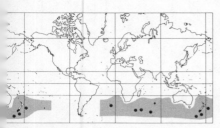

31. Northern Giant Petrel, 24.6,7

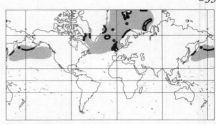

32. Northern Fulmar, 25.11

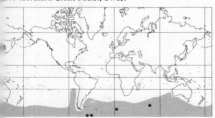

33. Southern Fulmar or Silver-grey Petrel, 25.11

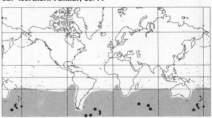

34. Cape Pigeon or Pintado Petrel, 25.11

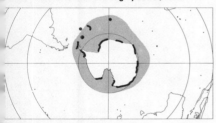

35. Snow Petrel, 25.11

36. Antarctic Petrel, 26.11

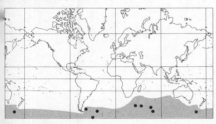

37. Blue Petrel, 26.11

38. Broad-billed Prion, 28

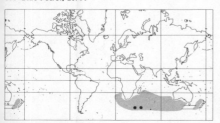

39. Salvin's Prion, 28

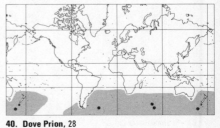

40. Dove Prion, 28

41. Thin-billed Prion, 28

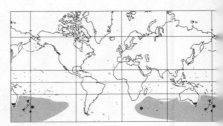

42. Fairy Prion, 28

43. Fulmar Prion or **Thick-billed Prion, 28**

44. Brown Petrel, 28.10

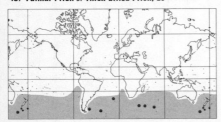

45. White-chinned Petrel, 29.7

46. Parkinson's Petrel, 29.7

47. Westland Petrel, 29.7

48. White-faced or **Streaked Shearwater, 29 8**

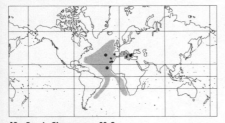

49. Cory's Shearwater, 30.9

50. Pink-footed Shearwater, 30.8

237

51. Pale-footed Shearwater, 30.8

52. Great Shearwater, 31.9

53. Wedge-tailed Shearwater, 31.7

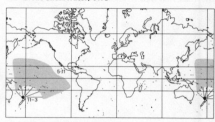

54. Grey-backed Shearwater, 31.8

55. Sooty Shearwater, 31.8

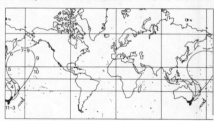

56. Short-tailed Shearwater, 32.8

57. Christmas Shearwater, 32.7

58. Manx Shearwater, 32.9

59. Levantine Shearwater, 33.9

60. Balearic Shearwater, 33.9

61. Townsend's Shearwater, 33

62. Newell's Shearwater, 33

63. Black-vented Shearwater, 33.9

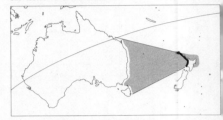

64. Fluttering Shearwater, 33.10

65. Hutton's Shearwater, 33.10

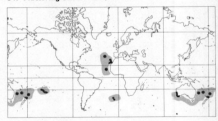

66. Little Shearwater, 33.9

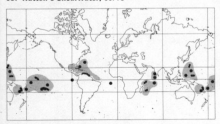

67. Audubon's Shearwater, 34.9

68. Persian Shearwater, 34.10

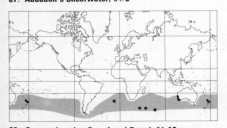

69. Great-winged or Grey-faced Petrel, 34.10

70. White-headed Petrel, 35.11

239

71. Schlegel's Petrel, 35.10

72. Solander's Petrel, 35.12

73. Murphy's Petrel, 35.12

74. Peale's Petrel or Mottled Petrel, 36.12

75. Kerguelen Petrel, 36.11

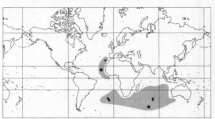

76. Soft-plumaged Petrel, 36.10

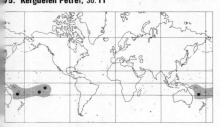

77. Tahiti Petrel, 37.12

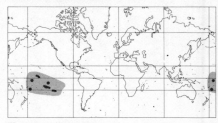

78. Phoenix Petrel, 37.12

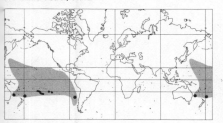

79. Kermadec Petrel, 37.12

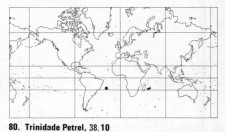

80. Trinidade Petrel, 38.10

240

81. Herald Petrel, 38.10

82. Black-capped Petrel, 39.10

83. Hawaiian Petrel, 39.12

84. White-necked Petrel, 38.11

85. Barau's Petrel, 39.10

86. Bonin Petrel, 40.12

87. Black-winged Petrel, 40.12

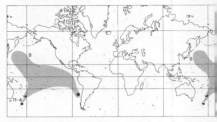

88. Cook's Petrel, 42.12

89. Stejneger's Petrel, 42.12

90. Pycroft's Petrel, 43

241

91. Gould's Petrel, 43.12

92. Collared Petrel, 43.12

93. Jouanin's Petrel, 43.9

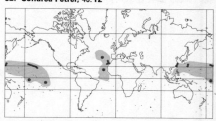

94. Bulwer's Petrel, 44.9

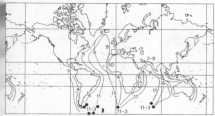

95. Wilson's Storm-petrel, 46.13

96. Elliot's Storm-petrel, 46.13

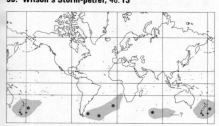

97. Grey-backed Storm-petrel, 46.14

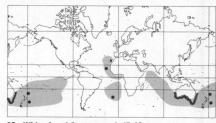

98. White-faced Storm-petrel, 47.13

99. White-bellied Storm-petrel, 47.13

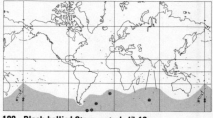

100. Black-bellied Storm-petrel, 47.13

101. White-throated Storm-petrel, 48.13

102. British Storm-petrel, 48.13

103. Least Storm-petrel, 48.14

104. Galapagos Storm-petrel, 48.13

105. Madeiran Storm-petrel, 49.13

106. Leach's Storm-petrel, 49.13

107. Swinhoe's Storm-petrel, 50.14

108. Tristram's Storm-petrel, 50.14

109. Markham's Storm-petrel, 50.14

110. Matsudaira's Storm-petrel, 50.14

11. Black Storm-petrel, 51.14

112. Ashy Storm-petrel, 51.14

113. Hornby's Storm-petrel, 51.14

114. Fork-tailed Storm-petrel, 51.14

15. Peruvian Diving-petrel, 54.14

116. Magellan Diving-petrel, 54.14

117. Georgian Diving-petrel, 54.14

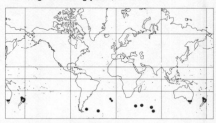

118. Common Diving-petrel, 54.14

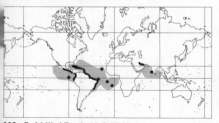

119. Red-billed Tropic-bird, 57.15

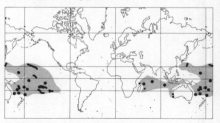

120. Red-tailed Tropic-bird, 57.15

244

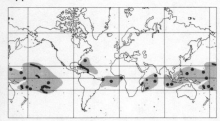

121. White-tailed Tropic-bird, 57.15

122. White Pelican, 59.16

123. Pink-backed Pelican, 60.16

124. Grey Pelican, 60.16

125. Dalmatian Pelican, 61.16

126. Australian Pelican, 61.17

127. American White Pelican, 61.17

128. Brown Pelican, 62.17

129. Chilean Pelican, 63.17

130. Northern Gannet, 65.18

131. Cape Gannet, 66.18

132. Australian Gannet, 66.18

133. Blue-footed Booby, 66.19

134. Peruvian Booby, 67.19

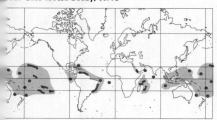

135. Blue-faced or **Masked Booby**, 67.18

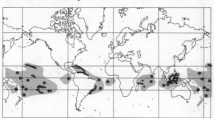

136. Red-footed Booby, 68.19

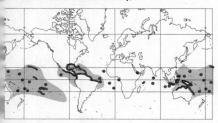

137. Brown Booby, 68.19

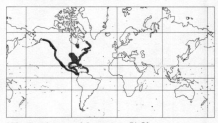

138. Double-crested Cormorant, 71.21

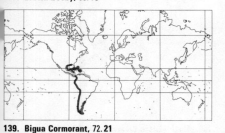

139. Bigua Cormorant, 72.21

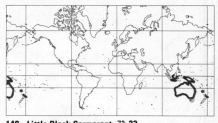

140. Little Black Cormorant, 72.23

246

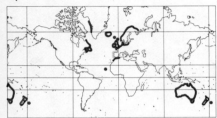

141. Common Cormorant, 72. **20,23**

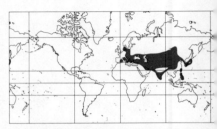

142. Common Cormorant (Continental race), 72. **20**

143. White-necked Cormorant, 72. **20**

144. Indian Cormorant, 72. **23**

145. Cape Cormorant, 73. **20**

146. Socotra Cormorant, 73. **20**

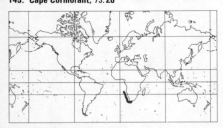

147. Bank Cormorant, 73. **20**

148. Japanese Cormorant, 73. **20**

149. Brandt's Cormorant, 74. **21**

150. Shag or **Green Cormorant,** 74. **21**

151. Pelagic Cormorant, 74.21

152. Red-faced Cormorant, 74.21

153. Magellan Cormorant, 75.22

154. Guanay Cormorant, 75.22

155. Pied Cormorant, 75.22

156. Black-faced Cormorant, 75.22

157. Rough-faced Cormorant, 75.22

158. Kerguelen Cormorant, 76

159. Red-legged Cormorant, 76.21

160. Spotted Cormorant, 77.22

248

161. Blue-eyed Cormorant, 77.22

162. King Cormorant, 78

163. Little Pied Cormorant, 78.22,23

164. Reed Cormorant, 79.23

165. Javanese Cormorant, 79.23

166. Pigmy Cormorant, 79.23

167. Magnificent Frigate-bird, 83.24

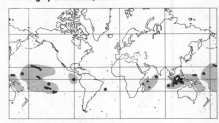

168. Great Frigate-bird, 83.24

169. Lesser Frigate-bird, 83.24

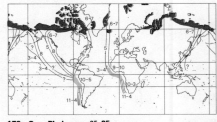

170. Grey Phalarope, 85.25

249

171. Wilson's Phalarope, 85.25

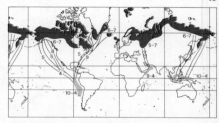

172. Red-necked Phalarope, 85.25

173. Yellow-billed Sheathbill, 87.25

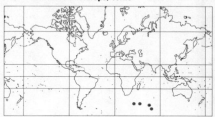

174. Black-billed Sheathbill, 87.25

175. Great Skua, 89.26

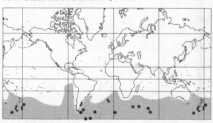

176. Southern Skua, 90.26

177. McCormick's Skua, 90.26

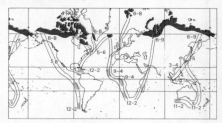

178. Pomarine Skua, 90.26

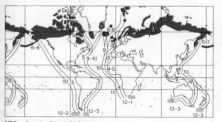

179. Arctic Skua, 90.26

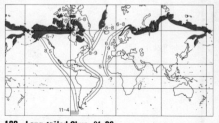

180. Long-tailed Skua, 91.26

181. Pacific Gull, 93. 27,34,40

182. Magellan Gull, 94. 30,38

183. Ivory Gull, 94. 33,39

184. Grey Gull, 94. 30,38

185. Heermann's Gull, 94. 30,38

186. Red Sea Black-headed or White-eyed Gull, 95. 32,37,40

187. Aden Gull, 95. 32,37,40

188. Simeon Gull, 95. 30,34,38

189. Japanese Gull, 96. 27,34

190. Audouin's Gull, 96. 29,35

251

191. Ring-billed Gull, 96.**28,35,40**

192. Common or **Mew Gull,** 96.**28,35,40**

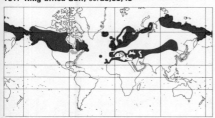

193. Herring Gull, 97.**28,35,40**

194. Thayer's Gull, 97.**28,35**

195. Lesser Black-backed Gull (Scandinavian race), 197.**27,34,40**

196. Lesser Black-backed Gull (British race), 97.**27,35,40**

197. California Gull, 98.**28,35**

198. Western Gull, 98.**27,34**

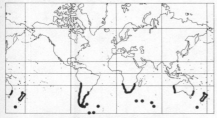

199. Southern Black-backed Gull, 98.**27,34,40**

200. Slaty-backed Gull, 98.**27,34**

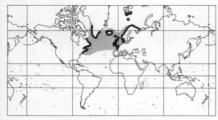

201. Great Black-backed Gull, 99.27,34,40

202. Glaucous-winged Gull, 99.29,35

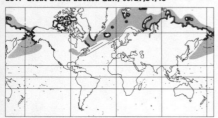

203. Glaucous Gull, 99.29,35,40

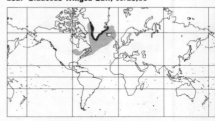

204. Iceland Gull, 99.29,33,35,40

205. Kumlien's Gull, 100

206. Great Black-headed Gull, 100.32,37

207. Laughing Gull, 101.31,36

208. Indian Black-headed Gull, 101.32,37

209. Grey-headed Gull, 101.30,36,38

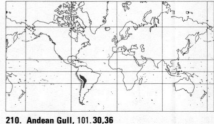

210. Andean Gull, 101.30,36

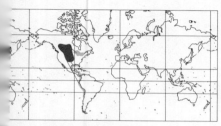

211. Franklin's Gull, 102.**30,31,36**

212. Silver Gull, 102.**29,38,40**

213. Black-billed or **Buller's Gull**, 103.**29,38**

214. Mediterranean Black-headed Gull, 103.**32,37**

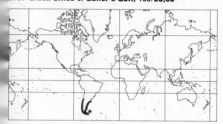

215. Patagonian Black-headed Gull, 103.**31,36**

216. Northern Black-headed Gull, 103.**28,31,32,37,40**

217. Bonaparte's Gull, 104.**31,36**

218. Slender-billed Gull, 105.**29,37**

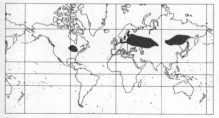

219. Little Gull, 105.**31,32,37**

220. Chinese Black-headed Gull, 105.**31,37**

254

221. Sabine's Gull, 106.**33,39**

222. Ross's Gull, 106.**33,39**

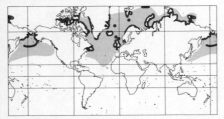

223. Common Kittiwake, 106.**33,39**

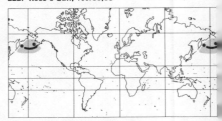

224. Red-legged Kittiwake, 107.**33,39**

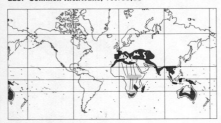

225. Whiskered Tern, 109.**44**

226. White-winged Black Tern, 109.**44**

227. Black Tern, 110.**44**

228. Large-billed Tern, 110.**45**

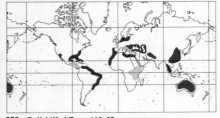

229. Gull-billed Tern, 110.**43**

230. Caspian Tern, 110.**41**

231. Indian River Tern, 111.45
    Black-bellied Tern, 114.45

232. South American Tern, 111.42

233. Common Tern, 111.42,43

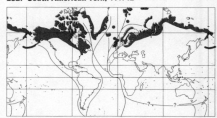

234. Arctic Tern, 111.41,42

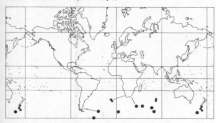

235. Antarctic or Wreathed Tern, 112.42

236. Kerguelen Tern, 112.42

237. Forster's Tern, 112.42

238. Trudeau's Tern, 113.43

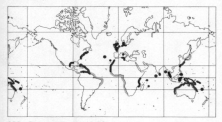

239. Roseate Tern, 113.42

240. White-fronted Tern, 113.43

241. White-cheeked Tern, 114.42

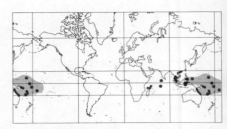

242. Black-naped Tern, 114.43

243. Aleutian Tern, 114.44

244. Spectacled Tern, 115.44

245. Brown-winged or Bridled Tern, 115.44

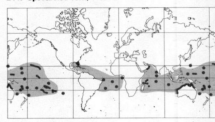

246. Sooty Tern, 115.44

247. Fairy Tern, 116.43

248. Black-fronted Tern, 116.43

249. Amazon Tern, 116.45

250. Damara Tern, 117.43

251. Chilean Tern, 117.43

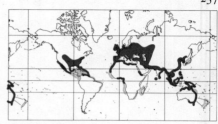

252. Little Tern, 117.43

253. Crested Tern, 117.41

254. Royal Tern, 118.41

255. Lesser-crested Tern, 118.41

256. Chinese Crested Tern, 118.41

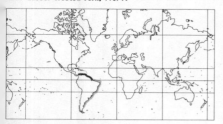

257. Cayenne Tern, 118.41

258. Elegant Tern, 119.41

259. Sandwich Tern, 119.41,43

260. Inca Tern, 119.44

258

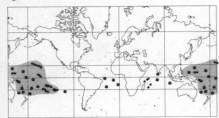

261. White Tern, 119.43

262. Blue-grey Noddy, 120.44

263. Common or **Brown Noddy, 120.44**

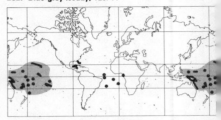

264. White-capped Noddy, 120.44

265. Lesser Noddy, 121.44

266. Black Skimmer, 123.45

267. African Skimmer, 123.45

268. Indian Skimmer, 123.45

269. Little Auk or **Dovekie, 125.46**

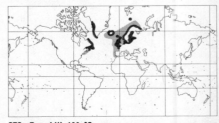

270. Razorbill, 126.46

259

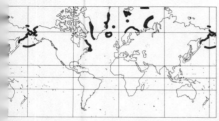

271. Brunnich's Guillemot or Thick-billed Murre, 126.46

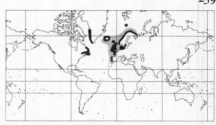

272. Common Guillemot or Murre, 127.46,48

273. Black Guillemot, 127.46

274. Pigeon Guillemot, 127.46

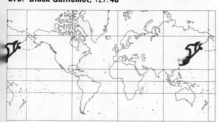

275. Spectacled Guillemot, 127.46

276. Marbled Murrelet, 128.48

277. Kittlitz's Murrelet, 128.48

278. Xantus' and Craveri's Murrelets, 128.48

279. Ancient Murrelet, 128.48

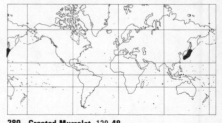

280. Crested Murrelet, 129.48

260

281. Cassin's Auklet, 129.48

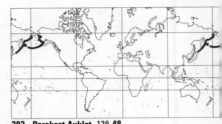

**282. Parakeet Auklet, 129.48
Least Auklet, 129.47,48**

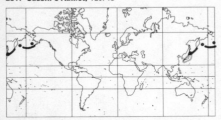

283. Crested Auklet, 129.47

284. Rhinoceros Auklet, 130.47

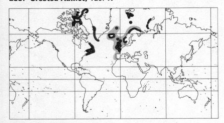

285. Atlantic Puffin, 130.47

286. Horned Puffin, 130.47

287. Tufted Puffin, 131.47

SEABIRDS OF THE BRITISH ISLES

INTRODUCTION

About 200 species of birds nest in the British Isles. Internationally, the most important part of the avifauna is the two-dozen or so breeding seabird species – more, and for many species in greater numbers, than in any other European country.

The reasons for this varied and abundant seabird fauna are not difficult to find. The long coastline provides a great variety of different nesting habitats: rocky cliffs for Guillemots, Razorbills and Kittiwakes, rocky stacks and islands for Shags, Cormorants and storm-petrels, vegetated islands for Puffins, Manx Shearwaters and Great Black-backed Gulls, sand-dunes and beaches for terns, salt-marshes for Black-headed Gulls, coastal moorlands for skuas, and so on.

More important still, the coastal waters are equally varied, being generally shallow (though in the west the deeper waters beyond the Continental Shelf are not that far distant) and rich in fish. Many areas contain abundant populations of small fish such as sand-eels, sprats and the young stages of herrings, which form the main diet of so many British seabirds. These fish are particularly abundant in the surface layers of inshore waters during the summer months, when they are joined by the young stages of several species whose adults spend most of their lives on the sea floor. In winter, the amount of surface living zooplankton, and the fish which prey on it, are considerably reduced, and those seabirds, notably the terns, which catch their food by means of a shallow dive, migrate south to areas where food resources are more reliable.

In general, except for the coastal feeding gulls and terns, the majority of British and Irish seabirds breed most commonly in northern Scotland and western Ireland. The sites of their breeding colonies are determined not only by the availability of suitable nesting sites but also by the availability of rich food resources close inshore. Particularly in the case of the auks, which pursue their prey under water, the colonies are situated frequently on (or on islands just off) major promontories and headlands, where strong tidal currents bring large numbers of surface living fish close inshore.

The geographical position of the British Isles is such that nearly all the seabird species of the temperate eastern North Atlantic breed here; the only ones nesting in similar latitudes in Europe that are absent are the Little Gull and Caspian and Gull-billed Terns. Three species (Leach's Storm-petrel, Great and Arctic Skuas) are confined to northern Scotland, and three more (Red-necked Phalarope, Black Guillemot and Common Gull) are virtually confined to Scotland and Ireland. The remainder breed throughout almost the entire latitudinal range of the British Isles. As mentioned earlier, most tend to be more numerous in the north, the only exceptions being the Manx Shearwater, Lesser Black-backed Gull and Common, Roseate, Little and Sandwich Terns which have their largest colonies in England and Wales rather than Scotland.

A marked feature of seabird breeding populations in the British Isles is that most species have increased during the present century. The few exceptions are the Little Tern, now one of the scarcest of all our seabirds, whose nesting beaches have become increasingly disturbed by man, and three of the auks, the Guillemot, Razorbill and Puffin. Various reasons have been put forward to account for these declines in auk numbers which have been particularly marked at their southernmost colonies; in the early 1970s Puffins in northwest Scotland decreased markedly too.

One important mortality factor, particularly for the Guillemot, has been oil pollution, which kills many thousands of individuals every year. Other more insidious kinds of marine pollution, in the form of various persistent toxic substances used in industry and agriculture and dumped or discharged indiscriminately into the sea, have been recognised in recent years. When more than 12,000 Guillemots were washed ashore dead in the Irish Sea in autumn 1969, several of the bodies examined were found to contain high concentrations of various industrial pollutants, including polychlorinated biphenyls (PCB's) and various toxic metals. While the deaths of the birds could not be attributed with certainty to poisoning (other stress factors such as moult, gales and possible food shortage were also at work), it is possible that these toxic substances are having sublethal (and occasionally lethal) effects on the birds. It is already clear that of all sea areas around the British Isles, the Irish Sea is the most heavily contaminated with toxic materials such as the PCB's and mercury. These materials are highly persistent and can accumulate in fish and seabirds to reach relatively high levels in their body tissues. They reach the Irish Sea from factories in industrialised north-west England through the direct discharge of effluents and from toxic wastes and sewage sludge dumped at sea. The slow rate of exchange of seawater within the partly enclosed Irish Sea does not facilitate the rapid dilution of these stable materials in the infinitely larger water mass of the open Atlantic. Levels of both mercury and PCB's in, for example, Guillemot eggs from some colonies in the Irish Sea average some twenty-five times higher than in similar samples from colonies remote from manufacturing industry, such as those in the Faeroes.

Yet, apart from the Little Tern, the auks and the Roseate Tern (which has slumped from 3500 to 600 pairs in the last few years) most British seabirds have increased over the last 70 years and appear still to be increasing despite increased pollution. Some increases, such as those of the Fulmar, Gannet, Shag and the larger gulls, have been spectacular. Many of the changes appear to have been due in one way or another to man's activities: in the cases of the larger gulls and the Fulmar to the provision of additional sources of food; in the case of the Gannet, and perhaps some other species, to the relaxation of persecution which was persistent and heavy at some colonies until towards the end of the 19th century. On the other hand, in the cases of marked changes among some other seabirds human factors do not seem to have played a major role, and the primary causes are often not known.

Of the 'Primary Seabirds' included in this book, and defined in its Introduction (p. xiii), 25 species nest regularly in the British Isles. These species are all listed in the Table opposite which sets out the type of habitat they occupy for nesting. All are colonial (though the 'colonies' of two species, the Red-necked Phalarope and Black Guillemot, tend to be rather loosely knit), and, as can be seen from the Table, most nest exclusively on the coast, where their distributions are determined primarily by two factors: the availability of suitable and safe places in which to nest, and the proximity of an abundant food supply within the optimum feeding range of the species in question. A few species, however, also nest inland in small numbers, for example Common Tern, Lesser Black-backed Gull, Herring Gull and Cormorant. A few others, for example the Red-necked Phalarope and Common and Black-headed Gulls have exclusively or mainly inland, or at least fresh-water, breeding distributions in the British Isles, though in winter they are wholly marine (absent from the British Isles in the case of the phalarope) or partly marine (the gulls).

Breeding species

STORM-PETRELS

Two species of these our smallest seabirds nest in the British Isles, the British Storm-petrel (p. 48; Pl. 13) and the much rarer and more localised Leach's Storm-petrel (p. 49; Pl. 13). They share a number of common ecological features. Both feed on small planktonic organisms obtained from the surface of the sea as the birds hover just above it. Both are migratory, wintering mainly in the Atlantic in tropical or more southerly latitudes (Storm-petrels ringed at colonies in Britain have been recovered off the coasts of west and south Africa), although there have been a few winter records of both species in British waters. Both choose to nest on remote and usually uninhabited marine islands lacking mammalian predators such as foxes, cats and rats, while to further escape the attention of avian predators, they arrive at and depart from their nesting burrows only during the hours of darkness. Both nest mainly in natural crevices among rocks or in cliff face scree, favourite sites of Storm-petrels being among the boulders of storm beaches (where in such places on Annet, Isles of Scilly, many hundreds attain a nesting density as high as one pair to the square metre) or among the remnants of old drystone walls on islands on which farming was abandoned many years ago (e.g. Skokholm, Pembrokeshire, and in Shetland).

Both species arrive back at their breeding quarters in April, lay single eggs in late May or June after a long period of nocturnal courtship at and over the colony, and have protracted incubation and fledging periods so that the chicks do not fledge until September or October.

The two species are hardly ever seen in any numbers in daylight around British and Irish coasts, and those that are observed are usually off western coasts rather than eastern ones. Periodically, as in 1881, 1891, 1899, 1908, 1917 and 1952, weather 'wrecks' of Leach's Storm-petrels have occurred in late autumn, when large numbers were found close inshore and many others were blown inland in a moribund condition.

Leach's Storm-petrel is one of the most localised of all British breeding birds and is largely restricted to four remote island groups off north-west Scotland: St. Kilda,

	Bare/rocky islands	Islands with soil/vegetation	Mainland seacliffs	Sand dunes	Shingle beaches	Coastal lagoons	Salt marshes	Coastal buildings	Paramaritime moors	Freshwater marshes, lakes
Fulmar	●	O	●					O		
Storm Petrel	●	O								
Leach's Petrel	●	O								
Manx Shearwater		●								
Gannet	●	O	O							
Cormorant	●	O	●							O
Shag	●		●							
Razorbill	●		●							
Guillemot	●		●							
Black Guillemot	●		●							
Puffin	O	●	O							
Kittiwake	●		●					O		
Great Black-backed Gull	●	●	O		O				●	O
Lesser Black-backed Gull	O	●	O	O	●				●	O
Herring Gull	●	●	●	●	●	O		O	O	O
Common Gull					O					●
Black-headed Gull				●		●	●			●
Sandwich Tern	O	●		●	●		O			
Common Tern	O	●		●	●	O	O			O
Arctic Tern	●	●		O	O				●	O
Roseate Tern	●	●								
Little Tern					●					
Great Skua									●	
Arctic Skua									●	
Red-necked Phalarope										●

TABLE: Nesting habitats of seabirds in the British Isles. Under each habitat type, ● denotes main habitat(s) of the species, O denotes less important habitats.

the Flannans, Sula Sgeir and North Rona. Being nocturnal the species is extremely difficult to census and the size of the total population, which is probably in excess of 2,000 pairs, can only be guessed at. Small numbers may breed on a few other remote north Scottish islands, for example on Foula (Shetland) and Sule Skerry (Orkney) where eggs have been found occasionally in the past. There are also a few old breeding records from western Ireland, but no positive ones more recently than 1906.

The British Storm-petrel has a much wider breeding distribution – mainly on western marine islands from the Isles of Scilly north to Shetland. As with Leach's Storm-petrel, the inaccessibility of the colonies and the problems of counting a nocturnal species make it impossible to assess the size of the total population, though it must run into tens of thousands. There is some evidence that the predation of adults by Great Black-backed Gulls has caused local population declines at some colonies, for example in the Isles of Scilly and in the Minch.

MANX SHEARWATER

This is a migratory species which, as has been shown by extensive ringing at British colonies, winters mainly off the Atlantic coast of Brazil, which is reached by an extremely rapid migratory passage in September-October. Birds return to the vicinity of their breeding colonies in early spring, some as early as late February, but come ashore only intermittently until breeding begins in earnest in late April. A single egg is laid and there are long incubation and fledging periods, most chicks departing in late August and September having been deserted by their parents about a week beforehand.

Manx Shearwaters (p. 32; Pl. 9) feed mainly on small fish – pilchards are especially important – which they obtain by shallow dives. During the early part of the breeding season off-duty parents may travel considerable distances to feed, those from colonies off the Pembrokeshire coast travelling even as far as the Bay of Biscay.

Most colonies are situated on soil-covered uninhabited islands off western and northern coasts. The birds excavate their own burrows or, more usually, occupy or renovate one excavated in a previous year. Like the two storm-petrels, arrivals and departures from the breeding colonies take place only at night, but even so at many colonies considerable numbers are killed and eaten by Great Black-backed Gulls. The species is, however, seen at sea much more often than the two storm-petrels. Around sunset, large rafts of shearwaters gather on the sea close to their breeding colonies waiting for dusk to fall, while their feeding movements often bring them close inshore where they can be watched passing by from suitable headlands in various parts of western Britain and Ireland.

Some colonies are very large – in all there are probably 130,000 breeding pairs on the Pembrokeshire islands of Skokholm and Skomer – but no assessment has been made of the total British population. Nor is it known whether the population as a whole is increasing or decreasing, though some smaller Scottish colonies and the one on Annet, Isles of Scilly, are known to have declined during the present century.

FULMAR

During the last 100 years and more the numbers of **Fulmars** (p. 25; Pl. 11) breeding in the British Isles, indeed in the North Atlantic generally, have increased enormously. Until 1878 the only British breeding station was St. Kilda, but in that year Foula (Shetland) was colonised and by the end of the century the species had begun nesting at other sites in Shetland and the Outer Hebrides. Since then it has spread steadily southwards and now, though the main population remains in the north, it breeds on nearly all suitable cliff bound coasts of the British Isles. Nest sites are typically on the higher parts of steep cliffs, often where the ledges have a covering of soil and vegetation.

Like the other petrels, the Fulmar is primarily a plankton feeder and is largely pelagic outside the breeding season. Over the years, fish offal and other waste thrown overboard from trawlers has become an increasingly important source of food for the species, and with the growth of the fishing industry it is this increased food supply which is believed to have enabled the Fulmar to expand its numbers so dramatically.

Although British Fulmars are known to range widely over the North Atlantic outside the breeding season (ringed birds commonly reach Greenland and Newfoundland as well as northwest Europe), the cliffs on which they nest are visited by some birds in nearly all months of the year. Indeed a feature of the species is the numbers of pre-breeders which occupy nest-sites for many hours at a time, and many new sites are prospected by these birds for several years before they actually breed. Fulmars do not lay eggs until they are at least seven years old.

GANNET

By far the greatest proportion of the North Atlantic **Gannet** (p. 65; Pl. 18) population breeds in the British Isles, where the total now numbers well over 100,000 nesting pairs. These are distributed among 14 island and one mainland breeding stations, the largest of which is the St. Kilda group, which at the last count held a total of 52,000 pairs. Four other colonies exceed 10,000 pairs – on Grassholm (Pembrokeshire), Ailsa Craig (Ayrshire), Little Skellig (Co. Kerry) and Bass Rock (East Lothian). Only three contain fewer than 100 pairs – the single mainland and English colony at Bempton Cliffs (Yorkshire) and recently established ones on the Flannans (Outer Hebrides) and Fair Isle (Shetland).

The whole North Atlantic population has undergone a steady growth in numbers during the present century, this growth being attributed to the almost complete cessation of the Gannet's exploitation by man as a source of food; during the 19th century man's persecution reduced the world population by about two-thirds. The only British colony which is still harvested is Sula Sgeir (Outer Hebrides), and here the numbers of young taken are now controlled.

Gannets lay a single egg in April and have long incubation and fledging periods, most chicks leaving the nest in August or September. Although many adults remain in British waters throughout the winter, a number together with juveniles are migratory, most of them spending the first year or two of their life off the coasts of west Africa.

Feeding, weather and migratory movements of Gannets can be seen off all coasts of the British Isles, though they are commonest off headlands on western coasts of Britain and in Ireland (especially during strong north-west winds in autumn) and least common in south-east England

COMMON CORMORANT AND SHAG

Both species are widely distributed on rocky western and northern coasts of Britain and Ireland, though they are much scarcer on eastern and southern ones, particularly in England between Yorkshire and the Isle of Wight. **Cormorant** (p. 72; Pls. 20, 23) colonies tend to be more discrete and localised than **Shags'** (p. 74; Pl. 21), and are usually situated in the open – on the top of rocky islands or on broad ledges high up steep cliffs – whereas Shags usually (though not invariably) choose to nest lower down on cliffs in rock cavities, amidst boulders or in caves. While Shags nest exclusively on the coast, there are single Cormorant colonies a few miles inland in Wales (Merionethshire) and Scotland (Wigtownshire) and there are also a few well inland on islands in lakes in Ireland. Unlike in the Netherlands and some other parts of Europe, however, there are no tree-nest colonies in Britain.

Both species feed mainly in inshore waters, the Shag mainly on small non-commercial fish such as sand-eels, the Cormorant on a wide variety of larger fish species, including flat fish, and, from estuaries and fresh-water, eels and trout. Because of this, it is an unpopular bird with fishermen and in many areas is heavily persecuted. Both species are relatively sedentary, some birds dispersing outside the breeding season to other parts of the British coast (and a few Cormorants to inland waters); young birds from Britain may move as far as the adjacent parts of the Continental coast, while some young Cormorants migrate south as far as Portugal. Every few years, during periods of winter gales and food shortage, numbers of Shags are blown inland and may be seen on lakes, reservoirs and other fresh water even in the middle of England. The Shag has been increasing in numbers in Britain in recent years, particularly on the North Sea coasts of northern England and southern Scotland.

Cormorants and Shags normally build bulky seaweed nests and lay clutches of three eggs. The breeding season varies from place to place (and not necessarily with latitude: Shags in Shetland nest earlier than do those in the Isles of Scilly, though the reverse is true for Cormorants) but eggs are usually laid about April.

SKUAS

Two species breed, the **Arctic Skua** (p. 90; Pl. 26) and **Great Skua** (p. 89; Pl. 26), both of which are confined to northern Scotland where they have increased in numbers during the present century. The increase in Great Skuas has been especially marked. Towards the end of the last century it was confined to Foula and Unst (Shetland), but since about 1920 it has spread to many other parts of Shetland and south to Orkney, Caithness and Lewis (Outer Hebrides) and in the last few years to Sutherland and St. Kilda. Arctic Skuas have increased somewhat less dramatically, though they are still slowly expanding their range; this is similar to the Great Skua's but extends slightly farther south to include Coll and Jura in the Inner Hebrides. Both species lay clutches of two eggs and nest in rather loose colonies on moorland, usually close to the sea but sometimes a few miles inland.

Skuas characteristically obtain much of their food by chasing other seabirds in flight and forcing them to disgorge their food. Great Skuas, in addition, frequently take the eggs and young of other seabirds, and they also feed on waste thrown overboard from fishing boats. Both species are migratory (a few Great Skuas, however, occur in British waters even in mid-winter): Arctic Skuas winter mainly in the Atlantic south of the equator (one Shetland-ringed immature having been found as far away as Brazil), while Great Skuas disperse widely over the North Atlantic (one ringed bird having reached as far as the Caribbean). In autumn there is a well marked passage of Arctic Skuas down both sides of the British Isles, but many fewer are seen passing north in spring, when the species is particularly scarce along North Sea coasts. Great Skuas are regularly noted on migration (usually in March-April and August-October) along the North Sea, Irish Sea and Atlantic coasts of the British Isles, but their numbers are usually small except off western Ireland where there is a substantial southwards autumn passage.

GULLS

This familiar and highly successful seabird family numbers six regular breeding species in the British Isles, or seven if one includes the Mediterranean Gull, a pair or two of which have nested in southern England during the last few years. Without exception, all have increased in recent years, in several cases spectacularly and to the detriment of other seabirds.

For the present purpose, they can be divided into three groups: the two smaller *Larus* gulls, **Black-headed** (p. 103; Pls. 28, 31–2, 37, 40) and **Common** (p. 96; Pls. 28, 35, 40); the three larger *Larus* species, **Herring** (p. 97; Pls. 28, 35, 40), **Lesser Black-backed** (p. 97; Pls. 27, 35, 40) and **Great Black-backed** (p. 99; Pls. 27, 34, 40); and the single member of the genus *Rissa,* the **Kittiwake** (p. 106; Pls. 33, 39).

Although there are several large coastal colonies of **Black-headed Gulls**, this species and the **Common Gull** breed mainly inland and indeed many must spend most of their lives away from salt water. Characteristically, Black-headed Gulls – by far the more numerous and widespread of the two – nest in dense colonies among aquatic vegetation growing in eutrophic shallow lochs and peat bogs; increasingly, large numbers now also nest on coastal salt marshes, particularly in south-east England and Hampshire. Common Gulls, on the other hand, are much more local, being restricted mainly to Scotland and Ireland, and nest in small groups, typically on small rocky islands in deeper fresh-water lochs.

Both species feed extensively on farmland on worms and other terrestrial invertebrates, while in winter they also feed in or near large towns (rubbish dumps being especially favoured) and roost at night on large lakes and reservoirs. Marine feeders tend to be restricted to littoral waters. The British populations of both species are relatively sedentary (though numbers of Black-headed Gulls, particularly young birds, do migrate as far south as Spain and Portugal) and their numbers are augmented in winter by tens of thousands of immigrants from many parts of northern Europe.

Of the larger *Larus* gulls, the **Herring Gull** is the most abundant and widespread. As in many other parts of its range, its numbers have increased enormously in the British Isles in recent years, and some colonies are now very large indeed. Three number 15,000 or more breeding pairs: Walney Island (Lancashire), first established in 1928 and where only 120 pairs nested as recently as 1947; the Isle of May (Fife), first colonised in 1907 but holding only 455 pairs as recently as 1936; and Puffin Island (Anglesey), where numbers appear to have reached saturation point by about 1960, and have begun to decline again during the past decade. Colonies are found in many types of coastal habitats and in the last 30 years the species has increasingly nested on buildings, particularly among the chimney pots of coastal towns and villages in south-west and north-east England. Herring Gulls feed mainly by scavenging, and an important factor in the species' general increase and expansion has been its ability to exploit the abundance of edible refuse now provided by man at rubbish dumps, fishing ports and harbours, especially in winter.

Lesser Black-backed Gulls have increased less dramatically, and in parts of northern Scotland have even decreased. Nevertheless several large new colonies exist, notably among the Herring Gulls on Walney Island where there are now over 17,000 nesting Lesser Black-back pairs. Several large colonies also exist on inland moors, notably in Lancashire and Perthshire. Unlike the two other large gulls, this species is mainly migratory, British birds wintering along the coasts of Portugal and north-west Africa, though a small but increasing proportion of the population remains in southern England. It is also less of a scavenger, a greater part of its diet in the breeding season consisting of invertebrates obtained from the shore or from arable land, as well as fish caught in inshore waters.

The third member of this trio, the **Great Black-backed Gull**, has an almost exclusively coastal breeding distribution in most parts of Britain and Ireland, though some colonies in Orkney and the Outer Hebrides are situated a few miles inland. It breeds chiefly on western and northern coasts but is gradually extending its range and has recently colonised parts of north-east Scotland, while a pair or two occasionally attempts to nest on the English east coast and in Dorset. The species has increased enormously during the present century in all parts of the British Isles. In England and Wales it now numbers about 3,000 breeding pairs, compared with about 2,000 in 1956, 1,200 in 1930 and under 100 in 1900. The largest colonies (or groups of colonies) at the present time are those in the Isles of Scilly (over 1,500 pairs), on North Rona, Outer Hebrides (1,500 pairs) and on Hoy, Orkney (over 2,000 pairs).

Great Black-backs take a variety of mainly vertebrate foods and at many colonies some individuals prey almost exclusively on rabbits and seabirds such as Manx Shearwaters and Puffins and also young gulls; the last named may include those of its own species, especially in colonies where the density of nests is particularly great. Many others obtain most of their food by scavenging around fish docks and fishing fleets, often going far out to sea to seek out the latter.

The increase of the three large gulls has caused various problems The predation by Great Black-backs of other seabird species, notably adult Puffins and Storm-petrels and the fledging chicks of Razorbills and Guillemots, has almost certainly caused population declines among these species at certain colonies, although it is known, in the case of the Manx Shearwater, that if a breeding colony is large enough and flourishing it can survive a considerable amount of gull predation. Aside from predation, gulls can, by sheer weight of numbers, crowd out other ground-nesting species. Thus the disappearance of terns from the Isle of May and Annet (Isles of Scilly) seems to be due to the fact that today all available nesting territory is occupied by gulls (Herring Gulls on the former island, Lesser Black-backeds on the latter) so that no room is available for the terns by the time they arrive back from Africa in late April. For these reasons, attempts to control the numbers of breeding gulls have been made on a number of island nature reserves, including Skokholm and Skomer (Pembrokeshire) and the Isle of May.

Unlike the other gulls, the **Kittiwake** is a maritime species, occurring inshore only when breeding or on weather movements, and inland only accidentally when sick or storm-driven. While the bulk of the population breeds on the North Sea coasts of Scotland and northern England, colonies are found on all suitable cliff-bound coasts of the British Isles. Nests are usually situated on tiny ledges on cliff faces, but in recent years, following a 70-year period of continuous expansion in its numbers, a few colonies have been established in north-east England on man made structures such as harbour walls and the window ledges of water-side warehouses. The only colony on the southern part of the English east coast was established on a pier pavilion at Lowestoft (Suffolk) in 1958, while even more remarkable has been the nesting since 1962 of a few pairs on a building overlooking the River Tyne at Gateshead (Co. Durham), more than nine miles from the sea.

Kittiwakes live almost exclusively on small fish and zooplankton taken from or just beneath the surface of the sea. Outside the breeding season it disperses widely over the North Atlantic, many British-ringed birds having reached Newfoundland and Greenland. Dispersive, weather or feeding movements occur off nearly all parts of the coast of the British Isles, especially during onshore winds in spring and autumn, but also on a smaller scale in other months of the year.

TERNS

Excluding the inland nesting **Black Tern** (p. 110; Pl. 44), which has made a few recent attempts to re-establish itself as a British breeding bird on the Ouse Washes (Cambridgeshire), and the **Gull-billed Tern** (p. 110; Pl. 43), which has nested in Britain on only one occasion (in Essex in 1950) five species of terns breed in the British Isles. All tend to nest on flat ground on low-lying, often sandy, coasts where inlets and estuaries provide shallow and relatively undisturbed waters in which small fish and crustacea living near the surface can be caught by means of an air to sea plunging dive. All except the Little Tern usually nest in large, dense colonies often with other tern species; all have clutches of two or three eggs laid in May or June; and all are highly migratory, wintering south of the equator, one of them, the Arctic Tern, going as far south as the Antarctic Ocean.

Sandwich Terns (p. 119; Pls. 41, 43) are the first to arrive back in spring (the first birds in mid-March). In Britain they nest entirely on the coast, but in Ireland there are a few colonies in the west of the country inland on lakes. Thanks to protection at many breeding sites, such as Scolt Head and Blakeney Point (Norfolk) and the Farne Islands (Northumberland), they have increased in recent years and the total population in Britain and Ireland now exceeds 10,000 pairs.

Roseate Terns (p. 113; Pl. 42) are the latest to arrive in spring (late April) and are entirely coastal. There are about 20 colonies, mostly on the coasts of the Irish Sea. The British Isles form the European headquarters of the species. Roseate Terns increased considerably during 1900–50, but have decreased again recently, from 3500 pairs in the mid-1960s to 600 pairs in 1977.

Arctic and Common Terns, while mainly coastal, do also breed inland, the **Arctic Tern** (p. 111; Pls. 41–2) now only in northern Scotland (on riverain shingle banks and on islands in lochs), the **Common Tern** (p. 111; Pls. 42–3) in small numbers in Scotland and, increasingly, on islands in gravel pits and other fresh-water in England. Less is known about their population sizes and status trends than for other terns. Common Terns number about 6,000 pairs in England and there are perhaps as many again in Scotland and Ireland together, with a few in north Wales. Arctic Terns are most abundant in northern Scottand, the bulk of the population probably being found in Orkney, but there is also a large colony on the Farne Islands (Northumberland). Both species may have decreased slightly in the last few decades.

Little Terns (p. 117; Pl. 43) nest only on the coast, usually on shinle beaches. Although there are over 100 colonies most of them are small and the total population is only 1,600 pairs. This is one of the few British seabirds known to be decreasing at the present time, this decrease being almost entirely due to disturbance at the breeding sites by holidaymakers. In reserves and other areas where the species is protected its numbers are being maintained.

AUKS

Excluding the flightless Great Auk, which became extinct in the middle of the 19th century, there are four breeding species, the **Guillemot** (p. 127; Pls. 46, 48), **Razorbill** (p. 126; Pl. 46), **Black Guillemot** (p. 127; Pl. 46) and **Puffin** (p. 130; Pl. 47). All except the Black Guillemot have decreased in the British Isles in recent decades. The decrease in the Guillemot population, particularly in the southern half of the country has been a cause of concern, as was a recent heavy decrease in Puffin numbers at several large colonies in north-west Scotland.

The one auk species which has not decreased is the Black Guillemot, which differs from the other three in several respects. It lives almost entirely in inshore waters; it has a more varied diet including a greater proportion of crustacea; it is almost entirely sedentary, being found only rarely in winter outside its breeding range; it is only loosely colonial, nesting individually in crevices amongst boulders low down near the sea; and it lays two eggs (not one). The bulk of the population is found in north and north-west Scotland (especially in the Northern Isles) and there are small numbers around most parts of the Irish coast. A recent gradual expansion in breeding range has occurred in the Irish Sea region, a small number of pairs having become established as far south as Anglesey since about 1962.

The other three auks feed almost entirely on fish, especially sand-eels, sprats and young herrings, which they obtain by means of a dive from the surface and an under-water chase in which the wings provide the main propulsion. All are highly colonial, and each shows a preference for a particular nest site (though some Guillemot and Puffin sites overlap with Razorbills'): Guillemots nest on narrow cliff ledges, Razorbills in rock crevices and beneath boulders, while Puffins burrow into soil. All lay eggs in May, but while some Guillemots and Razorbills intermittently land at their breeding sites from November or December onwards, Puffins, which are more pelagic in winter, do not return until March or even April. All incubate their eggs for periods of 32–42 days, but while the chicks of Guillemots and Razorbills leave their cliff sites for the sea after only 15–23 days (when flightless and weighing less than a third of their eventual adult weight), Puffin chicks remain in the nest burrow for seven weeks, during the last of which they have been deserted by their parents and live off their accumulated body fat. The chicks of Guillemots and Razorbills are accompanied out to sea by one of their parents, usually the male which then attends them for an unknown period of time, probably several weeks. In September-October the adults undergo a complete wing and tail moult, during which time they are briefly flightless. Adult Puffins, on the other hand, usually have their wing and tail moult in late winter or early spring.

Outside the breeding season, Guillemots and Razorbills disperse out to sea (though not normally into the pelagic zone), many birds reaching the coasts of continental Europe from Norway south to the Bay of Biscay, with some Razorbills going even farther south to west Morocco and into the Mediterranean. However, since Guillemots come ashore at their breeding colonies as early as November-December many adults must be relatively sedentary and remain at sea off our coasts throughout the year. Puffins are rarely seen from shore during the winter and presumably disperse well out to sea: birds ringed in Britain have reached New-foundland, Greenland, the western Mediterranean, and many parts of the Atlantic coast of continental Europe, particularly southern Norway.

The breeding distributions of Guillemot and Razorbill are very similar, though the former is much the more numerous of the two. Both species have declined during the last 30 years, particularly the Guillemot for which the numbers have been most heavily reduced at its southernmost colonies. Many thousands of Guillemots and Razorbills are killed by oil pollution every year and it seems probable that this has been the main cause of their declines in the south, where some colonies have been reduced by 90% since the 1930s.

The numbers of Puffins breeding at many southern colonies also declined markedly during the period 1920–50. Several colonies that once held many thousands of breeding birds now have fewer than 100 pairs (e.g. Annet, Isles of Scilly; Lundy, Devon; Ailsa Craig, Ayrshire) or none at all (e.g. St. Tudwal's Islands, Caernarvonshire). Around 1970, sharp decreases were noted in north-west Scotland, including on St. Kilda, the Shiants and the Clo Mor cliffs in Sutherland. The accidental introduction of rats was almost certainly the cause of the earlier declines at some island colonies, while at others oil pollution or increased predation by Great Black-backed Gulls may have contributed. But the chief reasons for the recent decline in north-west Scotland are unknown and for the time being it fortunately appears to have ceased.

RED-NECKED PHALAROPE

This rare summer migrant has a very limited breeding range in the British Isles and is restricted to a few small, shallow fresh-water pools and lakes in northern Scotland (notably Shetland) and Co. Mayo, Ireland. The total breeding population is only about 50 pairs, and even on passage it is rarely seen at sea around the coasts of the British Isles.

NON-BREEDING VISITORS

In addition to the breeding birds already mentioned, a further 13 species of seabirds are annual visitors to the British Isles, while 23 more (listed on pp. 274–5) have been recorded as accidental vagrants.

PROCELLARIIDAE

Two species which nest in the southern hemisphere, the **Sooty Shearwater** (p. 32; Pl. 8) and **Great Shearwater** (p. 31; Pl. 9), occur regularly in British and Irish waters, mainly in July-October, during their non-breeding season. Both species occur quite widely in the Atlantic just north-west of the British Isles in July-August and then move southwards down the west coast of Ireland and, during on-shore winds, southwest England, between August and early October. Small numbers, particularly Sooty Shearwaters, enter the North Sea. Another species, **Cory's Shearwater** (p. 30; Pl. 9) of the Mediterranean and Atlantic Islands, regularly disperses north in late summer as far as the entrance to the English Channel, and in certain years occurs in some numbers off south-west Ireland and south-west England; a few have been recorded as far north as Shetland. The **Balearic Shearwater** (p. 33; Pl. 9), the distinctive western Mediterranean race of the Manx Shearwater, also occurs regularly in the English Channel in autumn, a few passing north into the North and Irish Seas and sometimes reaching as far as Scotland.

PHALAROPES

Grey Phalaropes (p. 85; Pl. 25) occur annually on autumn passage, between late August and November, though their numbers are extremely variable. At irregular intervals, when strong westerly gales coincide with their south-easterly migration across the North Atlantic in September, large flocks numbering hundreds of birds occur off the coasts of south-west England and western Ireland; the largest flock recorded was one of 1,000 birds in the Isles of Scilly in September 1960. But in most years only very small numbers are seen, including ones and twos on parts of the English east and south coasts.

SKUAS

As well as the two breeding species, two other skuas—**Pomarine Skua** (p.90; Pl.26) and **Long-tailed Skua** (p.91; Pl.26) – are scarce but regular migrants in the British Isles. Pomarine Skuas occur in small numbers (rarely more than ten together) in spring and autumn off most coasts, though they are recorded most frequently off north Norfolk, Cornwall and around Ireland. Long-tailed Skuas are ever more uncommon, and are usually recorded as single birds in autumn off the coasts of Norfolk and Northumberland, though there are records from many other parts of the country. In recent years odd birds have sometimes remained for a few weeks in summer at the Arctic Skua colony on Fair Isle.

GULLS

Two northern species, **Iceland Gull** (p.99; Pls.29,33,35,40) and **Glaucous Gull** (p.99; Pls.29,35,40), are regular winter visitors, particularly to fishing ports in the northern half of the British Isles. Glaucous is the more common, some birds reaching southern England in most winters. Immatures of both species sometimes remain in Britain in summer. Another northern gull, the highly migratory **Sabine's Gull** (p.106; Pls.33,39), occurs regularly in very small numbers off south-west England and south-west Ireland, mainly during strong westerly winds in autumn.

Two other gulls are regular visitors. The **Mediterranean Black-headed Gull** (p.103; Pls.32,37), a pair or two of which have nested in recent years in southern England, occurs in very small numbers, chiefly on the east and south coasts of England. It has been identified in all months of the year, and individuals sometimes overwinter in the same locality for several years in succession. The **Little Gull** (p.105; Pls.31,32,37) has bred just once in Britain (on the Ouse Washes in 1976), and though others often oversummer here, it appears mainly as a passage and winter visitor, being generally most common and widespread in September-October. It occurs mainly singly or in small flocks (in the south often with migrant Black Terns) but occasionally in flocks of up to 100 and more, especially on the coast of Fife in late summer. Though most frequent on the English east and south coasts it is also recorded fairly frequently elsewhere in the British Isles, including inland.

AUKS

The arctic breeding **Little Auk** (p.125; Pl.46) is a winter visitor, occurring regularly and often in some numbers off northern Scotland during the months of November to February. Variable, but usually small numbers occur annually in the North Sea as far south as Norfolk, and periodically winter 'wrecks' occur, when moribund Little Auks may be found widely inland in Britain.

RARE VISITORS

The following seabird species have also been recorded in the British Isles as vagrants. A few, such as the Little Shearwater and White-winged Black Tern have been seen almost annually in recent years, but the majority have been recorded on fewer than ten occasions, some, such as the Black-capped Petrel and White-faced Storm-petrel, only once.

Black-browed Albatross	Bulwer's Petrel
Black-capped Petrel	Little Shearwater

Wilson's Storm-petrel

White-faced Storm-petrel

Madeiran Storm-petrel

Magnificent Frigate-bird

Wilson's Phalarope

Ivory Gull

Great Black-headed Gull

Laughing Gull

Franklin's Gull

Slender-billed Gull

Bonaparte's Gull

Ross's Gull

Whiskered Tern

White-winged Black Tern

Caspian Tern

Bridled Tern

Sooty Tern

Royal Tern

Brunnich's Guillemot

WATCHING SEABIRDS

Seabird-watching in the British Isles takes two main forms: first, observation at the breeding colonies, and second, observation from coastal headlands or islands where large numbers of seabirds pass by on migration or on feeding or weather movements. Since Britain and Ireland, together with their offshore islands, have over 10,000 km of coastline and numerous places where seabirds can be observed *en masse*, it is beyond the scope of this section to list each and every important seabird site. Many of the biggest breeding colonies, including the largest of them all – St. Kilda – are remote and inaccessible. The purpose of the map which follows on page 20, therefore, is to show a selection of diverse sites which are reasonably accessible to the public or at which 'bird observatories' provide accommodation for visiting bird-watchers staying overnight.

Two kinds of site are shown. Breeding colonies (marked ●) are generally best visited during the months of May, June and July – for most species the main breeding season. August is too late for many species (virtually all auks, for example, have gone to sea again by the end of July), though some, such as the Gannet and petrels, having long fledging periods, are still about until early September or later. Sea-watching sites (marked **x**) are mainly composed of headlands, where under the right weather conditions at appropriate times of the year, large numbers of seabirds can be seen moving past relatively close to the coast, or at least at distances at which they can be identified with binoculars or telescope. In general, strong onshore winds in autumn (and to a lesser extent at other seasons), especially if coupled with poor visibility at sea, provide the best conditions for large coastal movements of seabirds.

Finally, it should not be forgotten that cross-channel ferries across, for example, the English Channel and Irish Sea, and between Cornwall and the Isles of Scilly, often provide excellent opportunities for seeing seabirds in their natural environment – at sea.

DISTRIBUTION MAPS

Immediately after the map of sites are 24 individual maps showing the breeding distributions of the 25 species which nest in Britain and Ireland. (The maps for Guillemot and Razorbill are combined since their distributions are virtually identical.) No attempt has been made to map non-breeding distribution, but the captions indicate the time of the year when each species is present in British and Irish waters, and the coasts on which they appear.

BRITISH SEABIRD SITES

1 Hermaness, Unst, Shetland. Large seabird colonies on cliffs, including gannetry;
large puffinry on cliff top, and Arctic and
Great Skuas breeding on blanket moorland.

2 Noss, Shetland. Has Shetland's largest
gannetry, both skuas, and a large variety of
cliff-nesting seabirds. Can be viewed best
by tourist boats from Lerwick.

3 Fair Isle, Shetland (bird observatory).
Best known for rare terrestrial migrant
birds, but has fine seabird colonies including both skuas, all auks and the storm-
petrel.

4 Isle of May, Fife (bird observatory).
Huge Herring Gull colony (15,000 pairs),
also auks, including large puffinry.

5 Bass Rock, East Lothian. Large gannetry (10,000 pairs) at which a single
Black-browed Albatross has over-
summered in recent years.

6 Farne Islands, Northumberland. Large
and varied seabird populations including
Sandwich, Roseate, Common and Arctic
Terns, Puffins, Guillemots, Kittiwakes,
Fulmars, Shags, etc. Arctic Skuas frequent
offshore in autumn. Reached by frequent
day-trip boats from Seahouses.

7 Northumberland coast. Good autumn sea-watching from several headlands, including Cullernose Point and St. Mary's Island, with numbers of gannets, kittiwakes, skuas, shearwaters, etc., passing close inshore, especially during cyclonic northeast winds.

8 Flamborough Head and Bempton Cliffs, Yorkshire. England's only gannetry, but also large numbers of Kittiwakes, Fulmars, Razorbills and Guillemots. The headland provides a good vantage point for migrant seabirds in spring and autumn.

9 Scolt Head, Norfolk, and
10 Blakeney Point, Norfolk. Best known for their terns, including Sandwich and Common and two of Britain's largest Little Tern colonies.

11 Cley, Norfolk. Autumn seabird movements, notably of skuas (including Pomarine and occasional Long-tailed), small numbers of Sooty Shearwaters, and in November Little Auks not infrequently.

12 Dungeness, Kent (bird observatory). England's only established breeding Common Gulls, also Little and Common Terns, Herring Gulls. Offshore passage movements of terns (including Roseate and Black), Little Gulls, Arctic Skuas, Gannets, etc. Mediterranean Black-headed Gulls are annual visitors.

13 Selsey Bill, Sussex. Various seabirds offshore, especially terns, including Gull-billed almost annually.

14 Portland Bill, Dorset (bird observatory). Small numbers of breeding auks and other seabirds. Autumn movements offshore include shearwaters (especially Balearic), skuas, gannets, kittiwakes and terns.

15 Isles of Scilly. Great variety of breeding seabirds, including England's only Storm-petrels and Manx Shearwaters, Puffins, Razorbills, Guillemots, Fulmars, Roseate Tern and Common Terns, and huge Great Black-backed Gull colonies. Landing is prohibited on many seabird islands, but there are frequent boat trips around them in summer. Autumn sea-watching regularly produces skuas (including Pomarine), rarer shearwaters, Grey Phalaropes and Sabine's Gulls.

16 St. Ives, Cornwall. Excellent autumn seawatching during strong northwest winds, when large numbers of auks, Gannets, Kittiwakes and shearwaters and skuas pass very close inshore under the 'island'. Local sewage outfall has attracted rare gulls including Bonaparte's, Mediterranean, Black-headed, Sabine's and Little.

17 Lundy, Devon. Auk colonies, including Puffins, now much reduced, plus other common cliff-breeding seabirds.

18 Pembrokeshire Islands. Skokholm and Skomer (daily boat trips, weather providing, in summer from Martinshaven) famed for huge Manx Shearwater colonies; Puffins, Razorbills, Guillemots, Kittiwakes, Fulmars, etc.; large Storm-petrel colony on Skokholm. Grassholm, further offshore, has very large gannetry.

19 South Stack, Anglesey. Colonies of Guillemots and other cliff-nesting seabirds seen easily from lighthouse steps.

20 Walney Island, Lancashire. Site of Britain's largest gull colony – altogether over 30,000 pairs of Herring and Lesser Black-backs.

21 Ailsa Craig, Ayrshire. Large gannetry and many other cliff-nesting seabirds, though Guillemot, Razorbill and Puffin numbers now much reduced.

22 Rhum, Inner Hebrides. Various cliff-nesting seabirds, but chiefly noted for large Manx Shearwater colony near mountain top at 2,500 feet.

23 Handa, Sutherland. Huge Guillemot colonies (30,000 pairs) and large numbers of other cliff-nesting seabirds, including Puffins. Recently colonised by Great and Arctic Skuas.

24 Cape Clear, Co. Cork (bird observatory). Sea-watching site *par excellence*; often huge movements of shearwaters (including Great, Sooty, Cory's and occasional Little Shearwaters) and many commoner seabirds; even albatrosses are not unknown. Many other headlands in Ireland provide excellent opportunities for sea-watching.

NOTE: *Bird Observatories* Addresses of those providing accommodation can be obtained from the British Trust for Ornithology, Beech Grove, Tring, Hertfordshire, England.

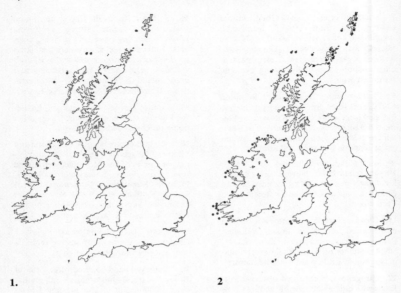

1.   **2**

1. Leach's Storm-petrel Summer visitor (April–October). On autumn passage most frequent off W. Ireland and S.W. Cornwall; annual in Liverpool Bay and off N. Norfolk; infrequent elsewhere.

2. Storm Petrel Summer visitor (April–October). Uncommon off British east and south coasts.

3. Manx Shearwater Summer visitor (March–October). Relatively uncommon off east and south coasts. Mediterranean race (Balearic Shearwater) reaches English Channel in autumn. Largest colonies are shown ■.

4. Fulmar Present all year. Bulk of the population is in N. Scotland.

5. Gannet Present all year, though young birds and some adults migrate south in winter. Fifteen colonies, of which five number over 10,000 pairs ⊡, five over 1,000 pairs ⊙ and five under 1,000 pairs ●.

6. Cormorant Present all year. Occurs off all coasts (also inland, especially in N. Britain) outside the breeding season.

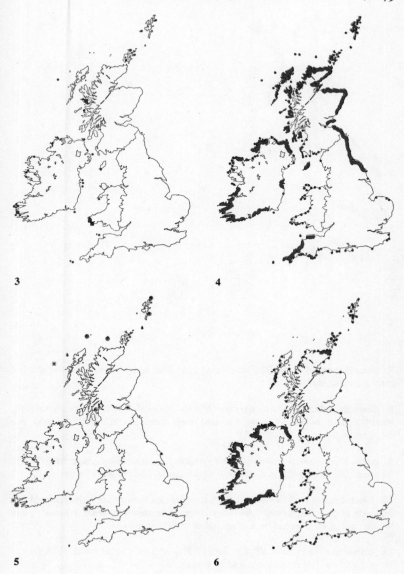

3

4

5

6

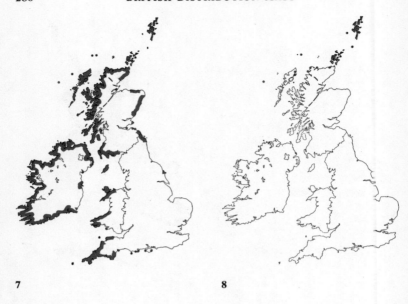

7   8

7. Shag Present all year. In winter occurs in small numbers off S.E. Britain, but only accidentally inland.

8. Great Skua Mainly summer visitor (March–November). All coasts on passage, usually small numbers, most frequent and numerous off S.W. Ireland and W. Cornwall.

9. Arctic Skua Summer visitor (April–October). Southward passage down North Sea and Atlantic coasts in autumn; less numerous and frequent in spring.

10. Black-headed Gull Present all year, in winter including many immigrants from northern and central Europe. An inland as much as coastal species in summer and winter, being widespread in S. England at the latter season.

11. Common Gull Present all year, including continental immigrants. Widespread (inland and coasts) on passage and in winter.

12. Herring Gull Present all year. Widespread in winter.

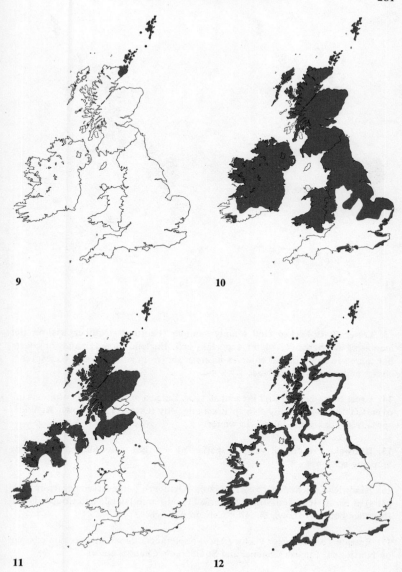

9

10

11

12

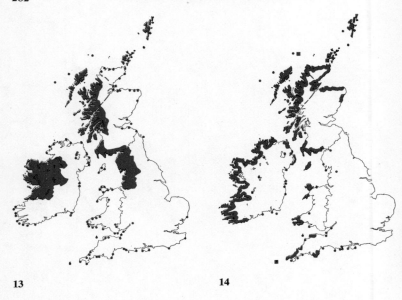

13   14

13. Lesser Black-backed Gull Mainly summer (February–October) visitor, but increasing numbers over-winter, especially in S. England. Breeds mainly on coasts but there are some inland colonies in areas shown in solid colour. Widespread, coasts and inland, on passage.

14. Great Black-backed Gull Present all year. Largest breeding concentrations (all over 1,000 pairs) at Scilly, North Rona and Hoy (Orkney) are shown ■. Widespread, all coasts and inland, in winter.

15. Kittiwake Present all year. Disperses at sea (but visits all coasts) outside breeding season.

16. Sandwich Tern Summer visitor (March–October). Largest colonies (over 1,000 pairs) at Scolt Head and Stiffkey (Norfolk) and Farne Islands and Coquet Island (Northumberland) shown ■. All coasts on passage.

17. Roseate Tern Summer visitor (April–September). Small numbers on passage on North Sea, English Channel and St George's Channel coasts.

18. Common Tern Summer visitor (April–October). All coasts (also inland) on passage.

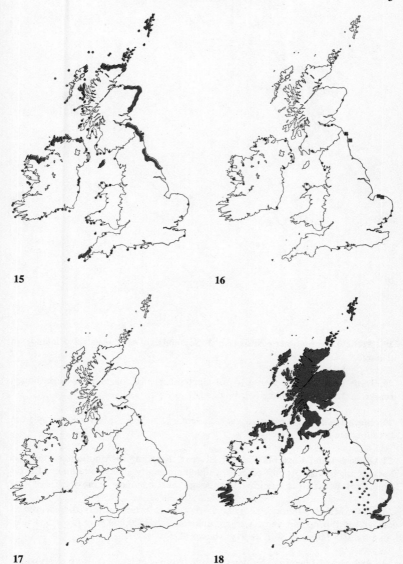

15

16

17

18

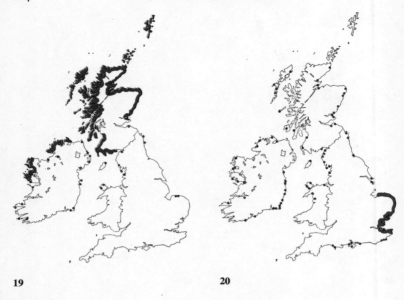

19   20

19. Arctic Tern Summer visitor (April–September). All coasts (also inland) on passage.

20. Little Tern Summer visitor (April–September). All coasts on passage though scarce in S.W. Wales and S.W. England.

21. Black Guillemot Present all year. Sedentary, inshore; rarely seen away from breeding areas.

22 Guillemot and **Razorbill** Present all year. Breeding distributions of the two species are similar. At cliff colonies Guillemots nearly always outnumber Razorbills. Present off all coasts in winter though most common in the west.

23. Puffin Mainly summer visitor (April–August) to inshore waters, though present out at sea throughout year. Largest colonies (over 20,000 pairs), on St Kilda, Shiants, Clo Mor and Sule Skerry, shown ■.

24. Red-necked Phalarope Summer visitor (April–September). Rare everywhere on passage though very small numbers are annual in autumn on East Anglian coasts.

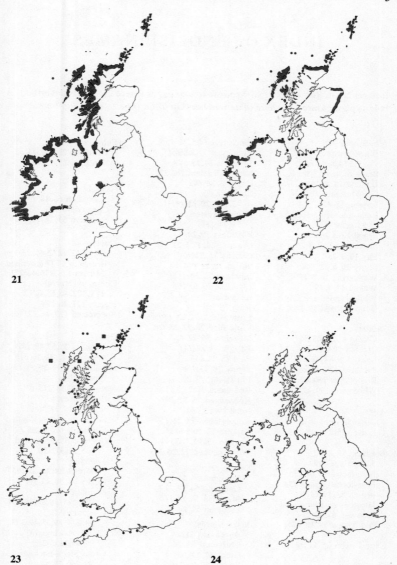

21

22

23

24

INDEX OF ENGLISH NAMES

References in Roman (normal) type are to text pages where the bird is described; in **bold** type they are to **colour plate numbers**; in *italic* type to *map numbers*.

INDEX OF SCIENTIFIC NAMES

References in Roman (normal) type are to text pages where the bird is described; in **bold** type they are to **colour plates**; in *italic* type to *map numbers*. Different subspecies are only indexed where their page, plate or map numbers differ.

Numbers in **bold** type refer
to colour plates

Albatrosses **3-6**

Penguins **1-2**

Petrels, Shearwaters,
Fulmars **7-12**

Diving Petrels **14**

Storm-petrels
13-14

Tropic-birds **15**

Gannets, Boobies
18-19

Pelicans **16-17**